Women and Domestic Violence in Bangladesh

After the independence of Bangladesh in 1971, the country has experienced large-scale transformations owing to national and international migration, urbanization, the development of many national and international non-governmental organizations (NGOs) and economic dynamism. Globalization and economic liberalization have created opportunities to develop sustainable social policies by strengthening the national economy of the country. Major progress has been made in closing the gender gap, and the Constitution of Bangladesh provides equality of status and opportunity to all its citizens irrespective of sex. However, domestic violence perpetuated against women is a common phenomenon in Bangladesh.

This book is a study about domestic violence against women in Bangladeshi society. It delineates, in particular, why and how some women become the victims of domestic violence in the changing socio-economic setting of Bangladesh. The author explores the multiple contexts in which domestic violence occurs by focusing on the everyday experience of women subjected to this violence. The book shows how changing socio-economic setting, urbanization and the growing demand for female labor influences the phenomenon and experience of domestic violence. It demonstrates that domestic violence is entangled in a complex web of institutionalized social relations that necessitates a structural and contextual understanding of the production of such violence in family, kinship and gender relations. Finally, it identifies factors that cause, perpetuate, and mitigate domestic violence or give strength to women to struggle and raise their voices or take shelter in the law against the perpetrators of domestic violence.

A novel contribution to our understanding of how gender relationships are differently constituted and contested in the everyday lives of Bangladeshi women, both in natal and affinal families, this book will be of interest to academics in the field of Sociology, Gender and Law and South Asian Studies.

Laila Ashrafun is Professor in the Department of Sociology at Shahjalal University of Science and Technology, Sylhet, Bangladesh.

**Routledge/Asian Studies Association of Australia (ASAA)
South Asian Series**
Edited by Duncan McDuie-Ra
The University of New South Wales, Australia

Published in Association with the Australian Studies Association of Australia (ASAA), represented by Ernest Koh, chair of the ASAA Publications Committee, Monash University, Australia.

Founded in 1986 to publish outstanding work in the social sciences and humanities, the SAPS entered a new phase in 2010 when it joined with Routledge to continue a notable tradition of Australian-based research about South Asia. Works in the series are published in both UK and Indian editions.

SAPS publishes outstanding research on the countries and peoples of South Asia across a wide range of disciplines including history, politics and political economy, anthropology, geography, literature, sociology and the fields of cultural studies, communication studies and gender studies. Interdisciplinary and comparative research is encouraged.

1 **Suicide and Society in India**
   Peter Mayer

2 **Women and Domestic Violence in Bangladesh**
   Seeking A Way Out of the Cage
   Laila Ashrafun

Women and Domestic Violence in Bangladesh

Seeking A Way Out of the Cage

Laila Ashrafun

LONDON AND NEW YORK

First published 2018
by Routledge
2 Park Square, Milton Park, Abingdon, Oxon OX14 4RN

and by Routledge
711 Third Avenue, New York, NY 10017

Routledge is an imprint of the Taylor & Francis Group, an informa business

© 2018 Laila Ashrafun

The right of Laila Ashrafun to be identified as author of this work has been asserted by her in accordance with sections 77 and 78 of the Copyright, Designs and Patents Act 1988.

All rights reserved. No part of this book may be reprinted or reproduced or utilized in any form or by any electronic, mechanical, or other means, now known or hereafter invented, including photocopying and recording, or in any information storage or retrieval system, without permission in writing from the publishers.

Trademark notice: Product or corporate names may be trademarks or registered trademarks, and are used only for identification and explanation without intent to infringe.

British Library Cataloguing-in-Publication Data
A catalogue record for this book is available from the British Library

Library of Congress Cataloging-in-Publication Data
Names: Ashrafun, Laila, author.
Title: Women and domestic violence in Bangladesh : seeking a way out of the cage / Laila Ashrafun.
Description: Abingdon, Oxon ; New York, NY : Routledge, 2018. | Series: Routledge/Asian Studies Association of Australia (ASAA) South Asian series ; 2 | Includes bibliographical references and index.
Identifiers: LCCN 2017059145| ISBN 9780815367765 (hardback) | ISBN 9781351256643 (ebook)
Subjects: LCSH: Family violence–Bangladesh. | Abused women–Bangladesh. | Poor women–Bangladesh–Social conditions.
Classification: LCC HV6626.23.B3 A84 2018 | DDC 362.82/92095492–dc23
LC record available at https://lccn.loc.gov/2017059145

ISBN: 978-0-8153-6776-5 (hbk)
ISBN: 978-1-351-25664-3 (ebk)

Typeset in Times New Roman
by Wearset Ltd, Boldon, Tyne and Wear

For my parents, my husband, Jasim, and my son, Anindya

Contents

List of tables viii
Preface ix

Introduction 1

1 Approaching *basti* life and a counseling center in Sylhet 18

2 Girlhood and marriage: perceptions and experiences of slum women 43

3 Liberating one's own space: in quest of self-identity and agency in everyday life 69

4 Women's married life and domestic violence in the slum 84

5 Unveiling domestic violence from the privacy of home 106

6 Legal battles at the counseling center: what do the women get? 128

7 Conclusions 147

References 154
Index 172

Tables

1.1	Occupations of the married women and men in the two *bastis*	40
1.2	Age structure, age at first marriage and number of children ever born to women of the two *bastis*	41
5.1	Happy wedding gifts of Moni Begum	110

Preface

Gender-based violence confronts women throughout the world, but it is a topic that has only come to prominence relatively recently in the social science research. Women themselves are often diffident about admitting in public that they have been the victim of marital and other domestic violence. Law enforcement agencies are often as male dominated as the wider society, and they are often averse to intervening in matters that are generally perceived to be "private." Domestic violence tends to be under-reported in police records, although surveys may provide ballpark figures of its incidence. This relative invisibility of domestic violence is particularly marked in Bangladesh and much of the global south more generally, where the collection vital statistics is often seriously incomplete and men and women alike tend to presume that husbands have the right to chasten their wives, including with physical violence if they see fit. Consequently, while we do know that domestic violence is extremely widespread, we still know relatively little about women's experience of domestic violence, how they develop coping mechanisms to survive and resist violence, and how they contend with agencies tasked with protecting them and ensuring their future security and well-being. It is onto this understudied terrain that I have chosen to direct my spotlight with respect to *basti* dwellers and a counseling center in Sylhet, Bangladesh.

This book began with the deceptively straightforward question: why and how do some women become the victims of domestic violence in the changing socio-economic setting of Bangladesh? It critically seeks to trace domestic violence against impoverished women in Bangladeshi society by paying keen attention to the different factors of inequality and subordination of women in their everyday lives. I have portrayed the position of womanhood in the lower socio-economic class in its social and cultural milieu. More specifically, I have shown the position of girls in lower socio-economic families and how the socialization of a girl is marked by tradition to make her a woman. I have studied how these women perceive and practice the stereotypical notion of gender relations, kinship and the marriage system in the patrilineal and patriarchal social structure. Hence, I have focused on how women are entangled with the dominant structural practice of the society. By the same token, I have also shown how some women become subjects and how their actions in practice contest the dominant structure.

This book is a qualitative and ethnographic work which has given me the space to explore the kind of issues that are amenable to questionnaire survey work. I have talked not just to victims of domestic violence but to other people in the neighbors, and spent time in a counseling center talking to practitioners as well as clients. Such qualitative methods do not normally permit generalization, but they do provide richer understanding of the processes that result marital violence and how people respond to it and address it.

The study reveals that in Sylhet district, women are now becoming encouraged to come out to the public domain and seek help from legal formal institutions and NGOs. It was promising to find out that these young women from the impoverished class are not only passive victims of domestic violence. They are now trying to express their demands and establish their agency and stop the violence against them. But this study also shows that when a victim woman raises her voice against domestic violence in the mediations in the counseling center she is certainly not challenging to the structures of the social system in which she lives. Rather I find most of the women are simply trying to improve their personal situation as a wife or daughter-in-law in their marital home. They do not want to file a case against the perpetrators of crimes against them for fear of breaking their marital bonds, insecurity, fear of more violence and social stigma. In this sense, their agency is not consciously intended to bring about social change by rejecting the status quo and the gendered relations of power. However, the efforts of the victim women to stand up against domestic violence in the counseling center has formed a sound basis for women's emancipation from violence and establishing human rights in the long run.

There are numerous people to thank and remember. Most of all, I am grateful to the almighty Allah, who gave me courage, energy and opportunity to write this book. I should like to thank those individuals who have given their countless acts of support, generosity and guidance. It would be impossible to convey my gratitude and respect adequately and difficult to pick out just one or two people for special mention.

My greatest debt is to Dr. Minna Säävälä, Department of Social and Cultural Anthropology at the University of Helsinki to whom I am humbly grateful. Many of the specific ideas on writing this book have emerged from her critical knowledge of South Asian social structure and culture, which I have drawn on amply in this book. She provided great feedback on my work by commenting on the early draft of the research proposal, during my fieldwork period, and by making me cautious at different points while I was writing the manuscript. She was also often ready to write letters of recommendation for various grants.

I want to offer my sincere gratitude to Professor Emerita Sylvia Vatuk, Department of Anthropology, University of Illinois at Chicago, USA, and Professor Patricia Jeffery, Department of Sociology at the Edinburgh University for their invaluable scrutiny and comments about my research. I am deeply grateful to Late Professor Karen Armstrong, Department of Social and Cultural Anthropology, University of Helsinki. I am indebted to her for giving me the opportunity to enroll and participate in the post-graduate seminars of Anthropology. Her inspiration, love and sympathy helped me a lot to complete this research.

I would like to thank Professor Sirpa Tenhunen for providing me with the opportunity to present my research proposal at the earlier stage in the conference of "Globalizing South Asia," Helsinki, 27.5–29.5.2010. In this connection, I would like to thank Professor Steve Derne, Department of Sociology, SUNY, Geneseo, for his suggestion as my research proposal commentator. I also benefited from Professor Lina Fruzzetti, Department of Anthropology at Brown University, USA, for her insights at an early stage of my writing when she read and commented on my research proposal and gave me suggestions for my fieldwork.

Special thanks are due to my friend and husband Professor Jasim for his tremendous encouragement and help for 24 years in shining my academic career. He always supports me in my pleasure and pain and keeps me fit for struggle to achieve the "best." I cannot repay his love, sympathy and care. I wish to thank my son, Anindya, for his endurance during the long period of time I was doing this work and for his love and dream to have a published book from mum. Your dream has been fulfilled, dear Anindya! I want to thank my mother Hamida Begum and father Dr. Ashraf Uddin Ahmed for their kind support for my academic life. I am really grateful to them forever.

I would also like to thank my respectable teachers from the Department of Sociology, University of Dhaka for encouraging me to pursue higher studies. I would like to mention Professor K. A. M. Saad Uddin, Professor A. I. Mahbub Ahmed, Professor S. Aminul Islam and Late Professor H. K. S. Arefeen. I also recall my well-wisher and uncle, the late Professor A. M. M. Sahidulla, Department of Mathematics at the University of Dhaka, for his endless encouragement and blessings for my academic upliftment. My appreciation is given to the reviewers of this manuscript who helped me to clarify my ideas. Many thanks are also due to Routledge editorial board, Dorothea Schaefter, Lily Brown and Duncan McDuie-Ra for publishing my research in the form of this book. Many thanks from the bottom of my heart!

Above all, my deepest appreciation goes to all the women who are central to this research. Trusting my intention, they allowed me to enter their lives and they shared their feelings. I wish to thank the personnel of the counseling center Bangladesh Legal Aid and Services Trust (BLAST), Sylhet, for their assistance and cooperation. I acknowledge my indebtedness to my victim sisters of domestic violence, clients in the counseling center, for accepting me and sharing their inhuman sufferings with deep confidence and trust. I can only hope that something of my love, sympathy and support for them come through in the stories that follow.

Introduction

In the United Nations Conference on Women in Beijing in September 1995, the subject of violence against women formed a significant part of the discussions. The mounting importance and detection of violence against women as a subject at the international arena was the product of almost two decades of organizing by women's groups in various parts of the world. As a result of these movements and discussions, the understanding on various forms of violence to which women have been subjected has gradually increased (McWilliams, 1998). Violence against women denotes universal male domination, although as a form of violence, it always has its local and cultural characteristics. The meaning of violence is shaped by competing sections of society, and violence against women is a contested field of relations where the boundaries of violence are continuously strived and debated. Definitions of violence against women are place and situation related, formed in specific circumstances and culture, rather than fixed. But routes of violence are often evidently patterned, and violence against women takes place in a particular time and space in a particular way.

This book is a study about domestic violence against women in Bangladeshi society. It delineates, in particular, why and how some women become the victims of domestic violence in the changing socio-economic setting of Bangladesh. As a Bangladeshi native researcher, I was inspired to do this research because after the independence of Bangladesh in 1971, the country experienced large-scale transformations owing to national and international migration, urbanization, the development of many national and international NGOs and economic dynamism.

Gender imbalance and women's poor educational, health and economic standing are some of the major issues in the development of South Asia, and for global development as well (World Economic Forum, 2009).[1] Still, the South Asian Woman as victim has been embodied in a structurally disadvantaged position, reflected in high maternal mortality, a skewed sex ratio at birth, a low labor participation rate for women, feminization of poverty, a high prevalence of domestic violence, victims of dowry murders, eve-teasing (sexual harassment in public) and rape, or many other gender-specific disadvantages such as female infanticide, sex-specific abortions and discriminatory food and health care practices (e.g., Jeffery, 1998; Agarwal, 1994; Agnes, 2002; Majumdar, 2003; Basu, 1999, 2015; Fulu, 2014).

2 *Introduction*

However, in Bangladesh, major progress has been made in closing the gender gap in school enrollments at both the primary and secondary levels, and interestingly, the gender parity index (ratio of girls to boys education) in primary education is already 103 and in secondary education a very high 117 (UNICEF, 2011).[2] The recent statistics (2005–2010) show that the youth (15–24 age group) literacy rate of both males and females are respectively 74 and 77 percent (UNICEF, 2010).[3] Also total fertility is declining: the Bangladesh Bureau of Statistics (BBS)[4] census data has found there is a rapid decrease in fertility rates, from an enumerated child to woman ratio of 807 in 1981 to 519 in 2001. Currently, many women from wealthy and powerful families are actively involved in politics, and Bangladesh has had a number of female heads of state. Many women are now members of the local government councils that have important responsibilities for rural and urban development. Because of rapid socio-economic mobility, many women from different socio-economic backgrounds both in the urban and rural areas are now working outside home, participating in training programs and educational institutions, accessing to and using credits and negotiating for control of resources. Traditionally, men have dominated migration flows, but the proportion of women is increasing and women currently predominate among internal migrants aged between 15–25 (NIPORT,[5] 2006). Women's participation in the education sector, involvement with government and NGO, internal migration to the urban milieu, labor participation in small-scale industries or large industries such as manufactured garments and apparel have created significant change in the social structure (White, 1992, p. 12; Kabeer, 2000, p. 60; Feldman, 2010, p. 307). These modifications give women the opportunity to share resources and places once restricted to them. These modifications also present women as self-regulating individuals who make choices and claim demands that contest with previous forms of labor control and subservience. These areas focus attention on women and their new role as a place for contesting previous and new social relationships and types of production, power and patronage (Feldman, 2010). According to recent statistics, more than 90 percent of the workers making up the garment industry labor force are women (ADB,[6] 2010). In this and other ways, women's positions have been noticeably altered by the freedom of mobility and economic empowerment. With the decline in family farming and the weakening of conventional family types, the effects of capitalist penetration have altered stereotypes of the Bangladeshi women. The material bases of "classic patriarchy" crush under the influence of new market forces, capital penetration in rural areas (Kandiyoti, 1998) or the process of unceasing immiseration. The crash of "classic patriarchy" results in the earlier liberation of younger men from their fathers and their earlier disconnection from the paternal household. This process implies that women are free from the control of mothers-in-law and head their own households at much younger age. Naila Kabeer (2000) has claimed that "while there has been economic gain involved, the increased physical mobility of women is negotiated within patriarchal bargains" (p. 60). As a result, the image of Bangladeshi women as mere helpless victims of tradition does not remain unaffected by social change. A static image of the Bangladeshi female as a singular, monolithic and subjugated subject in much of earlier developmental discussion has been criticized (White, 1992). The discussion on gender and development in Bangladesh is highly controversial and politicized.

Nowadays, there is a global discourse about gender equality and a global feminist activism and research that has been successful in incorporating women's rights and gender mainstreaming within the human rights regime. The pursuit of gender equality has been significantly approved as a central policy targeted by governments and international organizations all over the world. Equality has come to be perceived as a requirement not only for redistribution of material possessions or income but also for recognition of cultural identities and representation of particular points of view (Squires, 2007).

The Constitution of Bangladesh provides equality of status and opportunity to all its citizens irrespective of sex. The state has enacted several laws to safeguard the rights of women and to bring socio-economic change to their status. Several governmental and NGOs have launched development programs for the emancipation of women. However, in spite of all the legal provisions and development programs, women still remain in many ways in a structurally disadvantaged position in the country. According to the Gender Gap Index, the success of Bangladesh has thus far failed to translate into social development and equity to the extent we could expect from other developing Asian countries. For Bangladesh, the gender-related development index is lower than the human development index, indicating that an aggregated development masks gender inequalities. Of the 155 countries for which both indices could be calculated, 100 countries showed less disparity than Bangladesh. On the gender empowerment measure, which considers whether women are active in public and economic life, the rank of the country is 108th of 109 countries (ADB, 2010).

The leading newspapers of Bangladesh almost daily publish banner news of violence against women in various manifestations, i.e., physical torture by husbands and other affines, dowry-related deaths, homicides, suicides in the marital home, rape, and throwing acid in the face, which is a particular kind of violence against women that is found in Bangladesh. In an ideal world, everybody should have the opportunity to live their lives within a happy affectionate family, but we know that this ideal model of family connectedness does not always come true – family life may turn out to be a living hell for many wives, particularly young wives, who are structurally in a vulnerable and dependent position in societies with patrilineal and patrilocal kinship systems (e.g., Jeffery and Jeffery, 1996; Nazneen, 1998; Säävälä, 2001; Aura, 2008; William et al., 2011; Steele et al., 1998; Rahman,1999, 2001; Khan, Rob, and Hossain, 2001; Koenig et al. 2003; Bates, Schuler, Islam and Islam, 2004). Domestic violence against women in the marital home by affines ruptures the myth of the happy family and the home as an intimate and protective space. It makes women's lives vulnerable, scares the children who witness it and devastates their upbringing, and dehumanizes the affines who perpetrate it.

Human rights have been brought into question within transnational South Asian feminism. The vocal, observable and highly eloquent women's movements have contextualized gender concerns and investigated the overarching power of patriarchy upon the lives of women. State interferences have been invoked through continual campaigns to relief women from the clutches of the state (Agnes, 2002; Mahmood, 2000; Basu, 1999, 2015; Chowdhury, 2011). Now, the fact is that the topic of violence against women has been studied in myriad ways during recent years in Bangladesh. This topic has come to prominence relatively in social science research (Akanda and Shamim, 1984; Bhuiyan, 1991; Jahan, 1994; Hadi, 2000, 2005; Ali, 2002; Naved et al., 2002, 2005; Bhuiya et al., 2003; Bates et al., 2004; BIDS, 2004; Ameen, 2005; World Health Organization, 2010; UNICEF, 2011; William et al., 2011).

Domestic violence is entangled in a complex web of institutionalized social relations that necessitates a structural and contextual understanding of the production of such violence in family, kinship and gender relations. I therefore identify factors that cause, perpetuate and mitigate domestic violence or give strength to women to struggle and raise their voices or take shelter in the law against the perpetrators of domestic violence. Throughout this book, I have addressed the following questions:

1 How is domestic violence against women socio-culturally legitimated in Bangladeshi society?
2 How do women cope with violence or threats of violence against them? What kinds of agency do women have as victims of domestic violence?
3 How do women's changing economic roles affect the practice and legitimacy of domestic violence against them?
4 Does the public or legal arena provide opportunities for women to find justice and fight against domestic violence?

Research on domestic violence against women in Bangladesh

Today, domestic violence against women is understood to be a critical problem—one that occurs along many dimensions, takes many forms and arises under a range of different conditions. Violence against women has received growing attention and hence a number of studies have been carried out in Bangladesh, which found a high prevalence of victimization and domestic violence among women in Bangladesh.

Bates et al. (2004) completed a survey, in-depth interviews and small group discussions with married women in six Bangladeshi villages to explore the types and severity of domestic violence against them. They surveyed 1,200 women and found out that 67 percent had experienced domestic violence at some point in their marital lives and 35 percent had experienced it in the past years. They concluded that in rural Bangladesh, women's social and economic circumstances may influence their risk of domestic violence in complex and contradictory ways and those women who earned an income of any significance had increased odds for experiencing violence.

Naved and Persson (2005), using data from a population based survey of 2,702 women of reproductive age and 28 in-depth interviews of abused women, explored factors which are associated with domestic violence in urban and rural Bangladesh. According to this study, in both rural and urban areas, dowries or other demands in marriage make women's lives vulnerable to domestic violence. They found evidence of the intergenerational transmission[7] of violence in Bangladesh, a phenomenon well documented in other countries (Hampton et al., 1993). In brief, about 19 percent of urban women and 16 percent of rural women reported experiencing physical abuse in the 12 months prior to the survey. The study also reported that a lack of spousal communication and a lower age of women are related to domestic violence.

Ameen's (2005) intention was to explore the factors leading to wife abuse and whether the legal systems of Bangladesh tackle it adequately. As a lawyer, she emphasizes the legal rights of Bangladeshi women against wife abuse. Her study finds that women from all socio-economic backgrounds faced domestic violence, but the younger age groups (between 18–25 years) are more prone to become victims of domestic violence than other age groups. Ameen contends that uneducated or less educated women are humiliated and assaulted by their husbands and other in-laws more often than educated women. She also shows that early marriage raises the probability of unhappiness and consequent abuse in married life. Ameen states that an extended family household structure, maintenance problems, dowry demands and polygamy are the main reasons of domestic violence.

It is a common belief among some researchers (Schuler and Hashemi, 1994; Khandker and Latif, 1995) that if the disadvantaged women in Bangladesh become economically empowered through micro-credit involvement, they will face less discrimination and violent behavior in their families. However, some studies bring up the fact that micro-credit borrowers face more violent behavior from their husbands than non-borrower women. For example, Rahman (1999) in his ethnographic study found that 70 percent ($n=120$) of the women claimed that micro-credit involvement had increased domestic violence toward them. Chowdhury and Bhuiya (2001) studied data from 2,038 currently married women aged 15–55 years and reported a higher level of physical violence among micro-credit borrowers than among non-borrowers. This shows that the interaction between women's economic activity and domestic violence is less straightforward than would be expected, and it is in need of further scholarly attention.

Ahmed's (2005) study used a sub-set of data from a cross-sectional survey undertaken by BRAC-ICDDR, B in the villages of Matlab, Bangladesh. This study covered 422 currently married women, aged 15–49 years, from BRAC (a micro-credit organization) member households and 1,622 women from poor non-BRAC households. The study confirmed that 17.5 percent of women had experienced spousal violence and the proportion of victims was greater among micro-credit borrowers.

Bhuiya, Sharmin and Hanifi (2003) carried out a study on the nature of domestic violence against women in rural Bangladesh. Nineteen key informants were interviewed in order to collect data on domestic violence against women. Each key informant provided information about their ten closest neighboring ever-married women covering a total of 190 women. A significant number of women (50.5 percent) were battered by their husbands and 2.1 percent by other in-laws. It was found that those husbands who were less than 30 years old beat their wives more than middle-aged husbands. Women who borrowed from micro-credit organizations also had higher odds of being beaten by their husbands than non-borrowers.

Koenig et al. (2003) examined the determinants of domestic violence in two rural areas of Bangladesh. Basically, the researchers identified the specific contextual and normative factors that influence women's risk of becoming victims of violence. Through the Sample Registration System, the project collected data from 8,000 households and found that the effects of women's status on experiencing violence were highly context specific. Indicators of women's status at the individual level were membership in a savings and credit group and an autonomy score based on women's responses to five questions about their mobility, familial decisions making power and control of resources. It is evident that verbal abuse represents a very common experience among wives (79 percent) and 42 percent of women have sometimes experienced physical violence. Threats of divorce by the husbands were also reported by 18 percent of the female respondents. They found that in a culturally more conservative area women had a significantly elevated risk of violence, while in a less culturally conservative area women had a lower risk of violence.

In 2007, Wahed and Bhuiya carried out a study using secondary data sources on violence against women in Bangladesh. The common causes for domestic violence found in the study were questioning their husband's activities, failure to perform household work and care for the children, economic problems, refusal to give a dowry, the young age of a woman and lack of spousal communication. They also pointed out that a significant number of abused women remained silent about their experiences. They were afraid to break their silence because of the high acceptance of domestic violence within society, the fear of repercussions and of tarnishing their family honor and their own reputation, the fear of jeopardizing their children's and their own future, and due to the lack of an alternative place to stay.

In 2011, William et al., using data from the Urban Health Survey, a population based survey of 9,122 currently married women aged between 15 and 49, found that the prevalence of reported past-year physical spousal violence is higher in slums (35 percent) than in non-slums (20 percent). Slapping/arm-twisting and pushing/shaking/throwing something at the women are the most commonly reported acts of physical abuse. About every other slum woman believed that husbands should beat their wives under various circumstances, in contrast to 36 percent of non-slum women. Their results show that physical spousal abuse is a common event in slums and non-slums of urban Bangladesh. They argued that instant and long-term domestic violence against women is a critical social and public health concern.

Most of the previous studies on domestic violence against women in Bangladesh by and large are based on analysis of register and survey data or secondary sources. The quantitative approach usually involves large data sets that enable generalizations. However, there is reason to believe that such surveys do not reveal the whole picture: women may feel uncomfortable relating their experiences to interviewers, perhaps because of the lack of sensitive question wording and the lack of special training for interviewers. Survey methodology rarely gives the respondents and the interviewers' sufficient time and opportunity to build rapport and trust. Moreover, domestic violence is a multifaceted problem, and in Bangladeshi society, it is considered a private matter so in-depth research is very important to explore the inner causes that sustain, produce and reproduce domestic violence against women.

Throughout the book, I have constantly stressed the importance of context in explaining the emergence and persistence of domestic violence. In delineating the "context-specific explanation" (Dobash and Dobash, 1998), I present several cases and description for understanding of the particular context(s) in which violence occurs against young wives, narratives of violence and the formation of the identities of victims and perpetrators to allow readers to share violent experiences and causes, because these narratives fit categories in collective representations. In other words, collective representations of violence outline personal accounts of violence and collectively shared categories are used for structuring experiences of violence. I also depict an intensive study of a relatively kin-based society and reflect on the complex and intersecting net of specific and changing cultural beliefs and practices associated with the making of a woman and wife. Through an ethnographic portrait, this book encounters family law, domestic violence against women, and changing mediation practices in a non-governmental counseling center. The most important data used in this study is qualitative, and my approach is descriptive. The location of the study is Sylhet district, situated in the north-eastern region in Bangladesh. This book does not only give a description of the vulnerability of women to domestic violence in Bangladesh, but it also aims to understand the perceptions of women concerning domestic violence and their struggle against it in everyday lives. This book delves into the social, cultural and religious construction of gender relations and the factors associated with domestic violence against women in Bangladeshi society.

Gender relations, domestic violence and practice

Gender is seen as a cultural construction of sex roles, a definition of "masculine" and "feminine" and of the prerogatives of male and female, which produces inequality (Kimmel and Aronson, 2000). The meanings of gender vary from one society to another and within any one culture over time and over life courses. In some cultures, women are considered to be decisive and competitive, and others regard women as naturally passive, helpless and dependent. According to Kimmel and Aronson (2000), it is a culturally and historically bound function of power relations and the social organization of inequality between men and women, among different groups of women and men within any particular culture at any particular time.

8 *Introduction*

Feminists share a commitment to the centrality of gender, and they debate how to study it (Peterson, 2005, p. 499). Feminist anthropologists have introduced a strong gender dimension to kinship and marriage studies, best demonstrated in the work of Rubin (1996). Rubin (1996) traces the processes of the kinship system as not merely exchanging women but exchanging sexual access, genealogical statuses, lineage names and ancestors, rights and people – men, women and children – in solid systems of social relationships. She points out that not only are kinship and marriage always part of the total social systems and tied into economic and political arrangements, but also a political economy of sex.

Lerner (1986) showed that the exchange of women and the establishment of control over their sexuality preceded the emergence of private property, and this stage of transition resulted in women being reified; women's reproductive capacity was recognized as a resource and became the property of particular kin groups. Lerner, however, argues that it is not women who are reified but their reproductive capacity. She also argues that these developments enable the transition from horticultural to agricultural societies as control over women's reproductive capacity has an advantage with regard to the appropriation of surpluses over systems based on the complementarity between the sexes. While history as a transition/transformation of different modes of production proceeded to unfold, and would certainly have transformed the lives of women in a variety of ways, there was a certain basis upon which later developments were, in a manner of speaking, pre-scripted. Women might be more or less in the production sphere, provide labor in different ways, participate in different degrees in various spheres of activity, contribute to the creation of culture and seek to negotiate the circumstances of their lives, but their greater subjection to norms of sexual governance has remained a fairly constant feature through various kinds of transition in history – a kind of patriarchal despotism or a patriarchal equilibrium.

Gender is an ever-changing fluid collection of meanings and behaviors (Kimmel and Aronson, 2000, p. 3). To some scholars (Scott, 1988, p. 42; Kabeer, 2001), the essence of the definition rests on a vital connection between two propositions: one that gender is a constitutive element of social relationships based on apparent differences between the sexes, and two that gender is a leading way of signifying relationships of power. As a primary institution, the family is the first place where the reproduction of gender originates and where children are socialized into taking it for granted. Socialization theory (Stockard and Johnson, 1980; Walum-Richardson, 1981) complements institutional analyses by exploring the social learning experiences that shape people in general but particularly young children for the separate roles and institutional spheres of maleness and femaleness. Institutional explanations of gender differences often lay great stress on women's distinctive functions in bearing and caring for infants. This responsibility for mothering is seen as a major determinant of the broader sexual division of labor that links women in general to the functions of wife, mother and household worker to the private sphere of the home and family, and thus to a lifelong series of events and experiences very different from those of men. In this setting, women develop distinctive interpretations of achievement, distinctive interests and values, characteristic of and necessary skills for openness in relationships, "caring attention to others," and particular networks of support with the other women (wives, mothers, daughters, sisters, co-wives, etc.) who inhabit their separate sphere (Lengermann and Niebrugge-Brantley, 1992).

Feminist scholars (Ortner, 1974; Chodorow, 1978; Moghadam, 1990) argue that gender inequality is produced by marriage, kinship, parenthood and sexuality. They also use the term gender inequality to refer to "sexual division of labor" or "gendered division of labor" that highlights the asymmetrical arrangements within the household/family, community and society. In gender arrangements, men and women have differential access to political power, economic resources, and in the cultural and legal arenas. It also sketches out images of women that are fundamentally distinct from those of men. So gender relations may be seen as largely socially constructed and conserved over time and space. Moore (1991) notes: "[T]he relations of domination and subordination which are at the base of gender inequalities within the household cannot be explained as a simple outcome of economic inequalities ... gender relations are always involved with power" (pp. 8–9).

Male domination is reproduced not only by socializing women and men differently, but also by placing them in organizations and institutions in which specifically gendered norms and values predominate and by which both women and men are then evaluated and judged (Kimmel and Aronson, 2000, p. 5). In the discussion of gender, it is important to focus on the concept of patriarchy, which dominantly plays a significant role in gender relations in different societies. Patriarchy is not the unintended and secondary consequence of some other set of factors – be it biology or socialization or sex roles or the class system. It is a primary power structure sustained by strong and deliberate intention (Lengermann and Niebrugge-Brantley, 1992). Therborn (2004) states, "patriarchy refers to generational and to conjugal family relations or, more clearly, to generational and to gender relations" (p. 13). Patriarchy manifests the rule of the father and the rule of the husband. Through participation in patriarchy, men learn how to hold other human beings in contempt, to see them as nonhuman and to control them. Within patriarchy, men see and women learn what subordination looks like (Lengermann and Niebrugge-Brantley, 1992).

In addressing the question of gender relations and practice in rural Bangladesh a brief discussion of the practice theorists' perceptions of culture, structure and agency is needed. The objective of practice theory is to understand where the system comes from – how it is created and recreated – and how it may have altered in the past or be altered in the future (Ortner, 1994, p. 390). The specific aim of practice theory is to understand production and reproduction of power asymmetries in gender relations and people's activities in the social structure.

Bourdieu's work on *habitus* and *le sens pratique* has important implications for understanding gender identity and social structure. Bourdieu claims that large-scale social inequalities are set up, not at the level of direct institutional discrimination, but through the subtle inculcation power relations upon the bodies and dispositions of individuals (as cited in Jenkins, 2002, p. 75). In order to epitomize this idea, Bourdieu considers the case of Kabylia in Algeria, where he observed that men and women carried themselves in markedly different ways. There, women's bodies were oriented down in keeping with "[t]he female ideal of modesty and restraint" and men's bodies were oriented toward other men (Jenkins, 2002, p. 75). This process of corporeal inculcation is an instance of what Bourdieu calls *symbolic violence* or a form of domination which is "exercised upon a social agent with his or her complicity" (Bourdieu, 1992, p. 167 as cited in McNay, 1999, p. 99). The inclusion of the social into the corporeal is captured by Bourdieu's notion of *habitus* (McNay, 1999). Habitus are the "mental, or cognitive structures" through which people deal with the social world. People are endowed with a series of internalized schemes through which they perceive, understand, appreciate and evaluate the social world. It is through such schemes that people both produce their practices and perceive and evaluate them. Dialectically, habitus are "the product of the internalization of the structures" of the social world (Bourdieu, 1989, p. 18). They reflect objective divisions in the class structure, such as age groups, genders and social classes. A habitus is acquired as a result of long-term occupation of a position within the social world. Thus, habitus varies depending on the nature of one's position in that world; not everyone has the same habitus. However, those who occupy the same position within the social world tend to have similar habitus. The habitus allows people to make sense out of the social world, but the existence of a multitude of habitus means that the social world and its structures do not impose themselves uniformly on all actors (Ritzer, 1992, p. 578).

Bourdieu pinpoints *habitus* within the bounded structure between self and society, looking at the structure as an embodied state operating through schemes of perception, thought and action and which "functions as an immense symbolic machine" (Bourdieu, 2001, p. 9) endorsing masculine domination. Bourdieu shows how "masculine domination imagines a natural, self-evident status through its inscription in the objective structure of the social world," which is then embodied and reproduced in the *habitus* of individuals (as cited in McNay, 1999, p. 99). According to Bourdieu, masculine and feminine is the principal classification and social division. At any given time, for a given society, some decisions would fall in the domain of what Bourdieu (2002 [1977], pp. 167–170) calls "doxa" – that which is practiced as a self-evident and natural part of the social order, "which goes without saying and therefore is unquestioned, the tradition is silent, not least about itself as a tradition." In Bourdieu's (2002 [1977]) schema, change takes place "when the dominated have the material and symbolic means to reject the definition of the real that is imposed on them through logical structures reproducing the social structures (i.e. the state of the power of relations)..." (pp. 167–170).

Like Bourdieu, Giddens (1979, 1984) first developed an original version of practice theory in the 1970s, but he arrived there via a very different route. Where Bourdieu prided himself in grounding his theories in empirical research, Giddens is more concerned with the history of philosophy and social theory than with sociological data (Eriksen and Nielsen, 2001, p. 129). Despite it being argued that individuals are also products of structures, Giddens (1979) associates agency with power and autonomy, in contrast to powerlessness as dependency. Gidden's (1984) structuration theory provides an innovative framework for analysis of gender as a social structure with his emphasis on the recursive relationship between social structure and individuals. That is, social structures shape individuals, but at the same time, individuals shape the social structure. So, human agency and social structure are not two distinct concepts or constructs, but are two means of understanding social action. He envisages what he refers to as the "duality of structure," recognizing that on one side individuals undertake social action and interaction and employ their knowledgeable activities in various situations. But simultaneously, they create and follow the rules, use resources and social relationships that are produced and reproduced in social interaction. Structuration involves studying the ways in which social systems are produced and reproduced in social interactions (Giddens, 1984, pp. 25–26). So social structures exhibit a dual role in that they are "both the medium and the outcome of the practices they recursively organize" (Giddens, 1984, p. 25).

Ortner (1984) pulled together this range of loosely interrelated work under the rubric of practice theory. The practice theorists endorse the notion that people are not merely the products of culture; they are also the producers, neither absolutely free nor wholly dependent on social forces (Tenhunen, 1997). Ortner (1989) argues for:

> an active notion of structure, but her focus is more on actors' motivations. If actors do not pursue individual profit, what do they strive for? ... structure is a concept of structural contradictions-conflicting discourses and patterns of practice ... an actor being loosely structured, which gives an actor a multiplicity of motives.
>
> (As cited in Fruzzetti and Tenhunen, 2006, p. xvi)

Ortner (1989) concentrates on self-legitimatization, but she also considers other interests including manipulation of cultural schemas, challenging illegitimate authority and learning to improve life (ibid.).

In South Asian patriarchal social structures, patriarchy helps to subordinate women in gender relations, so that women's needs, work roles, capabilities in many ways are devalued vis-à-vis those of men (Jain and Chand, 1982; Mies, 1982; Batliwala, 1985; Jain and Banerjee, 1985). The society often practices seclusion, controls women's mobility and sexual freedom. The region's culture and society encourage male domination over females so women's oppression, discrimination and subordination to a large extent are embodied in everyday interaction. The concept of patriarchy as the rule of father and/or husband is not a sufficient concept to depict gendered power asymmetries in the South Asian context. Patriarchy is focused on the relations between women and men; it can also be produced between individuals of the same sex; for example, in the South Asian context, the relationship between mothers-in-law and daughters-in-law, and between sisters-in-law. From the relationship of these women, the whole gendered relationship of the household is determined (Agarwal, 1994). It has been revealed in numerous South Asian ethnographies that women's different life stages play a significant role in determining gender roles in the household, community and society (Säävälä, 2006; Kumar, 2006; Aura, 2006, Vatuk, 2006).

Studies depict that South Asian gender relations are maintained or changed through cooperation and conflict (Sen, 1990) or as a "contested image" (White, 1992, p. 12) in any given context, for example, the relationship between husband and wife, the mother-in-law and daughter-in-law in a family. But the gender relations between the two sexes – male and female – and between the individuals of the same sex are also interrelated to other social and cultural relations because they gain importance through them. The form and practice of gender ideologies can also differ between propertied and non-propertied households, between educated, less educated and illiterate men and women, between male to male and between female to female positioned in different social classes (Mohanty, 1991; Agarwal, 1994).

Gender roles and relationships are not concrete and fixed but are matters of controversy and debate. Women do not present as some essentially gendered, but their identity is worked out in society and is constantly under compromise and appraisal. Sharma (1985, p. 45) compares social science research to shining a torch around a darkened room: as one object is lit up, others are cast into shadow. The dominant discourse on women in Bangladesh means that the shadows thrown are not disorganized; they mirror a predominant set of values and interests (White, 1992, pp. 3–4, 144).

Like Sarah C White, in this study, I see gender as a "contested image" (Poovey, 1989), the content of which is not fixed but variable, continually being defined and redefined, shaped and reshaped, confront and stay away from confrontation by context and interest. The view of "contested image" is a very useful one in understanding discussions of women and gender in Bangladesh. I follow Ortner's (1996, pp. 7–17) practice theory as a "loop" for understanding the way in which subjects and practices are created, recreated and governed by "structures" and how women as subjects, and their actions in practice, reproduce and contest the "structures." Women are attached to particular social structures, but their lives and activities are not entirely governed by them. They are influenced by global as well as local forces beyond their control; however, by the same token, I show that they have their own ways of reconstructing their positions and making space and opportunities for themselves.

The legal framework of family relations

Several special laws have been enacted in Bangladesh in the last three decades to protect women from violence and discrimination and to establish their rights in the family and society. They are, in short, family laws, some parts of the criminal law, a suit for civil wrong and laws for matrimonial remedies. In its legal justice system, Bangladesh follows two sets of laws under the English Common

Law system. First, the general laws combine both criminal and civil laws and are applicable equally to all citizens regardless of their sex and religion. Second, there are sets of religious-based personal and family laws that follow the respective religions in matters of marriage, divorce, maintenance, child custody and inheritance.

Regarding the Muslim Family Laws, Bangladesh follows the Muslim Family Law Ordinance of 1961. Some subsequent reforms and modifications have been made to this law. The Muslim Marriage and Divorces (Registration) Act in 1974 made it mandatory to register all Muslim marriages. The Child Marriage Restraint (Amendment) Ordinance of 1984 increased the legal age of marriage for women from 16 to 18. In the general sense, what is meant by the law are those that are introduced by the state. But Hindu law, however, does not involve state statutes, but rather it is the enforceable part of the Hindu religion. After the emergence of an independent Bangladesh, the existing Hindu law is yet to be altered and is therefore archaic. No codification and reformation of traditional and customary laws have been made to give them a statutory form. As a result, the Hindu community is still governed by the traditional customary law. Marriage is a union which the Vedas regards as indissoluble. As long as the husband is alive, the wife is enjoined to regard him as her god, likewise the wife is declared to be half her husband's body, who shares with him equally the fruits of all his acts, good or bad.

Divorce can be validated in Bangladesh by Islam without the formal intervention of the courts. Muslim personal law allows for divorce when the vow of *ila* is taken by the husband, that is, the husband swears in the name of Allah not to mate with his wife for at least four months or an indefinite period of time. Further, a Muslim husband in Bangladesh can divorce his wife by simply pronouncing the word *talaq* (I divorce you) three times. Theoretically, the same proclamation can be made by the wife, known as *talaq-e-tawfeez*, but only if the husband delegates such power to the wife as part of the contract in the marriage deed. A wife may also initiate divorce, known as *khula*, or *mubara'at* only when there is agreement by both partners, but as part of this bargain, the wife has to return the *mahr* as settlement (Alamgir, 1977). When a *talaq* is given orally (by spoken words) or by a written document called a *talaknama*, to redress the discrepancies of local customs, the amended Muslim Marriage Act of 1982–1985 grants women the right to formally initiate divorce on the grounds of abuse, desertion and their husband's impotency at the time of marriage or later (Bhuiyan, 1985).

Divorce is not known to the general Hindu law, but married Hindu women have a right to separate residence and maintenance, the 1946 Act confers them some right in a few cases listed below: (1) If her husband is suffering from syphilis or leprosy and he was not infected by her, (2) If the husband behaves cruelly to her and the cruelty is such that there is a risk to her life, (3) If the husband deserts his wife without her consent, (4) If the husband remarries, (5) If the husband adopts a different religion, (6) Or any other legal ground. Though the Hindu Widow Remarriage Act 1856 has been passed, Hindu women did not get their right to remarriage again in Bangladesh (Firoze, 1996).

14 *Introduction*

In Bangladesh, following the Family Court Ordinance 1985, a wife can file a suit to obtain her dower and maintenance from her husband. A dower is a sum of money received by the wife from the husband as a consideration for the marriage. As per the provisions of Section 10 of the Muslim Family Laws Ordinance, 1961 where no details about the mode of payment of dowers are specified in the Nikanamah or marriage contracts, the entire amount of the dower is presumed to be payable on demand. A high dower is also fixed to prevent the husband from divorcing his wife capriciously. The amount of dower is usually divided into two parts, a prompt part, which is payable on demand, and a deferred part, which is payable on the dissolution of a marriage by death or divorce.

There are some special laws concerning violence against women have been passed by successive governments in independent Bangladesh. Almost in all cases so far, there were demands from women's groups, human rights activists, the media and society at large for passing such laws as if the enactment of new law would be the best answer against violence against women. In cases of domestic violence, a number of criminal laws may be relevant. These include the Dowry Prohibition Act of 1980, which was amended in 1982. Following this Act, dowries are prohibited in all forms, and practicing a dowry system is punishable by one to five years of imprisonment. According to the Act, a dowry refers to "the property and valuable security given or to be given as consideration for the marriage of the parties" (Bhuiyan, 1991).

The Cruelty to Women (Deterrent Punishment) Act of 1983 contained a provision that punishes a person with imprisonment for life or the death penalty for kidnapping, trafficking, abducting women, or causing death or attempting to cause death and rape. Along with the perception that the existing laws were not enough to deter violence against women, a new law was enacted in 1995: The Women and Child Repression (Special Provision) Act. This law broadened the crimes to be covered from the previous law, which included acid throwing and violence for dowry or dowry demand. Although this law provided provisions for tough punishments for violence against women including domestic violence, it did not mention what the role of the state would be to help victims of such violence. Also, the law did not prohibit the publication of pictures of the victims in the media. There were remedies compared to the earlier law in case the police delayed filing a charge sheet or if they raped victims in their custody. The latest and improved version of the law came into effect in 2000. The Suppression of Violence against Women and Children Act of 2000 superseded previous acts related to violence against women (Ali, 2002).

The most significant change in terms of the legal protection of women's interests in marriage took place in 1985 through the establishment of family courts by the Family Courts Ordinance. The family courts have jurisdiction over the dissolution of marriage, the restitution of conjugal rights, dower, maintenance, child custody and guardianship – as long as they can be treated as civil cases. If there are any criminal offenses involved in a case, then the case is sent to a criminal court. The family court is not entitled to consider other issues of family law, including inheritances (Monsoor, 1999). The family courts made legal systems available to many women who otherwise would not go to a regular court. However, women in Bangladesh, especially illiterate and less literate ones, are rarely aware of their legal rights. Furthermore, court procedures for family disputes, criminal suits against offenders and legal divorce and maintenance cases are expensive.

The fact is that in cases of criminal force or assault, the Penal Code provides a penal sanction. However, when this same offense is perpetrated by a husband or other in-laws against a wife it is not considered an offense in practice. When the assault is directed toward the wife, she is not advised or supported to prosecute the husband or other in-laws, rather she is advised and forced by both natal and affinal family members to seek mediation informally inside the family or to hide it as private issue for the honor of the family. For long-term domestic violence, the victim women may seek support from the ADR (Alternative Dispute Resolution), referring to a form of mediation (see Chapter 6). Moreover, women are reluctant to proceed under the criminal court because the evidence is hard to obtain as witnesses do not corroborate in domestic violence. Therefore, the general criminal law does not have a specific law for domestic violence against women. The only remedy available to them in case they are not willing to proceed to criminal charges is to seek a divorce under the Dissolution of Muslim Marriage Law of 1939. The civil law remedies include divorce and claims for a dower, maintenance and custody. Moreover, in cases of abuse, the wife can seek an injunction under the Civil Procedure Code, the Specific Relief Act or under the Family Court Ordinance, 1985 under Section 16a. However, these are ancillary to other proceedings. On the other hand, criminal proceedings include cases instituted for resorting to polygamy without prior permission and for demanding a dowry (Ameen, 2005).

But even now the law remains an important site of struggle for women in Bangladesh as it controls and constraints them in many ways. Smart's conceptualization of family law is important for understanding the Bangladeshi context. According to Smart (1982), the family is the most likely place where women face discrimination and oppression. Although the family law strengthens the benefits for women, women do not enjoy the fruits of these benefits. Because women are still economically and socially subordinate to men, the law also follows this notion of subordination. Moreover, patriarchal arrangements are supported by the law; this justifies the social and economic insecurity of women and designates women as the weaker sex. For example, in cases of domestic violence, the law is subject to uneven development in Bangladesh; it has benefited women to some extent, but there is still certain reluctance on the part of the law enforcers.

It is evident from the general and special laws for protecting women and establishing their rights that there is still much to be done to effectively deal with domestic violence against women. Still the non-enforceability, complexity and confusion regarding their interpretation and jurisdiction of these laws indicate their inability to deal with problems of domestic violence against women effectively. The criminal justice system should be modified and coordinated at all levels, otherwise, the imposition of severe penalties and the objectives of such imposition are bound to be frustrated. Without amending and consolidating existing legislation concerning violence against women, any promulgation of special legislation may not be able to meet this problem.

Outline of the book

This book comprises seven chapters. Chapter 1 covers the methodological aspects of the study. It delineates why certain methodology is used and the experiences and challenges as a native researcher in the field and the field research sites: the locality of the two slums and the counseling center. I also portray the detail causes of migration of the poor households to the slums and their coping strategies for earning their livelihoods, women's changing lifestyles in their quotidian lives and the changing socio-demographic structure in the slums.

Chapter 2 aims to focus on perceptions and experience of slum women on girlhood and marriage. This chapter starts by illustrating girlhood and then focuses on the socialization process that makes the perfect woman or the perfect wife. This chapter also explores the differences and similarities of slum women's perceptions on marriage and identity as "embodied culture"[F1] in Bangladeshi society.

Chapter 3 describes how migration, living in a new environment and urban lifestyle have changed some slum women's vision, pushed them to income-generating activities outside home, constructed their freedom and built alternative discourses of gender relations. This chapter also portrays working slum women's everyday struggles to construct and reconstruct their position to establish rights in their families, locality and society.

Chapter 4 describes why and how some slum women experience domestic violence. It also focuses on changing patterns of seeking help from domestic violence and changing the meaning of kinship in the urban setting. This chapter also presents slum women's views on divorce and different coping strategies and the struggle of some slum women against domestic violence.

Chapter 5 expands why and how married women face domestic violence by their husbands and other affines (mother-in-law, father-in-law, sisters-in-law and brothers-in-law) through some cases. The empirical data of this chapter as a touchstone portray different causes of domestic violence against women and their sufferings, and how at last they have placed this private matter in the public domain and come to seek formal legal support from a counseling center. I expand my analysis into examining why seeking informal help from their kin for domestic violence commonly fails. Why do the women come to a formal legal organization to seek help and what do they expect from this organization?

Chapter 6 describes how the counseling center BLAST tries to help women victims of domestic violence with the help of law and what the women victims get from the law. How this non-governmental legal organization modifies the traditional mediation (*shalish*) practices and has incorporated formal legal procedures in this system to give a voice to the abused women in the traditional patriarchal society in a quest for women's rights within the social and legal arena. It considers whether the women have benefited from the legal arena. Chapter 7 contains the concluding reflections of this study and contextualizes the findings.

Notes

1 Amartya Sen categorizes South Asian gender inequality in natality inequality, mortality inequality, basic facility inequality, special opportunity inequality, professional inequality, ownership inequality and household inequality (Sen, 2001). www.thehindu.com/fline/fl1822/1822 0040.htm.
2 www.A_Perspective_on_Gender_Inequalities_in_Bangladesh_UNICEF_Report_Oct_2011_Final_Rev.Pdf.
3 www.unicef.org/infobycountry/bangladesh.
4 Bangladesh Bureau of Statistics (BBS) summaries of the 2001 Population Census. www.bbs.gov.bd/dataindex/cens.us/municip.pdf.
5 National Institute of Population Research and Training, Bangladesh (NIPORT). www.phishare.org/files/7254_tr_o8_68.pdf.
6 Asian Development Bank.
7 The intergenerational transmission of violence means that children who have been physically abused or see family violence tend to grow up as abusive adults (Hampton et al. [eds.] 1993). So when a mother of a son or sons experience violence toward his/their mother by his/their father, some of them adopt this practice and later in their marital life, repeat this same behavior toward his/their wife or wives.

1 Approaching *basti* life and a counseling center in Sylhet

Research methods and the main sources of data

This section describes the research methods and data, explains how they were collected and analyzed and about the rationale of the choice of methods in this study. The most important data used in this research is qualitative, and my approach is descriptive. My aim in this chapter of this book is to provide an in-depth representation of family life and domestic violence perpetrated against young wives belong to lower socio-economic strata by their affines (husband, mother-in-law, father-in-law, sisters-in-laws and brothers-in-law) in Bangladeshi society. I have relied on a number of methods of data collection. For the in-depth study and in order to reach a certain extent of generalization, I have selected multiple sites as my study areas, what Miles and Huberman (1984) call cross-site analysis (they use the terms "site" and "case" interchangeably). According to Miles and Huberman (1984, p. 151), having multiple sites increases the scope of the study. By comparing sites or cases, one can establish the range of generality of a finding or explanation and, at the same time, pin down the conditions under which that finding will occur.

The fieldwork of this study is carried out in two *bastis* and in a non-governmental counseling center in Sylhet, Bangladesh. As my aim is to describe the everyday lives and domestic violence on lower socio-economic strata's women's life situations, I selected the two *bastis* to obtain in-depth information. In developing countries, populations have been rapidly shifted from rural to urban areas. These people are rapidly being absorbed into urban poor communities known as *bastis*. These urban poor communities often miss out on the benefits of urbanization – they lack most basic government services. Women in urban poor communities may be particularly affected, as they lack the safeguards of traditional kinship that are provided in rural communities (Patel and Burke, 2009). These women are more likely to become victims of violence. Of the various forms of violence against women, domestic violence in the marital home is most common and is a major contributor to poor physical and psychological health among women (Campbell, 2002; M. Ellsberg, Jansen, Heise, Watts and Garcia-Moreno, 2008). In the World Health Organization (WHO) Multi-country Study on Women's Health and Domestic Violence Against Women, the prevalence of domestic violence against young wives is lower in urban populations than in rural populations among the investigated countries (Bangladesh, Brazil, Peru, Thailand and the United Republic of Tanzania) (Garcia-Moreno, Jansen, Ellsberg, Heise and Watts, 2006). But several studies represent that marital violence among poor populations in urban cities of developing countries, especially in South Asia, is remarkable. For example, more than 17 percent of the 751 women had experienced physical violence in the previous year in a slum in Calcutta, India (Pandey, Dutt and Banerjee, 2009). The prevalence of physical violence was up to 80 percent among 400 married women in a low socio-economic area in Karachi, Pakistan (Ali and Bustamante-Gavino, 2007). The Urban Health Survey, a population-based survey of 9,122 currently married women aged between 15 and 49, found that the prevalence of reported past-year physical spousal violence is higher in slums (35 percent) than in non-slums (20 percent) in Bangladesh. Various factors were also reported as risk factors of marital violence in urban poor population, such as low income, limited education, insufficient diet, overcrowding, unsanitary conditions, alienation, social instability and insecurity, physiological and psychological stress (Aekplakorn and Kongsakon, 2007; Ali and Bustamante-Gavino, 2007). However, the number of these studies is very limited and none have simultaneously investigated the situation of marital violence among urban poor populations. In this respect, I consider domestic violence against young wives by affines among women in the *bastis* is necessary to be studied to seek new ideas and information to stimulate new thinking about this violence.

Mediation or "dispute" resolution is nostalgically associated with grounding in local culture, as opposed to the forceful homogeneity of law. Depicted as being "away from judge – (and judgment) oriented accounts" and focused on actors' "circumstances, goals, strategies and actions" (Comaroff and Roberts, 1981, p. 14), it offers the possibility to more fruitfully engage with why people acted in a certain way and to construct a satisfying resolution (Basu, 2015). I selected the non-governmental counseling center, which provides free legal support to victim women from both urban and rural areas. I attain the mediations (*salish*) to find out what strategies these women use to claim and obtain resources, protection, security and voice? How are rights and obligations of victim women understood and negotiated? In this study, the two sites help me greatly to understand the lives of women from lower socio-economic strata, the causes of domestic violence, their coping strategies and struggle against it. I collected data for the study from May 2010 to January 2011 and again revisited the research areas during January to March, 2016.

Mostly practical reasons drive me to select the research sites. I have been working as a faculty member at Shahjalal University of Science and Technology in Sylhet since 1999, and I know the area and local language. The *bastis* are near the university. A woman from the *basti* was working as a cook in the bachelor's dormitory of the university teachers and she ended up being one of my main research informants. In finding a counseling center to study the influence of formal legal procedures on domestic violence, some lawyers in the Sylhet Judge

Court with whom I am acquainted suggested to select the counseling center inside the court arena. Sylhet has turned out to be a very fruitful area for studying the changing pattern of gender relations in the family, community and society because of intensive internal and international migration, urbanization and modernization that can be observed there.

From the two *bastis*, I collected data through focus group discussions, participant observation, case studies and a survey. First, I conducted a household survey of 69 households – 42 households in Pirer Tila and 27 in Durga Bari *basti* – to map the socio-economic condition of the slum dwellers. I covered the following topics in the survey: the wife's age, the number of children in the family, the wife's occupation, her husband's occupation, the wife's and husband's education levels, and their places of origin.

After surveying the *bastis*, I conducted focus group discussions. I considered focus group interviews to be a fruitful method, because they help to investigate generally accepted and shared views in a social group (Denzin, 1986; Frey and Fontana, 1993; Madriz, 1997). Using focus groups also enables the researcher to gather large amounts of information in a limited period of time. It emphasizes the collective, rather than the individual, fosters a free flow of ideas, encouraging the members of the group to speak up. More importantly, focus group discussions are an appropriate method to collect data from a lower socio-economic class of women (Jarrett, 1993; Madriz, 1998). My main purpose in using focus group interviews in the *bastis* was to learn about slum women's perceptions and experiences on girlhood, gender relations, marriage practices, their views on the reasons for domestic violence and their coping strategies against domestic violence. In this regard, as a native researcher, I considered focus group interviews as a fruitful method that enabled the women of the *bastis* to unveil specific, sensitive and little-researched aspects of domestic violence.

The women were divided into focus groups according to age because age plays a significant role in the power relations among women and younger women would not have felt at ease to talk in front of women of the older generation. As far as I could tell, the groups managed to create an atmosphere of trust in which the women felt free to express themselves. I divided the women into two groups, one for those between 16 and 30 years of age and the other for those above 30 years. Because very few women had any formal education for more than a few years of primary school, dividing them according to their educational attainments was not necessary.

The women formed focus groups of five or six participants. With the exception of a few women, most participants spoke spontaneously and usually with ease. I avoided using larger groups because of the difficulties of handling the discussion and keeping the conversation around the topic of research, as the women were quite vocal and even argumentative at times. Moreover, larger groups make it more difficult for all the participants to have their opinions heard. I acted as the facilitator in all the focus groups. My being a native of Bangladesh contributed to participants' feeling that the facilitator was familiar with their way of thinking and understood their expressions and feelings. The sessions typically lasted for two hours or more. The focus group interviews were tape-recorded with the permission of the participants and later transcribed by me.

I had developed an unstructured interview guide to be used in the groups, although in many focus groups, the participants changed between topics spontaneously, which added a wealth of information to my research. The quotations that are used in this study are chosen from a variety of age groups and sessions. To express the exact feelings and perceptions some quotations have been minimally edited. The ages of the focus group participants are indicated in parentheses after each major quote. To include the differences between religious groups and beliefs, participant's religion is also mentioned in some quotes. To add proper meaning and clarification of expressions, Bengali words, sentences and phrases are also used in some quotations.

The transcribed focus group discussions were analyzed by the contents analysis method, separating statements to the various topics chosen as the central themes to be reported in the study. Five major recording units (the smallest body of content in which the appearance of a reference[1] is noted) have been used in the content analysis research: words or terms, themes, characters, paragraphs and items (Nachmias and Nachmias, 1997, p. 327). In summarizing content analysis, the material is paraphrased, which means that less relevant passages and paraphrases with the same meanings are skipped and similar paraphrases are bundled and summarized. This is a combination of reducing the material by skipping statements included in a generalization while summarizing the material on a higher level of abstraction (Flick, 2006, p. 313).

Case studies have become one of the most common ways to do qualitative inquiry. They are seen as appropriate when the purpose is to "understand some special people, particular problem or unique situation in great depth" (Patton, 1990, p. 54) and where one can identify cases rich in information – rich in that a great deal can be learned from a few exemplars of the phenomenon in question (Patton, 1990). The aim of case studies is the precise description or reconstruction of a case. The case that is taken as a sample would be significant for the research question (Flick, 2006). In the slums, I conducted 12 case studies on particular women's life histories and purposively selected eight of those cases to be represented here. I believe that these case studies will lead to a better understanding of the lives of women from the lower socio-economic strata. Data on the particular cases are derived from individual interviews, participant observation and informal discussions with a number of people and are reconstructed on the basis of these different sources of data.

Social scientists are observers both of human activities and of the physical settings (Angrosino and Mays de Perez, 2000, p. 673). In the fieldwork in slums, I observed the physical settings and human life situations, which are prevalent throughout the area. I described the slum sites as part of obtaining a prominent understanding of the women's lives after migration to different environmental settings and socio-economic situations in the urban milieu.

In the counseling center, I conducted case studies of 20 women, and from the cases, I selected seven case studies to be presented in this dissertation. In the women's cases, I have collected data on the victim women's place of birth, education level, occupation, socio-economic condition of the natal family, story of marriage, relationship with their husbands and other in-laws in their affinal homes, and causes and incidence of domestic violence. I chose these cases to describe both what is common and what is particular about the cases, as each case has important atypical features, happenings, relationships and situations. These women were interviewed in private because of the victims' feelings of shame and vulnerability. I did not use a tape recorder while I was talking with the victim women because the phenomenon of domestic violence is a very sensitive issue. Renzetti and Lee (1993, p. 6) stated that research on domestic violence is a sensitive research because it intrudes into the private lives or deeply personal experiences of the research participants. I talked with the women about their problem and the conversations were lengthy, lasting three hours or more. I made copious notes and transcribed the notes in more detail after the meetings with the women were over.

With the help of the counseling center's advocates, I attended and observed ten mediations (*shalish*) to learn about the position of women in the legal arena. I have sketched out four of those mediations cases in this study. Documentation of the mediations is based on copious notes taken during the situation and transcribing them in more detail afterwards in a field diary. Participant observation in the mediations has enabled me to transcend my own pre-conceived vision of domestic violence against women in Bangladeshi society and the legal support for women.

After participating in the mediations, I also conducted expert interviews. Flick (2006, p. 165) discusses expert interviews as a specific form of semi-structured interviews. Here, the expert interviews – as the participants were experts for a certain field of activity – are integrated into the study not as a single case but as representing a group's point of view. I interviewed six advocates and made notes during the interviews. These interviews were not recorded in order to create a feeling of trust and informality for the advocates. My aim was to learn the changes between the roles of expert and private person by bringing out personal opinions concerning gender roles in the mediations.

In value-free social science, codes of ethics are the conventional format for moral principles. As I was dealing with the sensitive issue of domestic violence in the marital life of women who are in a vulnerable position, I informed the study participant about the nature and consequences of the research prior to the data collection. Participation of the subjects in the research was voluntary.[2] Protection of respondent's identities by securing anonymity is essential according to the codes of research ethics (Christians, 2000, p. 139). For reasons of confidentiality, all the personal data of the respondents that could lead to identification was concealed or transformed and pseudonyms are used instead of the real names of the research sites. The counseling center is inevitably identifiable as there are so few such centers in Sylhet, but the cases depicted are not recognizable. Ensuring the accuracy of data is a fundamental principle in social science research. In this study, I maintained the accuracy of data internally and externally by keeping the subject's feelings and expressions, sometimes with their own voices. The translations from Bengali to English are done by the author and the originals are securely stored.

The experience of fieldwork as a native researcher

I would like to begin by discussing briefly how as a native researcher I got access to the different fields. I may add here that although I am a native to the area, it was not so easy for me to create an appearance of acceptance to the women of slums and counseling center in a class-divided, hierarchical society. I am a Bangladeshi, but as a fieldworker at the first impression to the research subjects I am an unwelcome intruder or an outsider. My middle-class background with a university education and faculty position in a public university creates a hindrance in the field. In the field, I had to go through various queries and questions regarding my work from time to time. The respondents considered me as a worker of a non-governmental organization or a high official of a government organization and some of them tried initially to ask me favors in cash and kind. When I explained my position as a researcher and that I am going to write a book about their lives, some of them negotiated with me to receive some personal benefit. In the *bastis*, some women's male family members asked me several times to arrange a petty job for them in the university (Srinivas, 1979).

As the study deals with the sensitive issue of gender relations and domestic violence against women by their affines, in this context, this proved difficult for me without conscious, personal rapport building. I had to search for an informant to get access for me into the *bastis*. I met with Morzina, a 28-year-old Muslim woman from "Pirer Tila" *basti* who was working in the bachelor's dormitory of university teachers. I went to the dormitory and gossiped with her for a few days while she was doing domestic chores for the male teachers. I talked with her about her personal life and about the other slum women. Without any hesitation, she shared with me many events of her personal life. To my pleasant surprise, I found her very cooperative and friendly, and I felt that my entrance to the slum in her company was the right tactic. With the help of Morzina, I was able to have an in-depth view into the life of women in the Pirer Tila *basti*: their experiences, perceptions, feelings, hopes and dreams. She helped a lot in creating trust, friendship and acceptance with the women in oral and embodied interaction with them. Morzina was a good source of information, views and gossip about slum life because her family has been living in the same slum for more than ten years. Moreover, her husband and she had a friendly relationship with the *basti* dwellers and were accepted by them because of their good manners. Constantly, she enriched my ideas related to slum women's lives.

One evening, Morzina took me to the Pirer Tila *basti*. She told me that I might meet most of the slum women in the evening because in the day time some women go to work outside home. That evening, Morzina's husband, Momin, was present in the house. He greeted me and assured me of his help in my fieldwork. He informed me that he had talked about my work with some men in the slum and there would not be any problem arising from my talking to the women. I felt pleased that the males accepted my presence in the slum.

When Morzina first introduced me to the *basti* women they were curious about my personal life. To satisfy their interest, I tried to present myself as a simple Bangladeshi woman. I touched their hands, cuddled their children and walked with them in the surroundings of the slum. They liked my simplicity and offered me a chair to sit in a small open place of the *basti* used for gossiping. It was then the rainy season and suddenly after half an hour the sun was hidden by a thick gray cloud. As it seemed that the rain would start very soon, Morzina asked me to sit inside her house. I went inside her house that was just a shanty room and sat on a cheap wooden bed. After a short while the rain stopped. Again, some women and their children came inside the room, those who did not find a place stayed outside and some children peeped through a small window, and the small room got crowded. Some women joked about me and about my presence in the slum. I then felt that I was a creature in my own native land. I became very sweaty that day, and my hair became wet with sweat. It seemed that I just came out from the bathroom after having a shower. Noticing my condition, some women started to laugh. Morzina's elder daughter came with a hand fan to fan me. I felt embarrassed about my condition and took the fan from the girl's hand and asked her not to fan me. The girl smiled at me and gave me the fan. I offered Morzina some money and asked her to bring some snacks and tea for the women and children. Morzina arranged snacks and tea with great pleasure. She made two big kettles of tea for the women and served them. She also gave me a cup of hot tea to share with them. We started to gossip together, and this occasion gave me the opportunity to get involved with the slum women and create a cordial rapport.

For two weeks, I spent every day from morning to dusk in the Pirer Tila *basti* either with Morzina or other women and arranged several tea parties. By staying in the slum, I got the chance to observe the everyday life of the *basti* in detail. I gained confidence through this involvement and started my research work.

There is another small *basti* of 27 households adjacent to the Pirer Tila *basti*. In this slum, all dwellers are low-caste Hindus and belong to the economically poor class. I was determined to know about the Hindu women because I did not find any Hindu women in Pirer Tila, but I felt that my religion and background might create an obstacle to obtaining access to the *basti* for my fieldwork. Again, I requested Morzina to introduce me to some Hindu women, but she replied that she only knew some women because she had to pass that *basti* two times a day when she went to work. But she did not enter inside their houses because they might not like a Muslim entering their houses. I lost hope of getting into the *basti* with Morzina and started to search for another form of introduction.

But within a week I got an unexpected opportunity to make contact with two Hindu women of "Durga Bari" *basti* with the help of Morzina. One morning, she took me to the *basti* and introduced me to Probasini and Purnalakshmi, who had been living in that *basti* for more than seven years. I told them that I was going to write a book about Bangladeshi women's lives, but it seemed that they did not understand anything about it or did not think it was important to them. To make it easy, I told them that I was also regularly visiting the Pirer Tila *basti* and talking with the women about their lives. I assured them that I would not create any problem in their family lives and they would only have to talk to me when I came to their houses (a discussion on this issue when studying a vulnerable group, as cited in Liamputtong, 2007). Then suddenly the ice was broken and they became less reserved toward me, they took me to their *basti* and introduced me to other slum women. That day, I stayed for some hours in the slum and gossiped with the women and children.

Probasini and Purnalakshmi told me to visit the *basti* in the evening and promised to help me to learn about their lives. I also preferred the evenings because most of the men were working away from home then or meeting in the tea stalls. Luckily, that day I met Probasini's husband, Profulla, a cobbler who was self-employed with a workplace in a street corner of a market place. He came to the house from the market place for some leather and shoe color. I greeted him and talked about my work. When he heard about my project, he became astonished because he didn't have any idea about research and nobody came to know about their lives. But he assured me nobody would create any obstacle in my work. When I was talking with Profulla, some women were standing near to us and listening to our conversation. After Profulla's departure, the effect of the conversation was evident and I felt that the women had become a bit more relaxed in my presence.

Then in addition to visiting the Pirer Tila *basti*, I also started to visit the Durga Bari *basti*. Day-by-day, I became more accepted among the Hindu women by sharing food, gossiping and taking photographs. This involvement provided me with an opportunity and context to learn about their life experiences and views.

When doing fieldwork at the counseling center, I had to follow more formal, institutional procedures. After my first visit, the coordinator told me to write an application about my fieldwork, which he had to send in the main branch of the counseling center in Dhaka. I submitted an application to him and attached a request letter from the coordinator of the Department of Social Research (Unit-Sociology), University of Helsinki, Finland, for permission. After getting the application, he gave me permission to start my work from the next day. As a public university faculty member, I was respected and obtained easy access to the counseling center. I got the opportunity to gather the life stories of victimized women and to participate in some mediation (*shalish*) during my field work. The counseling center operates its activities in four rooms: one is the coordinator's office, one is for an accountant and advocates, one is for a female assistant and the biggest room is the client serving room, where a male peon also sits. The coordinator asked me to select a room to carry out my work. I preferred to sit in the client serving room because the affected women and their family members sit in that room and mediation sessions take place in that room. The room is very simple with some wooden and plastic chairs and two big tables. In one corner, there is a table with a revolving chair for the coordinator or the advocates. There are some shelves and a cabinet full of victim women's files. In another corner is the peon's table and on a small shelf, there are tea cups, a thermos flask and a big aluminum kettle.

In the counseling center, my presence and queries to the victim women about their lives did not meet with any obstacles. Almost all women and their natal family members shared their problems with me without any hesitation. But I felt embarrassed if the victim women and their parents started to cry. In those situations, the environment became uncomfortable and for some time we all remained silent. In the counseling center, I gave emphasis to the contextual character of violence. I found notions of violence are persistently shaped and reshaped. Although marital violence is repeatedly represented as fixed and unchangeable, it is reproduced in certain social, cultural and discursive contexts.

The court arena is a crowded place where different types of people come for various reasons. So in all the visits to the counseling center, I had to be cautious about my every step in the court arena. Because I am a woman, all the people were curious about the fact I was there and what I was working on. Although there are many female advocates in the court, I was a subject of curiosity because of my different occupation and career. In the first phase of my fieldwork, my day was generally divided into two parts. This proved to be a good arrangement for the study. For some weeks, after having observed the slums' morning life, I started to go to the counseling center in the morning and slums in the evening. Generally, I stayed in the counseling center from 9 a.m. to 1 p.m. I followed this timetable because the clients visit the center during this time and the advocates arrange the mediations then. In the evening, I went to the slums because most of the women were in their houses, and they preferred to talk in the evenings. There are obvious differences between the two arenas of the fieldwork.

The field research sites

Bangladesh is a low-lying riverine country located in South Asia. It emerged as an independent and sovereign country on the world map on December 16, 1971, following its victory in the War of Liberation waged against Pakistan. Bangladesh is bordered by India to the east, north and west and shares a short border with Myanmar (Burma) in the southeast. Bangladesh has a population of about 146.6 million. It is one of the largest deltas of the world with a total area of 147,570 sq. km., and the country is crisscrossed with rivers and canals. The country contains the confluence of the Ganges (Padma), Brahmaputra (Jamuna), and Meghna Rivers and their tributaries, which empty into the Bay of Bengal. Of the total area of Bangladesh, agricultural land makes up 65 percent of its geographic surface, forest lands account for almost 17 percent, while urban areas are 8 percent of the area. Water and other land use account for the remaining 10 percent. The economy of Bangladesh is agrarian, although the share of agriculture to GDP has been decreasing over the last few years. Yet it dominates the economy and most of the rural labor force works in it. The country consists of six divisions and 64 districts[3] (BBS[4] 2010).

Bangladesh is a small country, but the population density in Bangladesh is one of the highest in the world (about 920 persons per sq. km.). Although over the last three decades or so, the rate of population growth in Bangladesh has declined from 3.0 to 1.4 percent per year, every year two million more people are added to the total of 146.6 million. Moreover, the per capita GDP is extremely low at less than US$2,000 per year (2005), which is considerably lower when compared with even some Asian countries: US$3,486 in India, US$6,572 in China and US$8,843 in Malaysia. High population pressure and severe environmental constraints put pressure on land resources (both agricultural and homestead land) every year. The acquisition of land for government development projects, housing, industrial and commercial establishments, river banks erosion, tidal bore, deforestation and drought are exacerbating the situation day-by-day (Jansen, 1987; Hossain et al., 2003; Afsar, 2000, 2003; Hossain and Bayes, 2009).

According to the 1996 Agricultural Census, the number of rural households was 17.8 million and of those 10 percent did not own any land at all, about a third did not own any cultivable land and approximately 60 percent possessed less than 0.2 ha. The growth of this landless group is noticeable all over rural Bangladesh. In rural Bangladesh, those people who own no agricultural land or very little are not capable of managing their livelihood in the rural structure. Nowadays in this context, rural-urban migration is the most prevalent form of migration in Bangladesh. Rural life in Bangladesh is changing fast. Now people are far less dependent on agriculture and related work. Because of poverty and a lack of better jobs, people are increasingly dependent on non-farm livelihoods and moving from their original places of birth. Internal migration researchers in Bangladesh (Jansen, 1987; Hossain et al., 2003; Afsar, 2000, 2003; Hossain and Bayes, 2009) have found that the migrants prefer to stay in the neighboring villages in the primary stages of their migration and then move to towns. The migrants at the initial stage of migration earn their livelihood from wage employment and various non-farm activities, and after acclimatization to city life, they search for informal sector jobs, such as rickshaw pulling, hawking, day labor, construction work, etc. (ibid.).

After Bangladesh's independence in 1971, internal migration throughout the country accounts for about two-thirds of urban growth. The skilled, semi-skilled and unskilled workers from rural to urban areas scattered from village to villages and small towns, district to district and from division to division (Jansen, 1987; Hossain et al., 2003; Afsar, 2000, 2003; Hossain and Bayes, 2009). Internal migration is now considered to be a notable factor contributing to the ubiquitous phenomenon of urban surplus labor, which is a serious contributor to urban unemployment problems (Todaro, 1993, pp. 263–286; Afsar, 2003). In the urban areas, most migrants are young males, but the scenario has changed significantly by the migration of young female laborers to work in the ready-made garment factories of Dhaka city and other metropolitan areas (Afsar, 2003).

The flow of the rural-urban migration process can be characterized in two ways. First, from the previous studies (Van Schendel, 1981; Jansen, 1987; Kuhn,

2000), it has been revealed that the families with insecure or unguarded rural livelihoods migrate from their own villages/birth places (*desher bari*) to supplement and enhance their incomes with rural economic activities. In this context, the individual migrants avoid the vicious debt cycle by using their incomes to keep their agricultural activities alive and protect their households against economic crises (Afsar, 1994; Kuhn, 1999). Second, families with deteriorated rural livelihoods migrate with their family members to search for new sources of income and security (Roy et al., 1992; Momin, 1992).

Most of the cases of family migration seen in Bangladesh are closely linked with some complex circumstances: in-secured financial condition, relative poverty and deprivation, lack of employment and income opportunities, environmental crises, land disputes, vendettas and the loss of agricultural land due to poverty, indebtedness and the shortcomings of the inheritance system. Because of rural-urban migration, Bangladesh has experienced one of the highest urban population growth rates (around 7 percent) in the last three decades compared to a national population growth rate of about 1.5 percent per year (Islam, 1996). Moreover, thousands of people live in over-crowded slums or public spaces in almost every major urban center of Bangladesh (Anam et al., 1997). The existing estimation of the BBS' "Sample Vital Registration System" shows that lifetime internal migration has increased significantly. The proportion of lifetime migrants doubled (from 3.4 percent to 7.4 percent) between 1974 and 1982 and reached 10.2 percent in 1991 (BBS, 2000). It also shows that around 46 percent of the total migration has occurred from rural to rural areas in the 1990s and approximately 40 percent of male migrants have moved from rural to urban areas and 33.4 percent from urban to urban areas. By the same token, more than 56 percent of women have migrated from rural to rural areas and 28 percent from rural to urban areas (Afsar, 2003).

My area of research is in the Sylhet Division situated in the northeast of the country and with its hills and basins it constitutes a distinctive region in Bangladesh. It is made up of four districts: Sylhet, Sunamganj, Moulvibazar and Hobiganj with a total population of 7.94 million according to the 2001 census. It is flanked by the Indian states of the Meghalaya in the north, Assam in the east, Tripura in the south and the Bangladesh districts of Netrokona, Kishoreganj and Brahmanbaria in the west. Geographically, it is a land with a vast flood plain along with numerous *haors* or extensive marshes. The plain is broken only in the northern and eastern sides by clusters of little hillocks called *tillas* and intersected by a network of rivers. The climate of Sylhet is tropical monsoon with predominantly hot and humid summers having high rainfall from June to September and a relatively cold winter (Alam et al., 1999, p. 73; Karim, 1999, pp. 134–135).

Sylhet is known as an area of saints, with the mausoleum of the great saints Hazrat Shah Jalal and Hazrat Shah Paran. Hazrat Shah Jalal and his 360 companions played a significant role in the spread of Islam to the entire area during the fourteenth century. Remittance is the key element of the economic growth of the city and also the region. The money is mainly sent by emigrants of Sylhet living abroad, particularly in the United Kingdom, Middle East and America. The people of Sylhet are known as Sylheti, and the Sylheti language is the main language spoken in the city as well as throughout the division and is considered to be a dialect of Bengali (Ahmed and Motahar, 1999, pp. LVII–LXVIII).

In Sylhet, since the beginning of the twentieth century, the trend of migration (both internal and out migration) has increased, and now in Sylhet city, there are several slums. People from neighboring districts came in large numbers.[5] Sylhet experienced an increase in population after 1911. This increase occurred due to a large flow of immigration throughout the whole of the British period, because at that time, a large number of laborers for the tea gardens came to Sylhet. Besides, a large number of landless people of the thanas of Barhata, Atpara, Mohonganj, Durgapur, Itna and Ostogram of Mymensingh district migrated to Sylhet. Actually, this shows that in the past, because of the easy availability of cultivable land and river, ponds and canals a large number of families migrated to Sylhet and earned their livelihoods doing agricultural work, the fishing business, cane work/handicraft, the coal business, the stone business and working in the tea gardens as laborers (Rahman, 1999). The flow of migration, which started during the decades after 1911, has continued to the present. Like other urban areas of Bangladesh, as a divisional city, Sylhet is facing urban population pressure and the slum population has greatly increased in Sylhet city. These people live in deplorable situations with a lack of basic facilities, such as safe water, sanitation, health services, a clean and hygienic environment, poor housing, an electric supply, etc. In Sylhet, there are 756 slums and the mean slum population size is 129 and the establishment of new slum settlements is continuously increasing.

The *bastis*

The aim of this section is to highlight the changing life of migrated women in the *basti* and the environment and livelihood of the locality. I have sought answers to the following questions: Who comes to live in urban *bastis*? What are their educational backgrounds, socio-economic conditions, lifestyles and skill levels?

The BBS (1999) defines a *basti* as: "A cluster of compact settlements of five or more households that generally grow very unsystematically and haphazardly in an unhealthy condition and atmosphere on government and private vacant land." Here, I want to use Bengali term *basti* to highlight the real meaning and scenario of *basti* according to the Bangladeshi social structure.

Bastis are the result of the "over-urbanization" in Bangladesh after independence. This over-urbanization is seen here as overcrowding in the sense of densely populated, precarious urban slums with high concentrations of poverty and vulnerability. Here the term "over-urbanization" is derived from the experience in Latin America, which was seen there in the 1950s. After over-urbanization in Bangladesh, there was a rapid expansion of large urban centers without having absorbing capacity that incorporated immigrant laborer with insufficient skills in the modern sector. This absorption generated large, under-employed and unemployed urban populations who depended upon the informal sector. They suffered from insecurity of income and lack of services and spread slums in urban areas (Afsar, 2000; Uddin, 2003; Rashid, 2007; Hossain, 2007).

I have selected two *bastis* for my field research; one is "Pirer Tila" and the other is adjacent to it is known as "Durga Bari." Both *bastis* are near the Shahjalal University of Science and Technology in Sylhet city.

Pirer Tila *basti*

The Pirer Tila *basti* is situated on high land. As this *basti* is near a *mazar* (shrine) of a local *pir* (saint) so it is here named Pirer Tila. There are 42 houses in the Pirer Tila, which were built on the inherited land by one of the sons of the late local *pir*. This *basti* is a linear settlement consisting of two rows of houses overlooking a narrow unpaved lane and also some scattered congested settlements. Almost all the families that I visited live in small single-roomed dwellings. Inside the room, each resident performs all the activities such as eating, cooking, sleeping and leading their daily domestic lives. Here, some rooms are "semi-pucca" (South Asian expression meaning a semi-permanent construction) and some are tin-shed rooms made of split-bamboo-frame walls and corrugated iron sheet, and the floors are made of mud. The tin-shed rooms have no windows or ventilation system and dangling doors are made of scrap wood. The semi-pucca rooms are constructed of brick and mortar, and a thin cement layer covers the packed earth floors. Some rooms have small windows and some have integrated ventilation passage through the walls. The lanes among the rooms are so congested that from one room to other room there is only four-fifths of an arm's span space between the rows. Domestic life may be visible from one room to other room, so the *basti* dwellers hang dull dirty curtains to conceal their private lives. The rent for a semi-pucca room or tin-shed bamboo frame wall room ranges from TK600 to 1,000 (US$9–US$14) per month.

Open drains run down through the middle of each lane so that people tend to walk down them with their legs straddling the drains. There is no open space in front of each room, so people sit on the sill of the doors and perform different domestic activities, such as chopping scrap wood, sewing old torn clothes, suckling babies, etc. There is no permanent drainage or sewage systems, so on rainy days, the entire slum is flooded with filthy water and excrement. Most of the time, filthy water seeps into the rooms, and because of this, the packed earth floors become muddy and it is hard to walk on them. In these circumstances, people make stepping-stones from bricks inside the rooms and lead their regular domestic lives with difficulty. Generally, on average, five to six persons reside in each of the shanty rooms. They manage their daily cooking arrangements by separating a corner with a plastic cover along with split-bamboo matting (*basher bera*) and some cover a small place near the door with a brick wall. They cook in *matir chula* (a stove made of mud) with firewood, dried leaves and branches of trees, abandoned paper, left over wood-pulp (*kather gura*), and they rarely use kerosene stoves for cooking food because kerosene is very expensive. But sometimes in the rainy season when the floor gets wet it becomes impossible to cook outside in the *matir chula*, and they have to use a kerosene stove for cooking. Most of the time, women and children are busy gathering broken thin dried branches of trees and dried leaves for fuel from the nearby university area (320 acres) and its surroundings.

In Bangladesh, almost all of the *bastis* have poor access to water and sanitation services (Uddin, 2003; Afsar, 2000; Rashid, 2007; Hossain, 2007). In Pirer Tila, there are no private water supplies and toilet facilities. There are only two tube-wells in the open space of the slum, and sometimes one of the tube-wells does not work. In the early morning, women and children from a long queue collect drinking water from the tube-wells. There is no specified time in a day for each household to use these tube-wells, so it always creates problems, and sometimes, some household members quarrel over water. On the first day, I visited the *basti* and saw two women quarreling near a tube-well late in the morning for water collection. Water collection is a typical event in the Pirer Tila *basti*. Sometimes, daily life proceeds with negotiation and cooperation and sometimes with brawling and hostility. While I was standing near the tube-well, my informant Morzina smiled at me and told me that if I spent some hours in the *basti* I would see quarrel and altercation for water collection frequently.

There are only two toilets for the 42 households in Pirer Tila. These are located in the corner of a row of households. The condition of the toilets is indescribable. One toilet has no roof and other toilet's roof collapsed during torrential rains. It is very hard to imagine how nearly 200 residents can manage with these two toilets, but as they have no alternative, they have to use these. There are also two open toilets at the back of the scattered households of the slum, where people have made a bamboo platform and surrounded them with pieces of quitted gunny bags for their personal privacy. Most of the time, men and children urinate in open spaces, but it is really hard for the women to use open spaces, and usually female residents queue for the toilets or they use the open toilets.

The *basti* has legal electrical connections and all the households have at least one electric bulb. Some tin-shade split-bamboo-frame households have no electric fans, but most of the semi-pucca households have electric fans. Three houses of the 42 houses have black and white televisions and only two houses have color televisions, but almost all the houses have a radio. There are six adult women who have mobile phones, but I don't know about the men. The women who do not own mobile phones go to the nearby grocery shop to use a public phone. Occasionally, some houses hire a video cassette recorder to watch *Dallywood* movies (Bangladeshi cinema) and *Bollywood* movies (Hindi Cinema). Then some neighbors gather together to watch the movies, basically women, adolescent girls and children sitting together and young and adult males sitting in a group.

The extent of poverty and vulnerability of the houses is very visible from the *basti's* daily life and environment. During focus group discussions and in-depth interviews with married women, I often saw rats, cockroaches and hens running across the floor. People of the *basti* usually have a few cheap possessions, one or two *chouki* (cheap wooden beds), *almira* (a cupboard), *alna* (a cloth hanger), *mora* (a bamboo made stool), a table, chairs, kitchen utensils, some glass crockery, etc. The rooms are dirty as every activity of daily life is performed in one room. The bed sheets and pillow covers are dirty and have a filthy odor, and are old and torn, while some beds have no bed sheets. Most of the households have small children and they urinate on the bed and floor and sometimes defecate. These rooms have no ventilation system so a fetid smell always exists in the rooms.

In the first day of my focus group discussions, I had planned to arrange a gathering in a small open space. But as it is the rainy season and raining off and on, my informant Morzina and other women suggested arranging the discussions inside. Morzina asked me to use her room for the discussion. This house is like other households of the *basti*; it possesses the same quality and standards. She lives in a semi-pucca room and has made cooking arrangement outside the room by hanging a plastic curtain along a split-bamboo fence. That day, her mother-in-law was cooking the lunch, she prepared a very small quantity (500 gram) of cabbage leaf *vaji* (fry) for seven persons together with coarse rice. Together with her husband, four children and mother-in-law, Morzina lives in the same room. There are two *choukis* (cheap wooden beds); she sleeps in one with her husband and their two-year-old youngest daughter and her mother-in-law sleeps with the three older children in the other bed. There is no comfort and privacy, but there is no option for Morzina and her family.

Households are considered as poor and vulnerable when the members have scarcity of resources to fulfill their basic needs and services to achieve a reasonable minimum level of welfare (Rakodi, 2002). Almost all of the migrants face severe problems and discomfort in their low-cost housing, physical insecurity, insufficient delivery of basic services and subsequent health problems. But poor housing conditions and an unhealthy environment affect women more than men because comparatively they spend more of their daily lives within their homes and settlement. Like the women, small children also bear the major brunt of the environment impact (Uddin, 2003; Hanchett et al., 2003; Pryer et al., 2005; Rashid, 2007; Hossain, 2007; Rana, 2009). Due to dirty environment and poor nutrition, skin infections are rampant among the slum residents throughout the year. When I was doing field work at that time, I noticed some women and most of the children had scabies (*khujli*) and boils (*fora*) on their bodies and heads. Some were also suffering from fly-borne and respiratory illnesses.

Durga Bari *basti*

The land of Durga Bari *basti* is owned by a Hindu man. The land owner does not live near the *basti*. Every month he comes to collect the rent for the houses. There are 27 houses, where low-caste Hindu families reside. According to the caste system, they belong to the *Sudras*, an untouchable category, and are cobblers by profession. Their occupation is considered by society as lowly and polluted work. Although most of the men are not engaged in their caste occupation, some are engaged as casual, unskilled day laborers doing such tasks as earth work (locally called "*mati kata sromic*") or a rickshaw pulling. This *basti* is adjacent to the Pirer Tila *basti*. Though there are no conflicts between the Hindu and the Muslim families, there is an invisible dividing line between the two poor slums.

The Durga Bari *basti* is in a poorer condition than Pirer Tila *basti*. The surrounding environment is dirty. Hens run across the yard and frequently enter the houses. On the roof of the houses, women spread small fish to dry in the sun. In the middle of the yard, dwellers hang their wet clothes on lines. There is very small space for free movement. The shanty dwellings are constructed in L-shape and they have a tin-shed and split-bamboo-frame walls. There is a long narrow veranda in front of the houses. In the middle of the open space there is only one tube-well and two toilets for 27 families. In each of the households there are approximately four to five inhabitants. They do not cook in front of their households. In the summer and winter seasons, they cook in a shared *matir chula* (a stove made of mud) under a shed made of straw. As there are 27 families, sometimes women quarrel with each other about their turns to use the *chula*, and most of the time the quarrels start before lunch. Probasini, a woman living in the slum, told me about an incidence of the everyday life of the slum. She described that one day she became very angry with Indumoti, who was frying *sutki* (dry fish) on a low fire and it was taking a long time. It was near lunchtime. Probasini got scared because she had not yet cooked lunch for her husband. Every lunch time her husband came to have lunch at home and then took an afternoon nap. According to Probasini, if she could not prepare lunch for her husband, he would scold her. So she scolded Indumoti with some abusive names. After that they started to quarrel. This type of altercation is a regular scenario in the *basti*.

Like Pirer Tila *basti*, there is also a legal electricity connection in the Durga Bari *basti* and in every house there is only one bulb. Most of the houses have a radio, but only two houses have black and white television sets. Everybody has some cheap wooden furniture, kitchen utensils and women have small gold jewelry, which they received from their natal family as wedding presents. In every house there are photographs and idols of Hindu deities. At dusk each day, all the woman worship (*puja*) for the well-being of their families and a long life for their husbands. There are several China rose (*joba*) trees in one corner of the *basti*, the women and children pluck flowers from the trees and offer them as sacrifices along with sugar and rice grains to the idols. "We don't have enough money to arrange fruits in plates of worship (*puja-er thala*), we try to make the goddess happy with our small capacity," said Anjali, a woman from the Durga Bari *basti*, while I was observing her worship (*puja*) from outside her house. Dusk at the Durga Bari *basti* comes with rituals of worship to the goddess. After passing the sleepy night, the dwellers again engage in everyday life.

Migration from village to *basti*: the causes left behind

The aim of this section is to describe and analyze in detail the causes of migration of the poor households from their birth places (*deser bari*) to the new environmental settings and their coping strategies for earning their livelihoods, and women's changing lifestyles and vision in the new settings. In this regard, I asked some general questions to the *basti* women: Why did the *basti* dweller women migrate from their native place (*deser bari*) and affinal village (*shosur bari*)? How do their families earn their livelihoods? How have they settled in the new environment?

Some residents of the *basti* have lived for many years in the *basti*. The twin imperatives of marriage at a young age and a family burden when they were quite young appeared to compel many of them to leave their birth places to earn their livelihoods. All the *basti* dwellers in my study have the experience of spatial mobility, and they have some positive and negative memories related to their native place (*desher bari*) and affinal village. Most of the women had moved with their husbands after marriage, so they had experienced spatial mobility twice: First, after marriage they left their natal family and native place, and second, for various reasons they were forced to leave their affinal villages. This displacement had forced them to adapt to the new environment and it had changed their lifestyles. The *basti* dwellers, both women and men, who came to live in the city, have experienced displacement in order to earn a meager livelihood. Their sense of place has to be renegotiated in significant ways. The *basti* women and men imagine and negotiate their identities and rights in their daily life, not only by reference to their birth place, kinship connections and experiences in the previous residence, but equally in relation to the new surroundings and experiences.

After learning about the migration history of the *basti* women, I found that most of them come from the greater Sylhet division – Sunamganj, Habiganj, Derai – and most of them had migrated approximately eight to 10 years ago. Those who had migrated from the nearby divisional districts – Mymensingh, Netrokona, Brahmanbaria, Jessore, Rangpur – tended to have been living in Sylhet for a longer time, approximately 10 to 20 years. My ethnographic data suggests that people are forced to migrate for various reasons, but the causes have to be understood in relation to culture, context, gender and lifestyles. I have noted some specific causes for migration including poverty and the lack of work in their native villages (*desh-er bari*), river erosion and loss of land, land disputes in the native village, illegal acquisitions and eviction from the land, and being abandoned by the family for love marriages.

Nasimon Begum (35 years) narrated her prolonged sufferings of poverty and vulnerability, which was caused by river erosion. She explained that her homestead land was near to river and within two years the river eroded 55 percent of her homestead land. Moreover, every rainy season the family faced the unbearable hardship of devastating floods. With one handicapped child and four kids, the family was in a pathetic condition. In the rainy season, there was water everywhere and the family lived on a wooden platform in a hut. The family used to make the platform with a *chouki* (cheap wooden bed) and Nasimon cooked using a kerosene stove once a day. All seven of the family members sometimes lay down and sometimes sat on that platform. The floor of the hut was flooded and outside the hut there was a small boat. Sometimes poisonous snakes came inside the room. All night Nasimon could not close her eyes for fear for her kids, she was certain that they would fall into the water and die or a poisonous snake may bite them. The family had no food and no money during the rainy season. Finally, the couple decided to migrate to Sylhet city with a great hope to stay alive.

Like Nasimon, most of the climate migrants of Bangladesh face the same problem. From the analysis of the impact of the 1988 flood migration the increased rate of family migration (a married man and woman from the same household moving together) is visible in Matlab of Chandpur district, which lies in the floodplain of the Meghna River System, and is in the recurrent flooding areas of coastal and other districts such as Faridpur, Barisal, Noakhali and Sirajganj. Migration has most typically occurred not among the landed households who experience land damage and loss, but among the previously landless households who can't manage to remake their loss of property and fail to cope with labor market disruption, price fluctuations and increased competition for formal and informal credit (Kuhn, 2000). Actually, internal migration is an essential option in the life of people from turbulent environmental zones, where floods, cyclones and hot season droughts mean that "belonging" can never be guaranteed. Samaddar (1999) writing about Bangladesh says that the country is "an insecure environment, inhabited by insecure families, and these vulnerable families are continuously dreaming about escaping poverty and natural calamities ... has made Bangladesh a land of fast footed people" (pp. 83–87).

Land disputes are an integral part of rural society and sometimes disputes over land become a powerful weapon or alternative mechanism to secure the inheritance of land or means to capture land (Arens and Beurden, 1977; Jansen, 1987). In one case, a man who had four marriages, set up a will for special plots to his "favorite" sons and divided his land unequally. His orphaned son, whose mother died just after his birth, suffered the consequences of being left without inheritance. To describe this situation, his wife Hosneara (27 years) said that they came from Kishorganj. For seven years, they have been living in this *basti*. Her husband and she had migrated here with great sorrow. Her husband had homestead land in his native village (*deser bari*), but the couple couldn't live there because of a land dispute. They have a strong desire to go back to Kishorganj.

Actually, as most of the actors of rural to urban migration are related to agricultural work and village life, their identities always bear a "fluid notion of identity" because for them rural areas are not only a place of living and their importance lies not merely in the land itself, but also in the livelihood, the culture and the identity provided by the village. Their decision to migrate is always guided by the hope and desire to rebuild the family's linkage, support and honor through agricultural tradition and resources (Khun, 2003). Here in Hosneara's narrative, it is also clear through that she has a strong urge to go back and establish her future family life in her village surroundings. So after living for seven years in the slum, she does not feel any attachment to the urban surroundings and is always searching for her past identity.

Thanks to women's education, their access to mobility outside the private, domestic domain, media exposure and availability of information, some women are breaking the established social norms and values in society and embracing new ideas and values in their lives. Nowadays, love marriages are not exceptional in Bangladeshi society, although they are still undesirable and punishable in many families and in the larger society. In Bangladesh, an arranged marriage is still the idealized form of marital alliance (Jahan, 1994; Ameen, 2005), and most of the time, this kind of arranged alliance takes place among the high born lineages for their self-interest (Jahangir, 1979; Jansen, 1987). Although there exists no caste system among the Muslims in Bangladesh, traditionally, Muslims make a distinction between the ashraf (high born/respectful) and the ajlaf (low born/disrespected, synonymous to the Bengal atraf), which is a common division of status (Arefeen, 1982; Jansen, 1987). In this connection, Fahima (17 years) is a good example from Pirer Tila, she stated:

> I am from a poor family so my in-laws did not accept me as their son's wife. After marriage they forced their son to take a divorce. As their son did not listen to them, they did not allow us to enter the house. I have a stepmother, who also did not give us any place to live. So with the help of my cousin's brother we are now living in this slum and my husband is now running a petty business with him.

For Fahima, there are two problems, first, the marriage is a love marriage and second, she is from a low born/disrespected family. Besides, she was raised in the stepmother's family, so nobody will plead for them.

People from the lower socio-economic classes after migration have no other alternatives for residence than *bastis* or low-rent housing. The studies of internal migration clearly indicate that the diversified job opportunities in the different cities and metropolitan areas "pulled" the rural poor and helpless peoples from their birthplaces (Skeldon, 1997; Afsar, 1999, 2000). The study revealed that both push and pull factors have caused migration of the *basti* dwellers. Most of the migrants were agricultural laborers or somehow related to agricultural-based work. After the loss of land, rural agricultural laborers have no options for remaining in agriculture and have to rush to search for work in the urban area. In this connection, Morzina (28 years) said that after marriage the couple lived in the village for two years and her husband tried a lot to succeed running a petty business, but every time he faced losses. Moreover, he had a very small plot of joint cultivable land with his other relatives, so for him his own village was not a good place for earning a livelihood. So he decided to migrate and decided to make Sylhet city their new home. Now they have been living in *bidesh* (outside of home country, local term to denote a living place instead of villages of origin) for ten years. Morzina's mother also now lives in this *basti*. They now have no link with the village home and have good relationships with some families in the *basti* and consider some of them as their *attiyas* (kin).

Various studies have revealed that almost all of the rural poor migrants generally settle in *bastis*, and prior to migration they contact their kin, friends and neighbors in order to secure a job with the help of their social networks (Afsar, 1999). Arjan de Haan's (2003) study on Calcutta's labor migration also shows the same pattern. Some *basti* women in my study expressed their frustrated feelings after migration. They found it difficult to survive in this big city and felt helpless, shelter-less, and unemployed. At first, they missed their lost village life, village home, relatives and neighbors. But after they became settled in the urban slum and found a source of income, they realized how awkward their positions had been in their villages. Now according to them, there is no way to return to their villages and they are rootless. They have nothing in the village and they only should try to stay alive in the city.

The concept of *attiya* is relative; relationships can also be established and produced through a code of conduct outside the boundaries of marriage and blood connectedness. The sharing of living space in a locality, living in the same village, working together in the informal or formal sectors, performing religious rituals in a specific mosque, temple or church and so on, all can establish the *attiya* relationship if one so desires (Fruzzetti, 2006, p. 4; Kumar, 2006, p. 78). This fictive kinship generates a code of conduct according to seniority and gender and grounds the depth of relationship according to reciprocity and help. In the *bastis*, women address one another by kinship terms, *apa* (sister), *buji/didi* (elder sister), *bhabhi/bou-di* (sister-in-law), *khala/mashi* (maternal aunt), *chachi* (paternal aunt) and so on, or by first names plus kin titles and by their elder children's names, for example, Moyner *maa* (addressing Morzina by her elder daughter's name) and occasionally by the addressee's husband's name, for example, Momin-er *bou* (addressing Morzina by her husband's name, Momin).

Like Morzina's family, most of the family migrants have few opportunities and incentives to maintain a social or economic presence in the rural area because their pre-existing social and economic belongings and resources offer them very little to return to their village. Those family members who remain in the rural area most of the time bear insignificant linkage of reciprocity, except for the parents. Ashura, a 32-year-old woman from Pirer Tila *basti* said, "In the *basti* if anybody is searching for work their neighbors also look for work for them so they can survive. If anybody wants to borrow a small amount of money, they will get it from their neighbors." This happens for poverty, insecurity and time constraint. So, family migrants try to build urban support linkages or alternative exchange networks to substitute for the loss of the rural support of their kin, friends and neighbors with urban friends or neighbors. Actually, spatial isolation is also responsible for this social isolation, which puts the family migrants in a new environment, ecology and economy and isolates them from rural settings and lifestyles.

The data reveals that many family migrants do not have special bonds with the village people and some express anger and irritation with village society for their failure to offer loans, help or temporary dwellings. Khun's (2003) findings also concur with the present study's findings. The women stated that in the village from October to April (Kartic to Chaitra-Bengali calendar months), there is no work, so seven months of the year are crucial for them. They cannot survive in the village if they stay there. Women do not find any work in the village in the public domain, and even if a woman catches fish for household consumption from nearby ponds or ditches, people call her a bad and shameless woman. But in the *basti*, it is possible for women to earn money outside home. Sometimes in the village even men do not find work for survival. Actually, they have migrated to the city because of poverty and a lack of work.

In the Pirer Tila *basti*, only a few households are extended families (six out of 69). In-laws do not live in most of the households because there is not enough space for them. Moreover, because of poverty, a lack of cultivable land ownership and a scarcity of work, the extended households, which are more typical of rural Bangladesh, have broken into nuclear domestic units in the urban slum setting.

In Pirer Tila *basti*, the women who work outside the home are engaged in poorly paid jobs in the informal sector, which mostly fall into one of these job categories: as a domestic helper, cooking in the bachelor's dormitory (*mess*), as a casual day laborer ("earth worker" – *mati kata sromic*) or in small-scale businesses. When I asked about their work preferences, more than half of the women preferred to work as a part-time domestic helper in the nearby households. Working as a domestic helper is considered women's work as it does not challenge the patriarchal social structure. Some women prefer to work as casual day laborers because sometimes it is hard to find work as a domestic helper and some mistresses behave very rudely to them. Some women expressed their interest in small business, but they did not have any capital for investment. I asked them whether they know about micro-credit lending, and some of the women had some idea about it. But regular payment of installments is very hard for the women because there is no guarantee of profits in small businesses. Moreover, they fear their husbands because they think their husbands would not help them to pay the installments and force them to take the money from their business for useless consumption (*baje khoroch*). In the slum women's account, women want to work for the happiness of the family, so if there is a danger of micro-credit lending, it is better not to get involved with them.

In my research *bastis*, women considered that nowadays women's participation in economic activities for earning livelihood outside the domestic domain is very important because only with their husbands' incomes it is totally impossible to meet their household expenses. Even though the women earn a meager income, they contribute significantly to their families' livelihood maintenance and nourishment. In the *bastis*, most of the working-class women contribute their full income to their households' maintenance. When I asked them about their working-class husbands and young sons' incomes and expenditures, most of the women strongly claimed that their husbands and sons work outside for the family. According to the women, males work to earn money for the family, but most of the males often spend a significant amount of their earnings for their personal consumption. They spend a good amount of money on snacks and meals outside the home, smoke cigarettes (*biri*), enjoy betel leaves (*paan*) and nuts (*supari*), and watch Bengali movies. But women do not eat outside their homes without their children. Some women, who work as domestic workers get food from their work places, but they never eat the food without their children; they bring the food home for the other family members (including their husbands). According to them, to a mother, her children are pieces of her liver (*kolijer tukra*) and apples of her eye (*chocker moni*), so it is impossible for her to eat without them. Sometimes in hard times, women do not swallow even a small bite of bread; rather, they fast and serve the food to their children and husband. It is only out of love, there is no self-interest; it is thought to be a characteristic of a Bangladeshi mother (*Banglar maa*).

In this section, I have focused on causes of migration and how the poor families try to survive in the urban *bastis*. In Chapter 3, a further discussion about slum women's working outside their homes will clarify the feelings of *basti* women about income-generating activities, security and independence.

The changing socio-demographic structure in the *bastis*

The food consumption pattern is very poor among the *basti* dwellers. They mostly eat rice in the morning as breakfast, and a few of them eat handmade bread. For lunch and dinner, they eat rice mainly with pulses, dry fish curry, potato curry and cheap vegetables. Most dwellers prefer to eat fish, but it is too costly for them, so they can only rarely buy fish. When they buy fish, they usually buy small poor quality types from local fish markets or from fish vendors at low prices. Most of them only eat any meat or poultry, fruit, milk and milk products once a month or sometimes not for a few months. Most of the young women were weak and they were seemed to be older than they actually were.

From different types of work, the *basti* women earn different wages. Domestic work brings monthly Taka 1,500–3,000, for cooking in the *mess* (bachelor's dormitory) a cook earns Taka 1,800–4,000, and daily wages for earth work range between Taka 150–200, but it is seasonal work and extremely hard, destroying one's bones and muscles. According to the respondents, very few women can save small amounts of money. For those who save, it is extremely hard since they have to spend Taka 800–1,000 for rent and food expenses per month. The husbands of those women who go to work regularly and take care of the family can save small amounts of money. But these small savings are also commonly spent on treatment when a member of the family falls ill.

In Pirer Tila, most of the men work as rickshaw pullers, day laborers, three-wheeler drivers or in petty businesses. Most of them are illiterate, only a very few of them have education between the first and eighth grade. Many of the women are illiterate or can only write their names. A very few women have between first and fifth grade school education.

Of the 27 women of Durga Bari *basti*, 13 women are housewives, seven women work as a casual day laborers, five women are running small business along with their husbands such as making local color for shoes, pickle (*aachar*) and *naru* (round shaped local sweets) and two women cook at the Hindu student mess. Almost all of the housewives say that they wish to work outside the home, but they have not been able to find any suitable work to do and some of their husbands do not like them to do "earth work" (*mati kata*). Some women wish to work as domestic helpers, but they could not find such work.

Almost all the men are cobblers, six men are rickshaw pullers, five men also work as seasonal daily laborers along with their caste occupation of being cobblers, and some men help their wives in small businesses. Only two men were jobless because of sickness or reasons of ill health.

In the Durga Bari *basti*, 12 women were illiterate or could only write their name, 10 women had education levels between grades one to three and five women were educated up to the fifth grade. Among the men, 10 were illiterate or

Table 1.1 Occupations of the married women and men in the two *bastis*

Women's occupation	Pirer Tila	Durga Bari
Housewife	13	13
Earth worker/day laborer	10	7
Domestic worker	10	0
Cook	6	2
Small business	5	5
Grocer	1	0
Total	45	27

Men's occupation	Pirer Tila	Durga Bari
Electrician	1	0
Bus driver	1	0
Rickshaw puller	8	6
Three-wheeler driver	7	0
Earth worker/day laborer	8	5
Vegetable vendor	8	0
Small business	3	0
Cobbler	0	14
Jobless	3	2
Total	45	27

Source: Present Study.

could only write their names, 13 were educated a level between grades one to three and four were educated up to class five. In the study area, not a single child was in secondary education. Most of them dropped out from school as they did not like studying, and they entered the job market to support the family and became victims of poverty and early marriage. In reality, these children are deprived of parental care, education, opportunity and other needs of life and ultimately they also succumb to the vicious circle of low-paid work and are trapped in the darkness of poverty. UNICEF's (2011) data about secondary education also depicts similar findings in the level of slums in Bangladesh. Some researchers (Hossain et al., 1999) argue that for low-income households, mobility from low to high-income occupations through human capital formation is limited in Bangladesh.

The ages of married males in Pirer Tila are between 23 and 55 years. Most of them are monogamous. Only one man is practicing polygamy. The ages of women are between 15 and 42. There are also six older widows living in the *basti* in their son's households. All the women were aged between 11 and 18 when they first married and the duration of their current marriages were between two and 30 years.

In the Durga Bari *basti*, the married women are between 20 and 35 years old. There are no old or widowed women. The women's age at their first marriages was between 12 and 21 years and the duration of the current marriage ranged between two and 20 years.

Table 1.2 Age structure, age at first marriage and number of children ever born to women of the two *bastis*

Variables	Pirer Tila number	Durga Bari number
Age		
12–16	1	0
17–21	8	4
22–26	10	10
27–31	15	7
32 +	11	6
Age at first marriage		
11–16	41	21
17–22	4	6
Number of children ever born		
0	0	0
1	3	2
2	6	3
3	13	9
4	10	5
5 +	13	8

Source: Present Study.

Notes

1 A reference is a single occurrence of the content element.
2 According to Christians (2000, p. 138), proper respect for human freedom generally includes two necessary conditions: (1) Agreement of subjects for voluntary participation and (2) their agreement must be based on full and open information.
3 Administrative units of the Government of Bangladesh.
4 Bangladesh Bureau of Statistics.
5 In Sylhet, there was an abundance of Khas land. Even in 1982, there were 203,640 acres of Khas land in Sylhet; at that time, land rent was also comparatively low in Sylhet. So, landless people of other districts were induced to migrate here (Rahman, 1999).

2 Girlhood and marriage
Perceptions and experiences of slum women

This chapter primarily focuses on various factors that are embedded in the culture, traditions and customs in Bangladeshi society that influence women's gendered life stages. The meanings of life stages that are related to age are embedded in the notion of time. Although age and time are universal constants that can be measured, an objectivist approach does not bear any meaningful understanding of what is meant by time or age or life stage (Östör, 1984, p. 282). Life stages are not only the passing of time and age in a chronological manner; instead, life stages should be understood through maturity of the body and mind in relation to culture and religion in the realm of social relationships that change according to cultural-constructed practices, rituals and experiences. Women's life stages in Bangladesh are marked by remarkable alterations in personal autonomy and influence, status and relationships. For example, in childhood and adolescence, girls' lives are controlled by their parents, grandparents or other elder patrilineal and matrilineal kin. After marriage, they become dependent on their husbands and other affinal relatives. Again, child birth brings change in the web of autonomy and power among women and ultimately senior womanhood considerably gain in terms of prestige, autonomy and power in the later stages of the feminine life cycle (Aziz, 1979; Kertzer, 1984; Mandelbaum, 1987; Das Gupta, 1995; Jeffery and Jeffery, 1996; Säävälä, 1997). Age dynamics, which arrange the different stages of life, create a situation where women in different life stages may not have the same access and opportunity, position or potential means of power for change. In Bangladeshi society, women experience vivid changes in their lives depending on their age and relation to the kinship structure. Because a woman is not supposed to stand alone in any stage of her life, her identity is wholly defined by her relationship to others: she is a daughter to her parents and granddaughter to her grandparents, she is a sister of her sisters and brothers, she is a wife to her husband, she is the daughter-in-law to her mother-in-law and father-in-law, she is the mother to her sons and daughters; she is related with her maternal and paternal kin by blood and with in-laws by affinity. So, a Bangladeshi woman is always considered as a "relational" person; this is central throughout South Asian kinship-based societies (Daniel, 1984, p. 9; Trawick, 1990, p. 252; Säävälä, 2001, p. 102; Aura, 2008, pp. 40–41).

44 *Girlhood and marriage*

This chapter will describe the *basti* women's perceptions and experience on girlhood in the natal family, which prepares a girl to become a woman and inscribes womanliness into her. From this point of view, I will describe the effects of urban migration on the notion of having girls in the families at slums, the socialization process of the girls, views on marriage arrangements and exchange, marital life, and kinship bonds with natal families after marriage.

Girlhood in a Natal family: mixed feelings

All the women in the *bastis* unanimously stated that to have offspring is very important because without a child, a couple's life is sad and bleak. They argued that a family without a child is considered as an object of pity. Although a male offspring is of major importance and the most welcome one, in Islam, the birth of a daughter is considered auspicious as well, and in the Hindu religion, a daughter is considered as *Lakshmi* (auspicious like the goddess Lakshmi). And there is also a Bengali proverb that, "If a daughter is born first then the family experiences prosperity." But with regard to girls, the women interviewed in the slums expressed mixed feelings. Most women in the *bastis* emphasized that people prefer a son to a daughter. I got the strong impression that nowadays parents often have a desire for a daughter only when they have had sons. Most of the women did not want to have more than one daughter due to constant supervision and need to protect them when a girl is an adolescent and the anxiety of the arrangement of a marriage to a good groom and a good family. A *basti* woman (around 35 years old) stated,

> I have two adolescent daughters. Now I can't even sleep properly because of their protection and marriage arrangements. I don't know when I can send them to good grooms…. On that day I can peacefully have a sound sleep.

The need for more sons is strongly expressed by the *basti* women by reference to the continuation of the patriline, which not only reflects the practical need of the patriline as a social support network in securing livelihood and old age care, but also for symbolic and emotional needs and values, such as the continuation of the family or its lineage (*bongsho*). In Bangladesh, blood (*rokto*) passes from the father to the child. Sons are seen to pass on their father's blood (*rokto*) to future generations, building and continuing patrilines, carrying "the light of the line-*bongshor bati*" (Kotalova, 1993; Uusikylä, 2000, p. 55). In Bangladesh, sons are considered as the portrayals of the father or grandfather and the bearers of the father and grandfather's lives.

The male child is cherished in all religious and social groups in Bangladeshi society. Among the Muslims, a son is welcomed to the world with a loud audible prayer of "Allah is great" with rejoicing; a daughter receives only a whisper, and sometimes she receives nothing at all. Bertocci (1974) notes that this kind of response regarding the sex of a newborn baby in Bangladesh influences the roles and behavior patterns that she or he will be born and "act out later in life." Kotalova (1993, p. 65), in her research in a village in Bangladesh, explores gender preference for male child claims that signs of preference are evident at the very moment of delivery. The announcement that a child has been born is immediately followed by the question, "A girl or a boy?" ... "To get a daughter, one's face blackens" and "having a son one is happy." In their research on girls in Bangladesh, Islam and Ahmed (1993, p. 29) found that all the women in their study from a lower socio-economic group in urban Dhaka city suffered from the son preference syndrome. The researchers claimed this was an indication of a deep rooted anti-female bias in social norms. Miller (1981, p. 13), in her study on North India, pointed to this type of preferential attitude toward sons instead of daughters as the power of culture to shape family attitudes that determine how children are treated differently depending on their sex.

The lives of the *basti* dweller women have changed in many ways due to rural-urban migration. Now most of the families are nuclear, and information is better available for women in various spheres of life. Women work outside home to earn a living and men work in various occupations, living in a crowded place with unrelated family (which is totally opposite to life in a village *bari*[1]), and they have less privacy. So, they experience and embrace new values and practices in their adjustment to the new setting. In all my visits to the Pirer Tila and Durga Bari *bastis*, I had a chance to observe many girls of various ages. Some small girls played with handmade dolls (*putul khela*) and toy kitchen utensils (*ranna bara khela*), which is considered to be girl's play in Bangladesh. Simultaneously, some small girls were engaged in household chores and looking after their younger siblings. Some adolescent girls were doing household chores and some were freely gossiping together. I asked the grown-up women about their perceptions of daughters because I thought that rural-urban migration might have changed their ideas of the value of a daughter. However, most of the Muslim and Hindu women stressed the high value of sons and referred to the patrilineal ideology, religious beliefs and rituals that give sons a particular role in securing afterlife to the parents and considerations of sons as future bread winners. The narratives from two different focus group discussions are given below:

> Rohima (a Muslim woman, about 40 years old): When I die, my sons will take my dead body to the graveyard on their shoulders. They will bear my *khatia* (bed for bearing a dead body), buy my *kafon-er kapor* (funeral cloth), arrange *milad* (religious recitation for the peace of the departed soul). The sons will go to my grave (*kobor*) and give soil. Those who have no sons are very unlucky, daughters cannot do this.

> Sita (a Hindu woman, about 32 years old): In our Hindu society, sons are very important and more desirable than daughters, not only because they maintain the lineage, but also for religious rituals for achieving heavenly life. After the death of parents, Hindu sons carry their parents' dead bodies on their shoulders while saying '*Hori Bol*' (religious recitation) and take

them to the *shasan* (cremation place) for burning the dead body for heavenly peace. But daughters can't do this: it is not permitted in the Hindu religion.

It is interesting to note that Islam and Hinduism generally provide women a position of honor and respect, but in the case of death rituals, both the religions exclude women from burial or cremation. Actually gender relations in the patriarchal structure are deeply intertwined with religious ideologies and practices.

In Bangladesh, like in the other countries of South Asia, a strong son preference also exists for similar reasons. Säävälä (1997, p. 161) mentions that also in rural South India, where son preference is less extreme than in the northern parts of the subcontinent, son preference exists so that almost all families would like to secure the birth of at least one son in the family. She found that in South Indian villages, sometimes the birth of a daughter might be regarded as a misfortune for the family whereas a son's birth is never considered to be a misfortune. In contrast to the generally more woman-friendly image provided by ethnographies of South India, Hegde (1999) depicted the violent tragedy of female infanticide in some South Indian rural communities due to strong son preference. She showed how gender ideologies place mothers in the dual roles of a victim and a murderer in two rural areas in South India. In her research area, both men and women shared the same preference for sons for many reasons, such as to ensure the perpetuation of the family name, to have a rightful heir for their property, for the parents' safe passage to the afterlife, to have a bread earner in the family, etc. So when the poverty-stricken mothers gave birth to a female child they became frustrated and considered it as a misfortune and burden and could reject the female baby through female infanticide or neglect. Subedi (1997) stated that in Nepal, some families consider female children as unwanted guests, because daughters are considered the property of others to be handed away in marriage.

Some *basti* women expressed an interest in having a daughter in the family for their valuable contribution to the domestic sphere and on emotional grounds. Some of them expressed doubts about their son's caring in their future old age because nowadays the scenario has changed and sons do not always look after their old parents (Ashrafun and Uddin, 2010). The following quotations of slum women vividly illustrate why daughters are needed in a family:

Morzina (a 28-year-old Muslim woman, a mother of two daughters and two sons): In the family along with sons at least one daughter is desirable. Daughters yearn for their parents. Even after the marriage, daughters think about their parents' family, and if possible they try to help their parents economically and emotionally. Now I am hearing from people that sons do not take care of their parents after marriage.

Probasini (a 28-year-old Hindu woman, a mother of two daughters and two sons): In a family, a daughter is also desirable. Parents love their daughters forever although they cannot look after them.... It is a heavenly bond. It is the rules of society that daughters will go to others' home after marriage.... Daughters are weak; all the parents know this. So, parents do not place any *dabi* (demands) on their daughters, their daughters' happiness is their happiness, their daughters' sorrows are their sorrows. As long as parents are alive in the world, they try to receive their daughters to *naior* (returning to the natal family after marriage annually for some days in some special occasion). In our slum, some women go to *naior* every year because at that time they can meet with their parents, brothers and other married sisters and they regain their joy of life in that reunion.

In the above narratives, the desire for having a daughter is expressed. In Morzina's account, deep feelings of daughters for their parents are visible. Probasini expressed her love and gratitude toward her parents for their endless self-sacrificing love and sketched the joyful feelings in *naior*. The symbolic value of *naior* in Bangladeshi society is extensive. In Bangladesh, under patrilineality and the patrilocal residence system, after marriage when a woman moves from her parent's house to her husband's house, this physical separation and relatedness with the husband's lineage may more or less sever a woman's ties with her natal family. This physical separation also makes it difficult for a married woman to claim her share of inheritance apart from other considerations. In Muslim law, a woman inherits half of what her brother inherits and one-eighth of her husband's property when he dies and if they have children. But in practice women hardly exercise their rights to property for practical reasons. Moreover, in most of the cases a Bangladeshi woman does not receive her inheritance directly from the natal family. For example, if she is divorced or separated and remains unmarried, her father or brother assumes guardianship over her (Chaudhary and Ahmed, 1980; Abdullah, 1982). If she claims her land, she may not get the necessary support from her brothers in times of need and may also find it somewhat uneasy to visit her brother's house for recreation (*naior*). Similarly, if she is widowed and abstains from remarriage, she has to stay under the guardianship of a male relative – her father-in-law, brother-in-law or with her oldest son. It is usually more advantageous for her not to claim her share.

The women from the lower socio-economic class in most of the cases belong to the landless class or have a very negligible proportion of homestead and agricultural plot. So these women's hope for land inheritance is always void, rather their marriage arrangement is a burden for the family. So after marriage, the only way to keep up a supportive relationship with their parents and brothers is to abstain from demanding any inheritance from the natal family (Chaudhary and Ahmed, 1980; Abdullah, 1982). Hindu women are not entitled to inherit patrimonial property in Bangladesh. In their marriages, their natal families provide them dowry according to their economic ability and caste position.

Some researchers (Chen et al., 1981; Islam and Ahmed, 1993) have pointed out the negative value given to daughters: from early childhood, girls are treated differently than boys and they face sex-bias in allocation of resources and opportunities. Chen et al. (ibid.) and Islam and Ahmed (ibid.) have argued that in households with limited economic and food resources, adherence to such values results in serious food deprivation among girls and mothers. In the majority of the impoverished households, the male members are served first and they are given larger quantities of food as well as food of better nutritional quality. Some rural households serve food to sons and daughters together, but the mothers still prefer to give their sons a larger quantity of food. Most of the time the daughters do not object; they are socialized to accept whatever comes to them. The mother teaches her young daughter from early childhood that it is all right for boys to demand additional servings of food while a girl should learn to not be demanding and to be satisfied with what she gets (ibid.). But in the *bastis*, I did not find the situation to be similar to the above-mentioned studies. The data suggests that among the *basti* women, there is no gender-based asymmetry in the consumption of food and health care provision. However, women expressed different feelings regarding the upbringing of girls by taking into consideration their future married lives:

> *When I was a child, my mother and grandmother taught me how to be satisfied with less food and material, so I learned from them and it worked very positively after my marriage. But nowadays, we do not practice these teachings in the case of our daughters. Our girls get as much food as our sons, but we think the girls should have more patience and a sacrificing attitude because when they will go to their husbands' houses they may live in a different environment that is not in our hands.
>
> (A 35-year-old Hindu *basti* woman)

> *I always teach my daughters to have patience. Sometimes they follow [my instructions] and sometimes not. But I think it is very important for their marital lives. Allah knows where and to which family they will go! But I never behave in a different way to my sons and daughters.
>
> (A 28-year-old Muslim *basti* woman)

What strikes me is that most *basti* women expressed the same opinion that a girl's childhood should be joyful without any kind of burden. However, they unanimously stated childhood is an important time to learn society's norms for future life. They compared women's lives with the earth: according to them, "like the earth women also should have such capacities of tolerance." In this respect, the women's feelings can be expressed by the concept "classic patriarchy," which was described by Kandiyoti (1988, p. 278): childhood socialization of girl children is central for shaping women's gendered inferior position and subjectivity in the marital home. In Kandiyoti's (1988) account, one of the characteristics of classic patriarchy is the patrilocally extended household, where daughters are given away in marriage at a young age to another household headed by their husband's father. In this household, a bride is not only subordinate to all the senior men (including her husband) but also to the mother-in-law and other senior females. The consequences of the patrilineal-patrilocal complex for women bring about diverse forms of control and subordination in gender relations that cut across religious boundaries in Bangladesh.

In the Pirer Tila and Durga Bari *bastis*, women's views concerning the issue of raising girls were uniform. Most of them preferred that a girl should have patience, knowledge of familial duties and household chores from her childhood. But in the *bastis*, I got the impression that some women had a negative notion about the traditional ideals of girl socialization as evident in changing patterns of ideals and practice:

> *I work hard for the well-being of my children. I do not differentiate between sons and daughters for food consumption and medical care. Whatever my husband and I can earn, we spend on the family. I always try to feed my daughters like my sons, this is my duty ... if they learn the hardship of life straight from childhood they would lose the love for their parents and joy of childhood.
>
> (A 28-year-old *basti* woman)

> *It is very bad to ill-treat daughters. I think there is no difference between a son and a daughter. If I can raise my daughter properly she will also look after me in future.... So I cannot punish my daughter as a mother ... I cannot deprive her of anything. According to my economic ability, I should care for my son and daughter similarly.
>
> (A 25-year-old *basti* woman)

Both narratives strongly focused on the practice of equal treatment toward daughters. I argue that the perception of some women may have changed from the perspective prevalent in rural areas. But unfortunately, this changed perception remains unpracticed in the collective behavior toward girls.

With respect to educational attainment, generally in the Bangladeshi families, sons get more parental attention than daughters. Institutional education, as an essential qualification and valuable asset in ensuring entry into the "formal" and modern job market, is perceived as a necessary resource for a son to acquire and develop. In the present study, because a daughter is seen as a future housewife and mother, I found that the need for higher-level institutional education is not felt so keenly. Particularly in the economically insolvent households of the slums, in most cases higher education is perceived as irrelevant and impossible for economic reasons. So the poverty-stricken parents do not take care of their daughter's higher institutional education.

From grade 8 onwards, the dropout rate for girls is much higher than for boys. In the slums in Bangladesh, the dropout rate for males is 10 percent while that of females is 16 percent. This is probably linked to early marriage (UNICEF, 2011). This study's ethnographic data also revealed a similar situation. The middle-aged slum women unanimously stated that girls' education is not important. They often considered their economic condition as well as the prevailing social environment as preventing girls from continuing in school. This is how the *basti* women expressed their views:

> We are poor people, so we don't think much about our daughters' education. If a daughter wants and the parents wish, then it is enough for her to study up to primary level education. Most families are unable to provide economic support for education.
>
> (A 30-year-old woman)

> Now the era (*joog*) is not good, it is *kolikal* (the bad time). The environment (*poribesh*) is not good in the *basti*. Eve teasing[2] (*titkari*) is very common in urban areas. So to keep the honor of the family, parents prefer their daughters not to be educated higher than the primary level.
>
> (Around 40-year-old woman)

A review of the literature (Papanek and Minault, 1982; Mizan, 1994; Khair, 1995) reveals that in Bangladesh, guardians preferred that girls should receive non-formal education at home, and the parents and other older people of the family wish that girls should learn domestic skills and virtues, such as obedience, docility and modesty. Women's modesty (*haya*) and physical chastity (*satitya*) are highly valued for the family honor (*ijjat*). If there is any talk (*katha*) and whispering (*kanakani*) about a woman in a family, then the family loses face (*mukh*) and its honor.

The steps to make a perfect woman is further ensured by the propagation of the ideal of the "good woman," who is symbolized by such mythical personages as *Sita* (for Hindus) and *Bibi* Rohima, *Bibi* Fatema and *Bibi* Ayesha (for Muslims). For Hindus, from *Ramayana* women should learn about *Sita*'s character that is regarded as the most esteemed exemplar of womanly elegance and wifely virtue in Hinduism. Such models teach men that simply by virtue of their masculinity, they are entitled to expect these virtues in women. When they marry, they look for these divine virtues of an "ideal woman" in their wives and are led to believe that without these super womanly virtues, the couple will face great dissatisfaction in marriage.

When I asked the *basti* women about girl's education, the Muslim and the Hindu women unanimously emphasized the need for religious teaching along with formal education. In their accounts, girls should have religious education. The women said that they had learned religious ideals and appropriate behavior from their parents and now similarly they try to teach these religious practices to their daughters. The Muslim respondents said if a Muslim girl has no religious education and does not know how to behave and move outside the home, she will get nothing in this life. The respondents put emphasis on the heavenly life. According to them, without prayer, reciting the Holy Quran or maintaining religious life no one can bring happiness to family life. Similarly, the Hindu women pointed out that to worship the household deity is the prime responsibility of Hindu women. Every day they worship Radha-Govinda to ensure the happiness of the whole household; Hindu girls should learn how to perform these rituals from their early childhood. Otherwise, it was thought they would not to be able to bring happiness to their family lives (*sangsar-jibon*).

Islam and Ahmed (1993) highlight the fact that in poor, Bangladeshi households, girls perform all types of domestic work, such as washing, cleaning, taking care of younger siblings, cooking, collecting cow dung and carrying water. But boys are more involved in out-of-home work like marketing and harvesting. This gendered division of labor can be found in almost all the houses in the slums. However, among the disadvantaged families in the slums, these formulations have somewhat changed and made the boys' and girls' spheres of work ambivalent. Nowadays, even girls may work outside the domestic sphere. This is revealed in Joygun's (a 32-year-old part-time domestic helper from Pirer Tila *basti*) narrative. She has four daughters and two sons, and she works as a part-time domestic helper in a nearby house. She always takes her nine-year-old daughter with her to her mistress's house to help her with the domestic work. She added that after coming back home it is very hard for her to do all the household work alone. Her 14-year-old daughter helps her to do all the household chores and looks after her younger siblings. Her 12-year-old daughter had been working as a full-time domestic helper in a Sylheti house for two years, and her monthly salary helps the big family a lot economically. Joygun's six-year-old daughter and seven-year-old son help her husband to sell *pitha* (sweet cake) and *aachar* (pickles) in the street.

As was mentioned earlier, a girl's chastity is very important for a family's honor, and from the ethnographic data of the present study it was evident that insecurity and vulnerability strongly limit the slum women and their daughters' lives. Almost all the women in the slum stressed that a slum environment is not safe for rearing daughters, and they considered the urban environment as more dangerous compared to rural areas. They pointed out that when a girl reaches puberty, it is very hard to look after her security and chastity as there is no privacy in the *basti* and different types of people live there. The following quotations highlight the reasons for tension:

> Nasrin (a 25-year-old woman): When a girl child reaches puberty, the parents in the *basti* have to start to think about her marriage. A grown-up girl should be always kept under strict surveillance (*choke choke rakha*) in the slum. But sometimes it is hard for parents to guard their daughters because during puberty the minds of the girls wander here and there. Different types of men can attract them, if a man talks nicely to a girl and gives her some gifts, she becomes fond of him.

> Rashida (a 22-year-old woman): There are different types of people in the *basti*; some males are *bodmais* (wicked) and some men even in their old age have *bodkheyal* (perverse propensity) and look obscenely at women. So in the *basti* it is difficult to raise a daughter.

Rashida shared a sad experience from her family. She narrated in a plaintive voice that her younger sister had married a bad guy through a love marriage.

Together with her parents she tried to control her affair but they failed. One day her sister fled from the house with her lover. She has been married for only two years and has no children, but within this short period she had been mistreated by her husband, and he did not allow her to keep in contact with her natal family. Rashida and her parents secretly tried to keep contact with her. From Rashida's narrative, all her anxieties about a decent future for her sister is depicted. Social and physical isolation is a characteristic of many violent marriages. One way for a violent husband to assert dominance and control over all aspects of the woman's life is to keep her isolated and dependent on his demands. Violent men often isolate their victims from family and friends and prevent them from working outside the home (at the same time becoming extremely demanding and critical about their expectations concerning domestic work). In some cases, fear and shame of detection lead victim women to voluntarily withdraw from social and family interactions as their injuries and psychological torture become progressively worse (Johnson, 1998, p. 43).

The women in the *basti* also considered the limitations of technology in their personal daily lives. They stated that although mobile phone networks give them an opportunity to stay in contact with their relatives and friends, it also brought its own problems. The women of the *basti* informed me that they are facing a new problem. Nowadays girls talk over mobile phones whenever they get an opportunity. Some women expressed their fear that girls steal money from their houses or from other houses and go to a nearby call shop to talk with their "lovers" on the phone. In the account of the *basti* women, this is a matter of anxiety for them.

Some *basti* women described the problem of mobile phone by telling a story of a Muslim woman they knew who lived in the *basti* with her young daughter. The girl once got involved in an affair with a Hindu boy over the phone. When the mother got to know about it, she severely beat the girl several times with the help of other family members, but the family could not control this relationship. Finally, they forcefully arranged the daughter's marriage to someone else and thought that after marriage the girl would end the relationship with the boy. But their endeavor failed, and even after marriage, the girl continued her relationship with her ex-lover over the phone, and when the husband found out about the relationship, he instantly divorced the girl. The girl returned to her natal family and then fled with the Hindu lover, but the boy did not keep his promise to marry the girl. Therefore, the girl again came back to her natal family, but due to this bad series of events, the family felt ashamed and left the *basti*.

Basti mothers are conscious about the difficulty of securing their daughters' safety, chastity and future happiness. They feel responsible for protecting their adolescent daughters' chastity from all dangers by controlling their movements, keeping an eye on their activities, maintaining their *pardah* (veil) and arranging their early marriage. In the next section, I will focus on why and how marriage has built up a significant life stage for women. What types of marriage exchanges are now practiced in *basti* areas?

Getting married: the ultimate destination for women

Raheja and Gold (1994, p. 147), in their study in India, mentioned that the significant representations of different life stages of women are built from the male perspective. They noted some examples of songs that were sung by both married and unmarried women together to express the ironic apprehension of the married life and oppressiveness of kinship ideology that split their identities. Katy Gardner (1995), also in her study in a village in Sylhet, Bangladesh, delineated similar expressions in women's marriage songs. But the researchers also noted that although the women's songs give a melancholic expression of separation and dividedness, their world is unimaginable without marriage and a family.

Marriage is a socio-sexual institution, a part of the wider institutional complex of the family (Therborn, 2004, p. 131). In Bangladesh as in all of South Asia, marriage is the most significant symbolic and practical event in the lives of both men and women and it sets in motion the building of a new family. The concept of family is central in the Bangladeshi context, and no one is considered to be a proper adult without marriage. Marriage creates a happy conjugal relationship, is a context for begetting legitimate children and creates in women a sense of fulfilling their gendered roles of wife, mother and daughter-in-law. It is considered as a beginning of a long path of destiny, ending in the death of a woman. The aim of this section is to present how marriage becomes a central theme in the life of a woman. To understand the different steps of marriage and its relevance for understanding domestic violence, I will concentrate on why arranging a daughter's marriage is considered a moral duty (*dharma*)[3] for parents of all classes and religious groups in Bangladesh.

Today *dharma* is variously translated as "law," "moral duty," "right action" or "conformity with the truth of things." But in each of its various manifestations, *dharma* relates to the ideal human life sequence. *Dharma* is the way through which a man approaches the virtuous goals of human life. The social feature of *dharma* is suggested in the etymology of the word itself, which derives from the root dhr (to uphold, to sustain, to nourish). *Dharma* is social cement; it holds the individual and society together. *Dharma* is not only the principle of individual action and social relations but also the ground plan of an ideal life phase in the sense that it defines the tasks of different stages of life and the direction for each stage (Kakar, 1981, pp. 37–42). In a broader understanding, *dharma* is related to order in society the domain of commonsensical truths, the schematic and symbolic aspect of social knowledge. As a practice, *dharma* enters the life of Bangladeshi people in many different ways: in their daily lives, religious rituals, sacrifice, marriage practices, behavioral patterns, different ceremonies, the practice of health care. In all its forms and practices, it is internalized, instrumentalized, negotiated and manipulated. So, in many practices, some of the beliefs of people contradict formal religious doctrines; the practices performed or followed by people are considered as the "tradition and culture of this land" (*desher achar, niom, riti-niti*), no matter which religion people belong to (Kotalova, 1993; Uusikylä, 2000). In this sense, the notion of *dharma* incorporates

Bourdieu's (1977, pp. 167–170) concept of "doxa," where the tradition of marriage practices as a *dharma* would fall in this category.

Marriage is a practically universal phenomenon in Bangladeshi society. It is a firm belief that a woman must be given (*bie dawa*) marriage at least once and her marriage should be arranged at the proper time. A woman's life is out of frame without marriage and without being bonded to a husband at an early age (Kotalova, 1993, p. 190; Gardner, 1995). Marriage is the ultimate destination for women in Bangladesh. It is the tradition of the society that almost all the women in their adolescence or in their youth have to leave their natal family and begin a new life as a wife in a new family. Marriage is considered as a *dharma* (right action) of womanhood. Among the Muslims in Bangladesh, cross cousin and parallel cousin marriages are not considered incestuous. As Muslims can marry cross cousins and parallel cousins, it can be considered as functional endogamy and endogamy of relation as defined by Levi-Strauss (1969, pp. 47–50). The Hindus in Bangladeshi society marry within their caste (*jati*). The Hindus in this society cannot marry their consanguine kin; this is different from the Dravidian kinship system in South India (Dumont, 1980).

Most women interviewed in the *bastis* had married before they were 18 years of age. There is a Child Marriage Restraints Act in Bangladesh, which prohibits the marriage of girls below the age of 18, but still such marriages are common (Islam and Ahmed, 1993; Jahan, 1994; Ameen, 2005). According to the Multiple Indicator Cluster Survey in 2006, 42 percent of women aged 15–19 were currently married; while in the Demographic Health Survey in 2007, it was 47 percent, and approximately a third of women aged 20 to 24 were married by the age of 15. Over 74 percent of women had been married before their 18th birthday. While the percentage of underage girls (before age 18) in marriage is 79 percent in the slums, the percentage in the rural area is nearly the same (UNICEF, 2011, pp. 29–30). When I asked the respondents about marriage and the time line of marriage of their daughters, most of the women from the *bastis* unanimously gave their opinion in favor of early marriage and considered it as their *dharma* (moral duty). They expressed their fear that if the daughters fall in love with boys it would destroy family honor. In their accounts, it is better to arrange for a girl to be married in her adolescence because nowadays the environment (*poribesh*) is bad, a girl's marriage arrangements should be begun at the onset of her menstruation because at this early age, females may be involved in misleading activities due to their budding sexuality. Furthermore, it is always difficult to get suitable grooms as their daughters get older.

In the *bastis*, although women work outside home to support the family, they do not have any wish that their daughters should support the family economically. They only hope that their sons would look after the family:

> It is a long tradition in society to arrange the daughters' marriages as early as possible after their menstruation. So whenever parents find a suitable family and a good groom, they do not hesitate. Most of us gave birth to our first child between the age of 12–15 years and we did not face any problem.

Our mothers, aunts, grandmothers gave birth to in there, so we think early marriage does not create any problem for a child birth.

(A 40-year-old Muslim woman from Pirer Tila)

The government will not take any initiative to arrange our daughters' marriages, do not pay the dowries or protect our family honor. We have to think about our daughter's early marriage.

(A 28-year-old Hindu woman from Durga Bari)

The Hindu women in the *basti* were concerned about inter-caste marriages and dowries. According to them, it is very hard to arrange a Hindu woman's marriage because they have to consider two matters at the same time: the caste system and a dowry. They said in their villages of origin, they saw some older girls who were still unmarried. According to them, although the older girls are very pitiable, they are eagerly waiting with the hope (*aasa*) of marriage, but because the caste system together with dowry demands their parents could not arrange marriages for them. The Hindu women added these girls suffer a lot, remaining either in their natal families or in their brothers' families. Their brothers' families treated them like "maid servants" (*dasi*) or "garbage" (*aborjona*). Even if parents stand to lose everything because of their daughter's marriage, they wish to arrange their daughter's marriage as early as possible. "We have to follow society's (*samaj*) rules. So from an early age we try to understand our daughters' future married life," explained a 31-year-old Hindu woman, after telling me about the problems of finding a suitable groom for a Hindu girl of the same caste.

There are a few *basti* women who have different views regarding the early marriages of their daughters, but they also fear to go beyond the existing practice. The following quotations highlight this vividly:

Morzina (A Muslim *basti* woman about 28 years old): It is very rude behavior of the parents to arrange their daughters' marriage so early because at that time the girl does not understand sexuality, conjugal life, child birth and rearing or household duties. Now every day, I have to enter the university to go to my work place, and I love to see the female students of the university. If it is possible for me, I will not allow my husband to arrange our elder daughter's marriage so early. Now I am dreaming about my daughter's education. But, oh! We are poor and living in the *basti*. It is very hard to fulfill our dream (she takes a deep-drawn sigh).

Sumi Begum (A Muslim *basti* woman of around 22): We are poor people and always have early marriages. Most of us give birth to our first child before understanding sexual life and conjugal relationship. So sometimes it becomes a curse for us, we have experiences of poor health, miscarriage and child death. In our *basti*, Parul (16 years) gave birth to two sickly girls that did not live for a month. Likewise, Meherun (27 years) has experienced two miscarriages and her four children have died due to various complications. If she again gives birth to a dead child or it dies after some days she will become mad (*pagol*) and people will call her *apoia* (inauspicious).

Morzina and Sumi Begum both pointed out their awareness of the desirability of girls to grow up before marriage and childbirth. They saw this as a reason to postpone marriage so girls should get some education (Morzina) and avoid health issues (Sumi Begum).

There is an important issue regarding the age difference between the husband and wife. In Bangladesh, the preferable difference is 6–10 years; in some cases it is higher (Chaudhury and Ahmed, 1980; Jahan, 1994). It reflects the attitude of the guardians toward marriage and gender relations in marriage; they believe that the grooms should be old enough to have the means of providing financial support for their wives. The gap in age lays a solid base for establishing the husband's superior status in the family, as age is recognized as a status indicator in Bangladeshi society.

However, in Bangladesh, women's early marriage and early motherhood is very important; the birth of a child gives a woman dignity, value and power in the family. So, in Bangladesh, it is also common that after marriage the mother-in-law, mother, elder sisters, aunts and women in the neighborhood encourage the newly married bride to give birth to her first child as early as possible because there is a strong belief that if a young wife becomes pregnant, there is a good possibility for her to have a male child, so they discourage her from using contraception after marriage. The guardians of the girl believe that a child can entangle a man with sweet love and fatherhood (Aziz, 1979; Kotalova, 1993; Islam and Ahmed, 1993; Uusikylä, 2000). In the slums, I found most of the families are nuclear, women are information updated, working outside home and more or less free from mothers' and mothers-in-law's interference in their procreation and familial decisions, but they strongly believe that child birth at a young age means giving birth to sons. Some young Hindu women said that although they are living in the nuclear family in the urban slum, still their mothers and mothers-in-law pressure them to give birth to children at a tender age. Unnithan-Kumar (2003, p. 177) also focused on mothers-in-law's pressure for having more children on the slum women of Jaipur city, India. In Pirer Tila, some *basti* women stated:

> *If a girl becomes pregnant earlier, she may give birth to a son because at that time her reproductive organs (*mati norom thake*) are strong.
> (A 30-year-old slum woman)

> *There is a proverb, *Joubon-e putraboti hou* (give birth to a son in your youth).
> (A 41-year-old *basti* woman)

As in the *bastis*, people practice early marriage. I asked them if they asked their daughters' opinion about the match before the wedding? The young *basti* women told me that at the time of their marriages, they did not know anything because their elder kin decided everything; still some *basti* families do not allow adolescent girls to talk with their parents and family members about their mate selection. Sometimes, they do not even understand the duty and responsibility of a wife. In the *basti*, Sabina (18-years-old, a Muslim woman) expresses her thoughts:

> I did not see my husband's photo or could not meet with him, but my husband found the opportunity to see my photo. My duty was only to agree with my parents and relatives' decisions and giving my consent. My mother forced me to agree with their decision. I do not support this type of attitude of parents toward their daughters' marriages; rather they should talk openly with their daughters.

However, in the *basti*, I found some young women who freely expressed their negative attitudes and argued that it is not necessary to ask the girls before choosing their spouses. They claimed that parents and the elder kin understand matchmaking better than young girls, and consequently it is not necessary to ask their views about the marriage. It is a long-term practice in Bangladeshi society that the girl should comply silently with what their parents decide. According to the slum women, parents never put their daughters in danger. If any mishap happens, the daughters have to understand that it did not happen because of their parents; rather it was written by Allah at the time of the girl's birth in her destiny. To these women, nothing is in human hands and nobody can control three events in human life: birth, marriage and death.

Against these accounts, some other young *basti* women informed me that there are some changes occurring in general opinions for the need to involve the daughters in marriage negotiations. Nowadays, both the bride's and the groom's families send photos of the prospective spouses to each other before marriage arrangements are made.

> My mother showed me the groom's photo and asked my opinion on the match. I felt ashamed and did not pay much attention to the photo and said to my mother, I have no opinion, you know everything about me so your wish is my wish,

stated Rohini (19-years-old) from Durga Bari *basti*. Another newly married Hindu bride, Rekha (18-years-old), recollected her marriage arrangements,

> My maternal aunt (*mashi*) brought the proposal for me. My parents agreed with the proposal and showed me the photo of the groom. My parents allowed me to talk with the groom in front of my aunt, but I could not say anything to him. I felt ashamed and all the time looked down at the ground. Even for a moment, I did not wink at his face.

The *basti* women said, at present, sometimes the groom comes to see his future bride with his father, kinsmen or friends. Most of the time, the bride entertains

58 *Girlhood and marriage*

the guests and the groom with sweets, and during this time the groom's party evaluates her beauty, knowledge and quality of work.

Shahnaz (about 26-years-old and married for 10 years), a woman from Pirer Tila *basti*, told me that if a bride and groom can meet and talk with each other before a marriage was fixed, it was very good for their future married life. As a result, nobody can accuse anybody in future if they encounter any problem. Moreover, the era has changed, so the practice of marriage arrangement should be relaxed and the guardians should be open-minded. They should not only follow the old practices; not all the old practices are good. She recollected her marriage arrangement thus:

> My husband came to see me before the marriage arrangements. He also talked with me about my study and religious practices along with his friends and relations. I served snacks to all the guests and answered their questions. After the wedding date had been set, my husband came along with his younger sisters and gave me some marriage gifts.

From Rohini, Rekha and Shahnaz's argument it is clear that new ideas and practices are becoming common day-by-day in Bangladeshi society and women are getting more freedom than in previous times to express their choices. Similarly, Gardner (1995, p. 164) in her study in a village in Sylhet, Bangladesh found already in the 1990s that many meetings were less conservative. Now, girls may be asked to speak with the visitors or serve them food. In very progressive households, the groom may be present, and the couple may meet before marriage.

With respect to love marriage, I find most women in the *basti* maintained strong reservations about them. To most of the women, it is considered to be the antithesis of an arranged marriage. According to them, a love marriage may bring uncertainty in a woman's life and the woman may be unable to find any support from her kin. As Fruzzetti points out, questions of honor and perceptions of love are at the core of the perceived difference between arranged and love marriages. Bengali ... marriage expresses devotional and physical love and the continuation of the kin group, *bongsho*, as its aim, but love marriages are perceived as expressions of mere physical love (Fruzzetti, 1990 [1982], p. 14).

But I perceived that nowadays in the *bastis* the question of love marriages is a quite common issue, although the parents do not take the matter positively yet. In the *bastis*, lineage does not play any significant role because all the migrated people in the *basti* belong to the lower socio-economic class and as a result to the same family background as well, love marriages in the slum occur on the same status line. Despite this, parents do not support this type of marriage because they think that when the girls themselves handle their marriages there is strong possibility of them making mistakes and destroying their whole lives. Moreover, when a younger sister intends marrying before her elder sister, it brings enormous problems for arranging marriage later for the elder one. In the Pirer Tila *basti*, a 32-year-old woman illustrates the point in the following way:

It is seen that if girls get married by their own choice they cannot lead happy family lives. We have seen that within a few years the girls face problems from their husbands or in-laws. If a girl marries according to her parents and elder kin's choice then if she encounters conjugal problems the guardians try to solve them by meeting with her husband, in-laws and elder kin. At that time her husband fears to give her a divorce and does not dare to do whatever he likes.

Marriage in Bangladesh is not a personal concern; it is an important transaction between two kin groups. Kinship and the institution of the family remain the most important forces in many cultures and are fundamental to understanding social life. Within kinship-based societies, the self must be conceived of differently, often as a corporate sense of identity within an ideal of extreme cohesiveness and less-articulated conflict (Dobash and Dobash, 1998). Marriage thus focuses on the unique transactions through which two kin groups become affine, and it is preferred that marriage should be arranged only between an equal man and woman (Kotalova, 1993; Gardner, 1995). Aziz (1979, pp. 40–42) mentions that in Bangladesh among the Muslims equal marriage is desirable, and this equality refers to such status indicators as birth or profession and sometimes both. In order to enhance the *man-ijjat* (the prestige and honor) of the husband and his *gushti*,[4] it is desirable to have a network of powerful or influential relatives. The most important factors in the selection of spouses are overall reputation, economic standing, education, beauty, etc. Fruzzetti (1990 [1982]) also speaks of the "matching of the lines" (with the aim of maintaining the equality and status of the respective families) as the main feature of West Bengali marriage transactions. Levi-Strauss (1969, p. 43) pointed out that marriage is an eternal triangle at all times and in all places so the groups play an important role in every marriage.

In Bangladesh, there is no restriction for the alliance among Muslims for cross cousin and parallel cousin marriages. But in the case of age, it is preferred that individuals should marry from his/her generation and possible spouses should be younger than an individual, if the individual is male. By the same token, if the individual is female, it is preferred that her spouse should be older than her. Similarly, an individual can make alliance with his/her brother's and sister's sons and daughters by arranging a marriage with his/her sons and daughters following age and generations. But at present, in Bangladesh, a well-qualified male of a less wealthy *gushti* may be able to marry a girl from a wealthy and more reputed *gushti*. Recently, the educational status of the bridegroom or bride has influenced the ranking and the upgrading of the status. A son from a lower class family holding a university degree and/or immigration status to a foreign country, preferably the USA or the UK, can upgrade the status of his *gushti* by marrying a daughter from a higher status *gushti* (Bertocci, 1974). In the Pirer Tila slum among the Muslims, I found there are some marriages within the kin group from both sides, maternal or paternal. But as the houses belong to lower socio-economic class, I did not find any marriage that influenced class rankings.

From the study data, it is revealed that most marriage proposals (*beye-er prostab*) in the *bastis* are made by neighbors, kinsmen (*attio-suajon*)[5] or *ghotok* (matchmaker). After the negotiations have been successfully completed, the marriage date is fixed. Conventionally, marriage comprises of the *akt* and the *rousmat*. In some, both stages are merged. The *akt* is the official part of the wedding, when the bride formally says *kobul* (I agree) in front of witnesses and the groom and the male representatives of both households register the marriage. Then both parties fix the date of *rousmat*; at the *rousmat*, the bride is taken to her husband's home. It is the day on which the transfer of rights to her from one household to another is actualized. Bangladeshi women's sense of self and belonging is profoundly affected by the shift in space they undergo at marriage and by their position in the two families natal and affinal. The whole ritual contains the familiar stages of marriage arrangement – *prostab pathano* (sending proposal), *bou dekha* (bride selection), *bor dekha* (groom selection), *paanchini kora* (agreement for the alliance with sweets) and fixing some ceremonial dates (*tarikh thik kora*), *akt anusthan kora* (the formal agreement of a Muslim bride in-front of witness), *rousmat* (separation of a Muslim bride from her natal family through a wedding feast arranged by her father or brothers for the *kutum*),[6] *bou tule neoa* (transition and integration into the new relation in the affinal family), *bou bhat* (arrangement of wedding feast by the affinal house of a newly married bride for the new *kutum*), *fira zatra* (bring back the newly married bride and groom to stay for some days in the bride's natal family), but the whole formalities of marriage arrangement depends on the economic abilities of both families.

The present study reveals that among the *basti* dwellers nobody has the economic ability to arrange all the formalities of a traditional marriage arrangement although they try their best to arrange happy weddings for their sons and daughters. But the women told me that in the *basti*, most of the time marriages are arranged with the help of elder neighbors because in city life families do not have the strong influences of their relatives. Maybe some have families in a nearby household of the same *basti* or in some other *bastis* in the same city, but it does not strongly influence the marriage process. In the *basti*, people try to strengthen the relationship with those persons who have given them a helping hand. As a result, most of the time, social networks extend beyond kinship ties. To highlight the importance of social networks in the slum, Afia Begum (a 40-year-old woman) says,

> I am looking after a grocery shop as a sales woman and I have also invested some money. But this grocery shop does not belong to me; the owner of the shop is our landlord. He always tries to help our family and considers my husband and myself as the silent guards of the *basti*. If anything bad happens in this *basti* we at once inform him or try to solve the problem with other elder people. Sometimes we collect rents and hand them over to him. He is like a shade in our life, we always obliged to him. He is the kin of our soul (*atmar attio*).

The importance of keeping social networks in the *basti* is highlighted in this story, which was told by Afia Begum. Once, a family of the *basti* tried to help one of their neighbors by arranging their daughter's marriage to one of their acquaintances. The girl's father was a petty businessman and the mother was a domestic helper. Both his guardians and the groom liked the girl and gave her 500 Taka as a gift (*salami*) and a gold ring of four annas (traditional weight measure). They did not demand any dowry. But the girl did not let it happen. The girl was having an affair with a boy so after the marriage arrangements, one night she fled from the house with 1,000 Taka. After some hours when her mother noticed that she was not in the toilet, she realized the girl had run away. The groom's side demanded the money and gold ring, but the girl's father could not return them. At first, the family that had negotiated the match tried to force the girl's family to give back the groom's gifts, but as they realized that the family has no capacity to return the money and gold ring, they asked the groom's family to forgive the girl's misdeeds and rescued the parents from dishonor (*ossoman*) and economic pressure.

In the *bastis*, I found marital conflict, domestic violence, men's multiple marriages and extra-marital relationships are frequent events. I asked the women, "Do you not take any information about a prospective groom's personal life before arranging a marriage?" Most of the women informed me that when the events leading to a marriage arrangement in the slum, most of the time the parents of the girls try to hide the issue of the marriage arrangement from others, because they fear some people may not want the best for them and destroy the future alliance by defaming their families and girls. As a result, the father or the elder brother of the girl tries to gather information about the prospective groom's personal life as quickly as possible. In addition, parents want to arrange their daughter's marriage as early as possible because they fear if they reject the marriage proposal or try to find out more personal information about the groom, it may create problems in finding another suitable groom later on. It is also common practice of the groom and his guardians to conceal the groom's personal life and bad points such as any previous marriages, divorce cases, love relationships and bad habits. So sometimes women only see the ugly and rude faces of their husbands and in-laws after marriage and then they can find no way to escape from the relationship. When I asked: 'You know about this misfortune very well, but why do you not becoming alert?' Here are some answers to this question from different focus group discussions:

> We are poor and non-literate people, so when we get a proposal for our daughter we become greedy.
>
> (A 28-year-old *basti* woman)

> Marriage is written in every girl's forehead at her birth. Nobody can alter it. We do not want bad luck for our daughters. But how do you understand people so easily? When a marriage proposal comes from the groom's side they behave very nicely with the bride's parents and kin. Sometimes they do

not even want anything from them. Most of the time, we only see their cruel faces after our daughter's marriage.

(A 40-year-old *basti* woman)

Marriage is always a happy event. How it is possible to understand that this happy and joyful event can turn into a dark and inauspicious event? It is very hard to understand. If you always think about the bad side of marriage, you cannot arrange a marriage for any girl.

(A 25-year-old *basti* woman)

People explained this situation by referring to their own ignorance, greed (the first quotation above), destiny (the second quotation) or being brutally deceived (the third quotation). They generally are of the opinion that it is impossible to avoid such problems with marriage partners, as the causes are out of their own control.

The transfer of a woman from her natal to conjugal home in the Bangladeshi patrilineal structure follows the course of a complex set of ritual actions designed to affect her transformation from "one's own" to her natal kin to "other" and "alien" to them (Kotalova, 1993; Gardner, 1995; Uusikylä, 2000). In the South Asian context, Trautmann (1981, p. 291) has characterized this cultural understanding of marriage and the "gift of a virgin" as a "patrilineal idiom of complete dissimilation of the bride from her family of birth and her complete assimilation to that of her husband." Dube (1988), in her discussion of the production of women as gendered subjects in the Indian patrilineal milieu, points out that a woman should be like water, which, having no shape of its own, can take the shape of the vessel into which it is poured, or that she should be like soft and malleable clay that has no form until it is worked into shape by the potter.

The situation of a new bride (*notun bou*) in a patrilocal culture marks the most critical stage of a Bengali woman's life, denoting the marginality of a woman newly married, newly arrived and settled into a household, which consists of virtual strangers, she comes from her *desh* to *bidesh*. The concept of *desh*, used to refer to one's country, village or region. *Desh* is fixed and unchangeable and is defined socially in relation to the place of origin and location of the patrilineage. The *desh* of a married woman is her father's village, not that of her husband's. A daughter never loses links with her natal house, even when she follows the code of conduct (*niom-kanun*) of her husband's *gushti* along with the rules and systems prevailing in his *desh* (Gardner, 1995; Uusikylä, 2000). The *notun bou* as well views her husband's household and community with the shifting perspective of an outsider and insider, constantly interpreting, negotiating and consolidating between these two positions and between two sorts of belonging – natal and marital (Kotalova, 1993, pp. 25–32, Gardner, 1995). A married woman in Bangladesh, depending on the relationship with the other individual, is usually addressed as *bou* (wife), *ma* (mother), *bhabi* (brother's wife), *chachee* or *mamee* (father's brother's or mother's brother's wife), *shasuri* (mother-in-law) and a host of other kin terms, but rarely by her given name. Even a woman's own children rarely mention her name in public whereas the father's name is always required for self-identity and other forms of recognition including schooling and legal inheritance (Noman, 1983; Khan, 1988; Mabud, 1990; Miah, 1992). But over time, a bride becomes accustomed to her position and assimilates with her affinal family.

However, for a woman, her natal family continues to be viewed as a place of refuge and of succor throughout her life and on the one hand, women experience continual feelings of "foreignness" in their marital home and feelings of longing for the natal kin on the other. The present study's ethnographic data also revealed the same feelings among the *basti* women. From the women of the two *bastis*, I found out that some of their parents and other natal relatives were living in the village and some in the city in other *bastis*. Most of the women, whose parents were still alive, have relationships with them, although these poor parents could do very little for their daughters, but emotionally this relationship is very important. The women said, their poor parents could not save them from poverty, but in the case of marital maladjustment, the women relied on their parents for solutions or for mental soothing. But in their accounts, nowadays the relationship with married siblings especially with brothers depends on two-way reciprocity. No woman depends on her poor brothers to help in her family livelihood but seeks help when she is facing marital problems.

Bangladeshi women always consider that they are physically and morally bound to their husbands and to their families. In Bengali culture, the relationship of husband and wife is considered as a "shared body" relationship in which the wife is the half-body of her husband (Inden and Nicholas, 1977, p. 99). The Bengali word and concept *ardhangini* refers to the wife as the other half of her husband's body (Rozario, 1992; Uusikylä, 2000). The women generally follow two virtues: patience and sacrifice. After marriage when a young woman goes to her father-in-law's house (*soshur bari*), everybody demands that she should be subject to the "law" of her husband, father-in-law and mother-in-law. She is expected to adjust quickly to her husband's household, although she is placed there under restrictions and has little or no say in decision-making. In the *soshur bari*, a woman's mobility is restricted compared with her parent's household. In Bangladesh, the relationship between mother-in-law (*shasuri*) and daughter-in-law (*bou*) is generally one in which the younger woman is in an inferior position; she is directly subordinate to her mother-in-law. On the other hand, there is remarkable warm behavior displayed by in-laws to their son-in-law because they expect and hope if they treat the husband well then the wife would also be treated well in her in-law's house. Indeed, *jamai ador* (looking after a groom in his in-law's house) has become an idiom in the language for special privileges and exceptionally kind treatment. The Hindus, among whom marriage is a sacrament, celebrate a special day in the year in honor of the son-in-law, called *jamai sasthi*, when the husbands of the daughters of the family receive new clothes and special sweets and seasonal fruits from the wife's family.

In this section, I have illustrated how marriage as a significant institution changes a woman's life and described the marriage arrangements. The next section will look at current marriage exchanges in Bangladeshi society, which both directly and indirectly influence the future conjugal life of a woman and create situations for potential domestic violence. How are dowries set for Bangladeshi women and why are they given?

Marriage and dowry in the slum life

Marriage is an integral part of life for Bangladeshi men and women. Each new marriage creates an alliance between two families, in a broad sense between two groups. This union is based on the central notion of exchange in Bangladeshi society where material goods, food and women are exchanged and in turn new possibilities for future marriages are opened up with each marriage bond. Generally, in Bangladeshi society except for some tribal groups, one group acts as wife-givers and other group acts as wife receivers. The wife receivers' group by and large is considered stronger and in a higher position than wife-givers group. The marriage ceremony is one of the key symbols of Bangladeshi society. In the marriage ceremony, feasts and gifts are exchanged from both the bride and the groom's sides, but these are periodical. But through marriage two families become affines or enhance their affinity by the bond of marriage so it is considered emotionally, economically and socially an extremely important event.

The practice of dowry or gift giving by the bride's family to the groom's family started in the Indian subcontinent in the second century BCE, and now it is seen as a social curse for the South Asian region (Ahmed-Ghosh, 2004). The concept of dowry in Bangladesh originated from an ancient Hindu custom; an approved marriage among Hindus has always been considered to be a *kanyadaan* (gift of a daughter). According to the Hindu *Dharmashastra* (code of religion), the act of *kanyadaan* is not fulfilled till the bridegroom is given *varadakhshina* (gift of the groom) in the form of cash or kind. This was out of love and affection and in honor of the bridegroom and the amount varied in accordance with the economic position of the bride's father. Similarly, the bride gets *stridhan*, which is property of the bride. These were meant to provide economic security to the couple in any adverse situation. Over time, these two aspects of Hindu marriage assumed the name of "dowry" (*joutuk*) (Javed, 1991; Ahmed-Ghosh, 2004).

In the present study, most of the *basti* women said that the practice of dowry is embedded as self-evident in society so natal relatives of women cannot escape from the practice. As a result, now gift giving in marriage is considered as a regular practice in the marriage ritual. According to the women, for the beauty of the wedding ceremony (*sounderja-er jonno*), every father, whether rich or poor, has to provide marriage gifts for his daughter's marriage. For a poor father, it is an intolerable burden; if the man has more than one daughter, the family falls into a vicious circle of poverty. But in many cases, the groom's family demands some gifts with little consideration to what the bride's family can afford. Moreover, sometimes after marriage, some grooms and their families place multiple demands for different material resources including cash. Most of the time, these situations are unanticipated by the father or brothers of the married woman; as a result, the family falls into vulnerable situation as they try to preserve the continuity and happiness of their daughter's or sister's marriage. The women were knowledgeable that forceful demands for gifts in the marriage of a daughter are called *joutuk* (dowry), but the girls' families never utter this word in front of groom's family or to others. They are afraid to utter this word and get into an argument with the groom's family because they think that by uttering this word they may be damaging their daughter's chances for a successful marriage.

Researchers (Rozario, 2001; Ameen, 2005) claim that in present day, drastic change has occurred in the marriage gifts in Bangladeshi society. Now in Bangladesh, the bride's family has to give valuable material goods to the groom's family as a marriage gift. It is considered a normal practice for the happiness of the girl's married life. But sometimes these kinds of transactions occurred by putting pressure to the bride's family and sometimes on the basis of negotiation. This kind of gift exchange is considered to be a dowry (*joutuk*). But from the side of the groom, they only provide clothes and jewelry for the bride for the marriage ceremony, and in most cases, the bride's family does not make any demands for any material resources. For the groom's family in Bangladesh, a marriage gift is explicably or inexplicably a ubiquitous means of social commerce. In the marriage negotiations, it becomes a major factor for all religions in Bangladesh, which makes demands on the bride's family for wealth instead of a father's voluntary gift to his daughter. Sometimes, if the girl's parents arrange their daughter marriage into a family of a higher social stratum, it creates serious vulnerability and a devalued status for the bride in her affinal household because her parents cannot provide all the dowry payments according to their agreement. Moreover, in the in-laws' house, the new bride is now not welcomed as a new member of the family rather her status is measured by the amount of dowry she brings from her natal family.

In the case of Bangladesh, Santi Rozario (2001) states that the shift from *pon* (bride wealth) to *dabi* (dowry) is linked to socio-economic changes and it has happened with the shift from an agricultural pre-capitalist cash economy to an urban-based, capitalist cash economy. Rozario does not point a finger at traditional culture for the emergence of dowry in the Bangladeshi marriage practice, rather she claims that socio-economic transformations are the main reasons that have made marriage commercialized and focused people's greed. According to her, another signifying reason for this rising demand of a dowry is the mounting unemployment level among young males in the country, especially in rural Bangladesh. As a result, the dowry is considered as an "investment" or capital to helping the groom establish future economic security, for instance, to help him with dowry money to open a business or send him to abroad to find a job.

Now it is not necessary to demand a dowry from the bride's family, rather it works silently in the process of marriage. As a result, if the natal family of the bride does not provide any dowry or fails to fulfill its dowry promise, abuse directed at the bride begins. Not only the husband but his parents and relatives remind the wife that the remaining payment is still due. Incidents of murder or attempted murder are regular news items in the country's daily papers. Most dowry deaths occur in the privacy of the husband's home and with the collusion of his family members. The courts have therefore admitted their inability to convict suspects because of a lack of proof. Sometimes, the police do not investigate the real causes of death (Ameen, 2005).

In their descriptions of marriage gifts, the *basti* women explained that in marriages, parents give different types of materials to their daughters' marriage according to what they can afford. They give furniture, bedding, kitchen utensils and groom's garments. These are currently the common gifts when a marriage is arranged in a *basti*. But now low-income parents are facing unbearable burdens on their resources for their daughters' marriage because the groom's side demand color televisions, refrigerators, expensive mobile phones, sofa sets, etc. Those parents who can provide these expensive materials along with regular marriage gifts can only hope for their daughters' conjugal happiness. They argue that as they are live in the city where they can observe the trends for marriage gifts set by the wealthy, they cannot but follow the trends. In Sylhet, they observe that rich people provide expensive marriage gifts for their daughters' marriages and they fill one or two trucks with different expensive household materials and appliances for their daughters' affinal families in order to maintain their daughters' prestige or to ensure their daughters' happiness. "In Sylhet, we have noticed that the marriage gifts of the rich men's daughters go by truck and poor men's daughters by cart," expressed a 30-year-old slum woman while discussing the problems of dowry practice in the marriage. According to the *basti* dwellers, to the rich people these are not dowry; these are maybe voluntary gifts and best wishes from parents to their lovable daughters for an auspicious conjugal bond and a new kinship alliance. The respondents tried to argue that by noticing the practice of the upper class, the poor people are now feeling greedy and forget what they can afford and try to give marriage gifts that are alarming and dangerous for their daughters. Happy and voluntary marriage gifts have now turned into a dowry, and they make marriage uncertain and inauspicious. The women said that now it is always publicized in media that dowries are dangerous for women's lives and they should be removed from the society. There are many advertisements, different types of drama and songs trying to influence people to stand against this social disease. But nobody tries to internalize these statements; rather everybody is practicing or bound to practice this tradition and tries to keep it alive in the society.

To highlight the sad experiences and feelings about dowry practice in an ethnographic (in-depth) interview, a *basti* woman, Noziron (around 32 years old) described her personal experience of dowry practice. She tearfully described her younger sister's life. She said her younger sister died because of pressure for a dowry. She lived in another *basti* of Sylhet city with her in-laws. They were not good people and very greedy. When she was married, their father gave a dowry of all the necessary household items. But the poor father could not provide Taka 20,000 which her sister's affines demanded just after her marriage. So her sister's husband and mother-in-law beat her inhumanly, and she could not tolerate this humiliation and committed suicide by taking poison.

In the Hindu *basti*, some women described problems of giving dowries in the Hindu community. Purnalakshmi (26 years) expressed her poor father's deplorable situation after the marriages of his daughters.

> Now without homestead land my father does not have anything. For the marriage and the dowry of our three sisters, he had to sell all his agricultural plots. He is now suffering from acute poverty. There is nobody to look after him,

she said in a sad voice. According to Purnalakshmi, now many Hindu families are selling their lands for their daughter's marriage and they fall into degrading situations. But the parents are bound to follow their moral duty (*dharma*), the rules of society (*somaj-er niom*), and are obliged to arrange their daughter's marriage for their *shomman* (prestige). While I was hearing the sad experiences and views related to dowry practice, Kamini (around 25 year Hindu woman) gave a contrasting viewpoint of dowry practices in Hindu society. In Kamini's account, the household items, jewelry and cash, which are given by the fathers of Hindu girls during marriage, should not be considered as dowries. She pointed out that if Hindu parents do not give anything at the time of marriage, the Hindu women will not get anything from them in future because Hindu daughters do not inherit property. In future, the brothers will not give them anything, after the death of the parents, the brothers sometimes forget their sisters. Moreover, without a dowry, women do not get a warm reception in her in-law's house. From her perspective, it is the tradition of the country that every woman gets some resources from her natal family when she marries and these resources bring honor to her married life. If any woman goes to her affinal house empty handed, she will be insulted and her affines may subject her to various forms of torture.

I argue that the diverse views of voluntary marriage gifts and dowry practices create new grounds for alternative thinking relating to marriage exchange in Bangladesh. In the two slums, sometimes women favor this practice and demand it as a manifestation of their prestige (*somman*) and honor (*morzada*) in the affinal family and an asset for the future (*bhabishyot*) of the family, but sometimes the women disapprove of dowries due to the poverty.

Conclusion

At the beginning of the chapter the question of the desire to have either daughters or sons in the family was looked into and the effect of gender preferences on the position of women from the beginning of their lives was deciphered. The study's ethnographic data revealed that different everyday practices and events put girls in an unequal position in their gender relations when growing up to be a woman. I found the women still having "doxic" (Bourdieu, 2002 [1977], pp. 167–170) views of the value of daughters, so that most of them preferred to have only one daughter in the family, and found it prestigious to have many sons, guiding their daughters to learn religious ideals and texts and household chores, control girls' mobility by ending their formal education after the primary or secondary levels, prefer and encourage their daughters' early marriage and motherhood. As the women migrated from the villages to the urban areas, to some extent they are forced to become aware of alternative values and practices in this new environment.

With regard to marriage practice, the giving of dowries appears to be widespread in both the *bastis*. Most of the respondents were aware of the problems of dowry practices, but they stated that nowadays the pressure to give marriage gifts to the groom's house had grown. In the beginning of marriage negotiations, gifts are bound to play an important role for the creation of future alliance. Although there is legislation prohibiting dowries and many people are also critical of the dowry practice, this practice is taken for granted and perpetuated and even strengthened in a patriarchal order of the predominantly agriculture-based society, even in the context of rapid urbanization in the globalized and commercialized era. Basically, from the study, it is highlighted that economic crises in an agricultural society, together with the growing demands of the commercialized economy, are noteworthy causes for the growing importance of marriage gift transactions and dowries even among the poor urbanites. The next chapter will focus on how young *basti* women negotiate their place in society and struggle to build their identities in the urban milieu.

Notes

1 *Bari* has some resemblance to the localized patriline (*gushti*), usually the houses where brothers from the same parents are living with their wives and children either in a joint family or in nuclear families. The *bari* may also include households without an agnatic link.
2 Stalking and sexual harassment.
3 Term adopted from Kotalova (1993, p. 44).
4 The kinship term gushti refers to a group of households or families who are agnatically related with the exception of in-marrying wives and out-marrying daughters. A common ancestry provides a sense of belonging that binds together the members of a gushti (Aziz, 1979, p. 24).
5 The kinship term *attio*, or *attio suajan*, refers to people or a group of people considered "kin." *Attio* can be a person related by blood or marriage.
6 The kinship term *kutum* refers to people related through marriage. A *kutum* relationship is reciprocal and *kutum* relatives have the most honorable status and should be received with hospitality when they visit each other's residences.

3 Liberating one's own space

In quest of self-identity and agency in everyday life

Among the *basti* dwellers of the research areas, there are many women who work outside home. These women participate in the "public" world as a work force and are proud of their ability to work. These working women are acting as agents and are manipulating the circumstances to their advantage and strategizing with the resources they have. The aim of this chapter is to address the range and diversity of the day-to-day experiences of *basti* women who work outside home, to show women as subjects and that their actions interact with the external structures and how the women resist and challenge the code of conduct expected from them. I examine what changes taking place after rural-urban migration, wage work, more freedom of movement outside the domestic sphere in the lives of women.

This chapter focuses on women's agency and helps to place women as active agents, rather than passive objects, who apply "independent authority and control" and confront "oppression and exploitation of women" by existing power structures and gender hierarchies therein (Kabeer, 2001; Parmar, 2003). Treating people "as agents" means giving them a chance to be heard and to be involved in collective evaluations and decisions' (Agarwal et al., 2003, p. 5). Archer (2000, p. 254) views this as the emergence of "social selves … which occurs at the interface of 'structure and agency'." Agency refers "to an actor's ability to have some effect on the social world, altering the rules or the distribution of resources" (Scott, 2001, p. 76). In conflicts of gender power relations, agency in its ability to counter structures of hierarchy and subordination may give rise to different degrees of empowerment. Women actors, both individually or collectively as part of a group, possess some degree of agency which may vary. Agency is situated. "A person's agency aspect cannot be understood without taking note of his or her aims, objectives, allegiances, obligations and in a broad sense the person's conceptions of the good" (quoted in Peter, 2003. pp. 17–18). "Agency highlights how acts themselves may have value" (Peter, 2003, p. 17). "Agency brings to the fore a broader conception of social choice … participation and inclusion in democratic decision-making" (ibid., p. 24). In this chapter, I see how does women's agency enable them to strengthen their bargaining power by taking into account their own perceptions and experiences?

Working outside home: women's voices from the *bastis*

The word work (*kaj*) has a particular meaning among the *basti* women. They unanimously consider income-generating work as *kaj*, but work that does not produce income in terms of cash or kind is not considered as work in the same meaning. They firmly believe that married women are bound to do household work (*ghorer kaj/sangsar-er kaj*) and consider the household as the inevitable center of their life. But to them household work is not considered to be work because it does not bring any significant change in their lives and does not emancipate them from poverty. In the two *bastis*, women constructed household duties as the obligatory part of life of a married woman. Although most of the poverty-stricken women desire to work outside home, there is not suitable work available in the urban informal and formal sector in Sylhet city. Many women explained how they decided to take jobs that would have been out of question to their husbands and in their native place. A young woman (around 23 years) said, "We work outside home due to poverty.... And in the urban area many women are working outside home."

The first thing I discover when I raise this issue about their working outside the household is a very critical question. Because in Sylhet city, there are a few options for women's wage work in the urban informal sector. Among the *basti* women, I found most of the working women are part-time domestic helpers in the well-off houses near the *basti* and work as daily laborers in the building construction or as earth workers (*mati kata sromic*). There are some women cooking in a bachelor's dormitories (*mess*), a woman runs a shop, one is a tailor, and another woman is running a small business with a woman inside the *basti*.

Work of honor, work of shame

Domestic helper work is considered to be suitable work for women of the lower socio-economic class although in the society it is considered as low status work for women. In Bangladesh, globalization, rapid urbanization and industrialization have created different economic classes, and in the upper-class, upper-middle-class and middle-class families, the dirtier and heavier household chores are shifted to part-time or fixed domestic helpers. In the Pirer Tila, women usually work as part-time domestic helpers and they make preparations for cooking, sweep and mop up the house, and wash cloths and kitchen utensils. They usually work for two or three houses at a time, and their monthly incomes vary from 1,000 Taka to 3,000 Taka (1,000 Taka per house). Although the payments are low, domestic helper work provides a steady income compared with building construction labor and earth work, which are of varying availability and most of the time these are seasonal work. Some domestic helpers consider their work very hard and their income is not enough to maintain their families, but they have to do this work as it is suitable wage work for women.

Although these women are uneducated or less educated, they have consciously contracted low-paid and less dignified work outside the home to earn their livelihood. But by the same token, they have realized their position and ability in the family and society and have feelings of some sort of empowerment. Take the example of Amina, a 29-year-old part-time domestic helper, who is now working in three households. After losing their homestead and cultivable land due to river erosion, her family moved to Sylhet city seven years ago and started to live in the Pirer Tila *basti*. Amina's husband started to work as a rickshaw puller, but because of his ill health, he cannot provide the family with any regular income. This economic insolvency and increased domestic violence by her husband pushed Amina to work as a part-time domestic helper, which changed her understanding of women's position and roles in the family and gender relations. Amina could not go back to the village because she didn't have anything there and there was no opportunity to earn livelihood. When she started to work, her husband became violent toward her. Sometimes he beat her. Amina's husband had been suffering from chronic blood dysentery (*rokto amasha*) and gout (*baat rog*) for a long time and taking different kinds of herbal and allopathic medicine to get rid of those diseases but nothing worked. But the man didn't try to understand his inability. Amina quarreled with him and didn't stop her work. She learned her rights as a woman and as an individual after she had started to work.

Cooking in a bachelor's dormitory is considered to be lucrative work for the *basti* women, but in the context of Bangladeshi society, it is a low status and less prestigious work for women, which sometimes tarnishes women's honor. But as the two *bastis* are near the university area, some women now do this work and earn a fair amount of money. Those who work in the bachelor's mess, try to establish a positive notion of doing work in this distinctive sphere. Aziza, a 35-year-old woman stated,

> we work in the educated men's and students' dormitories inside or near to the university; they are very good people, they never see us in other way and respect us as their relatives ... we never feel insecure there ... we got the jobs with the help of people we know.

Morzina (a 28-year-old Muslim woman) is now cooking in a mess for bachelors inside the university area. She has got the work through some of her husband's acquaintances. Her husband has given her permission to work there, and now she goes there regularly two or three times a day to do the cooking. Her husband is a part-time electrician and considered as a pious (*dharmic*) man in the *basti*. He is now letting his wife work outside home in the public domain not only because of poverty but to help him to side-by-side eke out their livelihood.

I find Morzina's husband to be well informed and modern. He is also not bound by religious superstitions and believes in women's freedom. So without any objections from the husband and covering her head with a *sarir acchol* (last long part of *sari*), Morzina goes outside in the unrelated males' domain. Moreover, she also keeps on good terms with some other unrelated men to find different types of help, such as borrowing money in the time of crisis, finding suitable work, keeping her in favor at her work place, etc. What strikes me in this respect is that by working in the university area, she is now dreaming about her children's education, delaying the marriage of her 12-year-old elder daughter, and sending her two sons to a charity learning center run by the university students. She has also bought an old color television using a loan of 3,000 Taka from her work place. When she goes to work, her mother-in-law cooks lunch for the family and looks after her small grandchildren. Morzina's income has changed the traditional power relationship between mother-in-law and daughter-in-law. Morzina's mother-in-law now accepts the changing pattern of the power hierarchy and helps her daughter-in-law to work outside the household area.

In my conversations with Morzina I asked her how she feels to work in a bachelor male dormitory. Morzina says: "In my working place they call me *khala* (maternal aunt), some call me *boin* (sister); they respect me a lot. I don't have any problem." I also got the impression from Morzina's subsequent conversation about her new outlook on working in the male space. She stated that her husband is poor, so he alone cannot earn enough to support his family. In this context, she is helping her husband and can take better care of their family. Before cooking in a bachelor male mess, she worked as an earth worker, which she found was not good for women's body and health. According to her, nowadays many women are working outside according to their abilities, skills, and education levels. So in this sense, she is not doing anything wrong, not going to any bad places and while working she stays within the bounds of modesty (*shalinota*) with her husband's consent. Moreover, her outside work does not create any obstacle to her everyday household activities because her old mother-in-law and elder daughter help to do the household chores. According to her, she is not doing any harm to society and not disobeying the religious bindings for women. She strongly emphasized that, "Bibi Ayesha went to the battlefield with Hazrat Muhammad (SM) and Bibi Khadiza was a business woman. So to me if a woman modestly goes outside her home, it is not a problem for the family."

Again I asked Morzina, "You not have any reservations about working in the bachelor's dormitory, but is it not dangerous traveling to and from work?" Morzina explained her position in the following:

> I have strength in my hands and shoulders so I do not want to sit idly at home. I think I have to work for a better future for my children; I work for them, for my family. I have saved some money from my salary and bought a pair of gold earrings (*kaner dool*), a nose pin (*nak fool*) and two cheap mobile phones for my husband and myself.... I feel happy when I see the happy faces of my children. We have also bought an old color television set. Now we can enjoy drama, Bengali movies, film songs, news, etc. All the happiness of my family is made possible only by my earning.

Morzina's case is significant in terms of showing the change in power dynamics between husbands and wives over the decision to work outside home in the changed space. In Morzina's case, her modest dressing and mobility, her husband's lack of concern about her work in the bachelor's dormitory and getting work through her acquaintances, make her feel safer. Morzina has achieved economic resources, freedom for mobility and can dream of a better future, so she does not ever wish to stop working. Moreover, employment not only increases a woman's financial well-being, but it can also increase her social capital and social networks, thus providing her with additional instrumental and emotional resources (Macmillan and Gartner, 1999; Kaukinen, 2004; Tenhunen, 2006). If the job is satisfying, employment may affect a woman's mental health through an increase in self-esteem, a reduction in depression and an increased sense of control over her life (Raver, 2003).

In Bangladesh, when a working-class woman looks for a job or works outside, the main concern for her and her family is that there should not be any rumors about her, tarnishing her honor. The norms of respectability and sexual protection are important concerns in women's decisions to work. So in the daily lives of working-class women, the main way to deal with these concerns is to find a job through a relative or acquaintance. Many women in the basti think that a workplace should be open and protected, so not to harm the women's reputations. Although some get a very minimal monthly salary and daily wages, the women firmly believe that to work in an open and protected space is more important than money. In the two *bastis*, I found friendship or we-feeling among some women being of material and emotional significance. This friendship, especially among some *basti* women, is a matter of practical importance for searching for work outside home to earn their livelihoods. Women call one another by fictive kinship terms and go to one another's house freely and gossip together. They sometimes share their private lives' pains and pangs and sometimes its happiness. Tenhunen also explores a similar scenario in her study of a slum in Calcutta (Tenhunen, 2006). In the present study, Korima, a 23-year-old, domestic helper states the following:

> Some women of our *basti* have not found work, they always ask us [working women of the *basti*] to help them and look for a job for them. We also try to help them, but sometimes it is really impossible to find suitable work.

As mentioned in Chapter 1, I focus on some examples that *basti* women come into conflict with each other in their daily lives when they try to get access to limited facilities and spaces (e.g., using the toilet, tube-well or stove). But I also get the impression from Korima's narrative that women's informal sharing in the neighborhood also created a feeling of solidarity among the *basti* women. Those women who are engaged in income-generating activities try to search for work for unemployed women, and in this way a sisterhood develops among the neighborhood women. Although it is hard to solve many women's domestic conflicts with their spouses or mothers-in-law, the women feel the sorrows, anxieties and pain of their peers. Sometimes they support abused women who are their friends and informally try to mitigate their domestic violence.

When a woman has economic resources of her own, she may feel stronger. Economic ability is thought to expand their choices and help women to become more free and independent and increases her bargaining power within the household and society (Sen, 1990; Nussbaum, 2000; Kumar, 2006, p. 69). In the Pirer Tila, Afia (a 40-year-old Muslim woman) is running a small grocery shop. People from the nearby households come to buy their daily necessities in the shop. According to Afia, "If any woman does any good work with modesty, it should not be a problem for anybody." In Sylhet city, a woman grocer is not yet a very common scenario, but Afia has taken on this challenge. Afia's courageous step to be a grocer can be seen as a radical step and the acceptance of her way of living by others can be seen as part of a modern outlook. I get the impression from the respondents that if women get family support they can overcome other patriarchal and religious barriers and cope with the new situations, and in the long run, they may break away from the traditional womanhood concept.

But these ideas of working women from the description within some *basti* households are not enough for understanding women's agency in their everyday lives. I think the best way to demonstrate this is to begin with some unique cases – the first case represents a woman who adopts a typical role to survive in the *basti*. The case of Beauty sheds light on a radical transformation of an ordinary Bangladeshi woman. She speaks in an alternative voice and is active in the creation of her own world. Beauty is a Muslim woman, whose marital life is divided into two episodes. In the first episode, she experienced a happy conjugal life, but after sudden widowhood, she lost all support and rights from her marital home and was ousted from it. In the second episode, she was forced to marry a widower by her parents, but her conjugal life was not happy; she faced violent behavior and cheating by her second husband and was divorced by him. From then she decided to live alone by discounting Bangladeshi social structure because a divorced woman may acceptably live only with her parents or brothers but not alone.

The second case shows how gender extends to the relationships, practices, and interactions that make up differences between men and women and differences among women because identities and positions of power are set in specific contexts. Women contend with the responsibilities, unequal exchanges, and ambiguities of affect in affinity as mothers-in-law, daughters-in-law, sisters-in-law. Yet both gender and affinity are experienced and negotiated in different ways depending on age and generation, relationship with spouse, access to resources such as wage work and money, having children and other factors. Domestic violence against young wives in Bangladesh is culturally rooted and produces and reproduces interpersonal concessions for positioning power in the context of multiple structured inequalities. In spite of the seemingly common nature of domestic violence, domestic violence in affinity entails complex and locally relevant modes of interpretation and understanding. Parul's case focus on domestic violence to incorporate the webs of power within which women find themselves or through which they might actively seek to alter their circumstances.

Case 1 A woman on her own: coping with crisis

Beauty is a 24-year-old pretty Muslim divorcee, living alone in the Pirer Tila *basti*. She was divorced by her second husband. Her lonely living in a *basti* in an urban setting presents a different scenario in the context of Bangladeshi culture and it is of course a challenge to the patriarchal social structure. She works as a part-time domestic helper and also as a helper in a tailoring shop. So every day she remains busy from morning to evening by working outside home. I wanted to know about her life, so one day at dusk I visited the *basti* and was sitting with Morzina near to her door. After half an hour she arrived at her house with her only daughter. She made her apologies for being delay in a soft voice.

Beauty got married according to the wishes of her parents in the age of 15 when she was in the fifth grade at school. Her birth place (*deser bari*) is in Sunamganj and her father was a petty farmer. Her first husband was a petty business man and her affinal village was near her birthplace. After her marriage, she lived in her in-law's house with love and affection. She never felt that she was a daughter-in-law (*bou*) in their family. Her mother-in-law was a very candid woman; she used to gossip, cook and work with her. Her husband was also a very good and sympathetic young man. At the age of 17, she gave birth to a daughter, but the family was not unhappy because it was their first grandchild.

But Beauty's happiness did not endure long, only after three years of married life she became an unlucky woman because she lost her first husband when her daughter was only one year old. Her husband died from an unknown disease after suffering only for two days. After his death, her mother-in-law could not tolerate her. Everybody in her affinal family blamed her as an inauspicious (*opoya*) woman. After her husband's death all at once the whole scenario of her happy family life broke like a mirror. Consequently, her father took her away from that house.

After some months, Beauty's mother and elder brother again arranged for her to be married to a widower who had lost his wife some years ago. The man also had a ten-year-old son. Beauty did not agree to this proposal and cried a lot arguing that she had a small daughter so she preferred not to get married again. But her mother became very angry and forced her to get married.

She finally agreed to marry again. Her second husband was a truck driver, and he lived in a sublet house in Sylhet city. After marriage, she went to him with a hope for a new family (*sangsar*); but she found that her husband was a promiscuous man so he was not happy with her. He used to go to brothels and had a habit of drinking local liquor (*deshi mod*). She was not happy with him and protested against his bad habits; so most of the time he beat her brutally. Within one and half years of her second marriage, the man lost all fascination with her and got married again to another woman. He brought his new wife home and divorced Beauty and gave her 200 Taka to go back to her natal home. Beauty became totally frantic and went back to her natal family. She was so upset with her life that she wanted to commit suicide by taking a pesticide. But one of her elder parallel cousins (*boro chachato bhai*) and his wife rescued her.

At that time, Beauty's cousin lived in Sylhet city with his family and he asked her poor father to permit her to go with them to search for work. At first, her father hesitated, but finding no other alternative, he gave his permission. This time she could bring her daughter along with her. However, I asked Beauty about her present life in the *basti* and this is what she said:

> Now for three years I have been living here in this *basti* in a rented shanty beside my cousin's shanty. I am now working in a household as a part-time domestic worker. They are good people and behave very nicely to me. I am also learning women's dressmaking in a tailoring shop. Now I am earning Taka 2,400 per month and eke out my livelihood by myself. At first I was afraid to live alone, but now I am capable. I feel that I have strength in my hands and feet, I think I am a human (*manush*). I will never marry again. I can now dream for my daughter; she is now going to primary school.
>
> INTERVIEWER: Does anybody disturb you in the *basti*? How do you protect yourself and your daughter?
>
> BEAUTY: Yes, there are some lecherous men in the *basti*, they look disdainfully at me. Some women also gossip about me. But I don't care now. At nights I sleep with a *boti* (a long knife with a short haft) near my bed-side. Besides, my cousin's two elder daughters also sleep with me in the night for protection. Moreover, very secretly I want to tell you that along with my *bhabi* (sister-in-law), I told some women in the basti that some bad supernatural spirits (*giin*) have possessed me. They are very rough so if anybody marries me they would kill him. I also wear a long, loose topcoat (*burkha*) and heavy scarf (*vari orna*) when I go outside to work to protect my honor. I always pray five times a day and recite the Holy Quran. People know it and consider me to be a pious woman.

In the example of Beauty, we can see how a young woman saved herself and started to live alone in an urban basti, constructed her freedom in relation to dominant cultural discourses, working in a tailoring shop and as a part-time domestic helper, doesn't want to remarry, is courageous and wants to rely on herself. To save herself from scandal and bad people, she also applies secret resistance, which is spirit possession[1] on herself, it is not normal to human and is ghastly and fearful. In Bangladeshi society, people fear super natural powers (*giin*) and believe that sometimes *giin* can catch human and reside in their bodies, and those who possess special powers given to them by *giin* can harm other human.

Michael Gilsenan (1982, p. 76 as cited in Gardner, 1995, p. 257) points out: "It is not the objective 'reality' of miracles which is interesting, but rather the fact that people believe in them." Crapanzano (1977, p. 7) has stated that, "Spirit possession may symbolize a magical route of escape from the burden of responsibilities accompanying an ideology of intensive individualism that is contradicted in the real world." Agarwal (1994, p. 427) also finds in Indian Rajasthan, village women sometimes claim to be possessed by a spirit, which demands satisfaction, in order to consume food items otherwise denied to them. A similar case has also been found by Khan (1983 as cited in Agarwal, 1994, p. 427) in the tribal belt of Pakistan. Beauty is a model of patriarchal repression, but now she is trying to protect herself by her secret resistance power and agency. Beauty's veil performs dual functions: It protects her honor and makes her feel safer. It acts as a symbolic armor protecting her from the risks of "unfamiliar and unrelated urban life," and in a "crowded basti environment." According to Kandiyoti (1988, p. 283) the veil (*pardah*) is a "traditional modesty marker," which symbolically identifies a woman's modest character and religiosity to everybody, including society at large.

Case 2 No place of her own: too great a risk?

From the first day of my fieldwork in the Pirer Tila *basti*, I noticed a sick and thin adolescent girl. She always wore a *maxi* (long gown type dress) and *orna* (long piece of cloth for covering the upper part of the body) and was busy doing her household chores. Her pale and gloomy face marked a sorrowful young lady's portrait in my mind. I wanted to know about her so I asked my informer, Morzina, to arrange a meeting with her. Morzina said it would not be good for Parul to talk with me inside Parul's house because she was living with her husband and mother-in-law and her mother-in-law was a bad woman. Parul is a frequent victim of domestic violence by her affines. I did not witness any incident of violence, but Morzina did. She informed me everybody in the *basti* knew that Parul was facing domestic violence, but nobody could do anything for her because they all feared that it may break the couple's relationship. Only when Parul shouted too much and her husband and mother-in-law beat her severely some women went to stop her violent husband and mother-in-law. So one afternoon Morzina arranged a meeting with Parul inside Morzina's house.

Parul's (16 years old) mother-in-law does not want to keep her as her son's wife because she had failed to give birth to any living children. Two of her daughters were stillborn. She was considered to be inauspicious by her mother-in-law. Moreover, the mother-in-law believed that if her son married again they would get dowry money to establish a small business. As a result, she was trying to influence her son and encouraged him to get divorced and remarry. Parul has a skinny and weak body after giving birth to two stillborn children in her adolescence. Her deliveries were very problematic and she had lost a lot of blood. Now her husband does not like her and looks for faults in everything she does. According to Parul, her husband is very lazy and he does not go to work regularly. Parul works as a domestic worker in a house nearby and her income maintains the family. But her husband and mother-in-law are not grateful to her, rather everyday she has to hear some filthy language and abusive words from them or experience violent behavior from their side. One of the conversations I had with Parul follows below:

INTERVIEWER (I): Don't you resist them when they beat you?

PARUL: Sometimes I also use foul language (*kharap khota*) when I can't tolerate any more but then they beat me more than usual. I cannot escape it. I hate my mother-in-law and husband very much for their inhuman behavior. So when she orders me to clean her *paan* (betel leaf) I do not clean it nicely when I find an opportunity to do that secretly. Sometimes she orders me to clean her *sari* with soap but I do not do it properly. I only wet the *sari* with water and hang it outside to dry in the sun.

I: Do you receive sufficient food in your house?

PARUL: No, I work and earn the livelihood but my mother-in-law and husband enjoy my income. Most of the time, they only give me a little food. In my workplace, my mistress usually gives me rice and curry to take home for lunch, but I never bring it home; I eat it there. Why and for whom should I bring rice? Nobody loves me; they always scold me and beat me like an animal (she starts crying).

I: Do you hand over your full salary to your husband and mother-in-law?

PARUL: (After crying for a while) I earn Taka 1,400 from my workplace and this is known by my husband and mother-in-law. So I am bound to give them all the money; otherwise they would beat me and stop me from going to work. I am afraid of losing this job because my mistress is very good to me. But sometimes my mistress gives me some tips on religious occasions and when she is pleased with my tidy household chores. This is my extra income; I never disclose it to my husband and mother-in-law and I secretly keep it as savings.

I: Why are you staying with them as they are so brutal with you?

PARUL: I don't want to stay with them; I want to go back to my mother. She knows everything about their torture but she instructs me to stay with them as long as I can tolerate their violent behavior. Because if I leave on my own, my brothers will not let me stay with them and all my kin and village neighbors will call me bad names.

Parul's suffering illustrates the complex ways in which existing patterns of domestic violence against women by affines are focused in Bangladeshi social structure. From the narratives of Parul, it is evident that although she understands that at any moment she can get a divorce from her husband and there is no sympathy and love for her, but she has to tolerate all the violence as long as the relationship does not end from the husband's side. In Parul's narrative, it can be seen that resistance to intra-family power structures in the extended family can take different forms. The oppressed are not always passive victims in their given situation and accept the oppression; they also try to resist oppression in many covert and subtle ways (Agarwal, 1994, p. 423). White (1992, p. 138) depicted a contested image of how a Bangladeshi village woman prepared tea with milk for herself and her female guest but served tea without milk to her husband and his friends, so that the men would "not think she has nothing better to do than make tea for them all day, and should be discouraged from returning."

Similarly from Parul's narratives, we see sometimes she disobeys her mother-in-law's order, does not properly do her mother-in-law's work, eats food outside home at her workplace without sharing with affines, hides her extra income from her mother-in-law and saves it.

I have discussed these two women's case, not because they are typical, but they could represent their agency, they are active and creative people involved in a continual flow of conduct in their structure.

Toward a new perception on pardah (a veil) and bargaining power

I asked the Muslim women in Pirer Tila *basti* who work outside their homes, how they maintain *pardah* (a veil) in their everyday lives. I found significant changes among the basti women about work outside home and religious practices. Most of the working women unanimously said that unquestioningly as Muslims they try to follow the verses of the Holy Quran and Hadith of prophet Mohammad (SM). But they also argue that although Allah has created them to conform to religious practice, he has made them poor so it is hard for them to follow the religious rules properly. Because of poverty, they could not stay in the house. In a focus group discussion some women said:

> If we always only think about *pardah* then how can we manage to secure food? Who will feed us? If I sit in the house because I am conforming to *pardah* nobody would employ me. I know that going outside without covering one's head is bad but I don't have any choice. I am an earth worker and my work is very laborious. I do not sit around. So if I wear a *burkha* (veil) I cannot do my work.
>
> (Azmeri, a 25-year-old woman)

> I know that according to *Hadith*, if a woman looks upon the face of an unrelated man it is a sin. To get forgiveness from Allah one should recite 100 times *Astagferullah* (Please pardon me), counting the *Tasbiah* (rosary). We are living in the *basti* together with different types of males and we have to interact with them. Now if we think about Hadith' rules, how many times will we recite *Astagferullah*? Allah created us poor, so of course he will forgive us.
>
> (Rafia, a 35-year-old woman)

It is noteworthy that Azmeri and Rafia both pointed out the mismatch between religious rules and poverty, their types of work (according to Azmeri) and the surrounding environment (according to Rafia). This is clear when we look at the forces behind the changing outlook about religion, we see by actively involving in income-generating activities, women are able to construct the idea and put into practice the identity of an autonomous individual. Moreover, it is reflected from the narratives that the level of religious belief has usually been connected with the social surroundings of women and their neighborhoods or close family members. I find that religious beliefs and practices are not a homogeneously inflexible set of rules, but a contested sphere in the lives of *basti* working women.

It is evident that because of migration to the city that individuals and groups have been changed by their exposure to modernity, and that women are now working outside the home in the public domain with unrelated men. But to me, alternative visions have also emerged in the minds of this group as they witness women's participation in the workforce outside home in the city. This notion of modernity can be related to Arce and Long's (2000, p. 2) definition of modernity. For them, modernity can be understood as "the new or emerging here-and-now materialities, meanings and cultural styles seen in relation to the notion of some past state of things." The change in consciousness of agents is considered to be the cause of the structural changes. Women's participation in the public domain and working in the informal sector can certainly be described as an agent of change in the social structure, and it can be related to modernity.

Gender roles and relations are not tangible and static but are matters of controversy and debate. Women do not exist as some essentially gendered, ahistorical group, but, like men, their identity is worked out in society and is constantly under negotiation and review (White, 1992, pp. 143–144). In this study, the example of women's agency can also be found from another quote. Hazera, (a Muslim woman, around 31 years old) is a casual unskilled laborer (an earth worker – *mati kata sromic*); she narrates her agency and bargaining power to control her economic freedom in this way:

> Sometime people use bad words to describe what we do when we leave home to earn a livelihood. Even some women in the *basti* say, "she is working outside as an earth worker after having three grown up male children." They hate me and sometimes laugh at me. But I don't bother; I want to walk along my path because I still have strength in my body. Nobody will feed me and my family members, people can only insult and criticize me. My husband also works with me as an earth worker; he is very simple (*sida*), when somebody in the *basti* criticizes me to him, he becomes furious and talks nonsense through one's hat to me. At that time, I also stand against him with my three sons and establish my right to work. We have been living in the *basti* for many years after migrating from our village, and during that time I have been trying hard to sustain our lives without bothering about anybody's comments. When I was young, I did this hard work with courage. So why should I not do it today? Moreover, it is a seasonal work, so who will feed us in the hard times when we do not get any work?

Increasing a woman's economic resources builds her agency to either bargain for a better situation for herself within the relationship or threaten to leave the relationship altogether and deprive the man of both her company and her financial contribution. Hazera's statement and strong standing against her husband

and criticism show that work and earning opportunities provide a woman with bargaining power and reduces her risk of abuse. She is not only working in a quest for freedom and empowerment but also to create the basis for an articulated ethos against opposition at home and outside, which are the key symbols of women's subordination in gender relations. Caplow (1968) points out that as children grow and mature, they gain increased interpersonal competence, knowledge and material resources. The power that they have is not sufficiently great to countermand their father's residual patriarchal authority and greater material resources, but coupled with the mother and other siblings, children might have a significant influence over decision-making. Indeed, even before the children are old enough to participate in such coalitions, they are assumed to be coalesced with the mother and constitute a resource for the mother in that she might bring up what is best for the children as part of any negotiations.

From the ethnographic evidences, I find that in the two *bastis*, women, who were working outside home say that they try to save some money secretly from their earnings. Although most of the women spend their earnings on their families' subsistence needs, sometimes they also meet their own needs from their secret savings. Abdullah and Zeidenstein (1982, p. 47 as cited in Agarwal, 1994, p. 425) observe in their many interviews with Bangladeshi village women that they covertly seek to gain access to some cash and material resources. Similar findings are also highlighted from South Asian scholars in a Calcutta slum in India (Tenhunen, 1997), Sri Lanka (Risseeuw, 1988), Bangladesh (Nath, 1984) and in Pakistan (Lindholm, 1982).

I found that in the *bastis*, some women are building their agency and working outside home and helping to maintain their family's livelihood, and some women still cannot join in these income-generating activities as they have not found any suitable work or because their husbands oppose and prevent them from getting a job. When they talked with me, they said decisions related to taking up work outside home are not solely dependent on the women themselves, they also depend on their husbands. The following quotations illustrate the obstacles to women working outside home:

> My husband does not allow me to work outside. Once I got a good offer from another woman of this *basti* to be a partner in a petty business, we wanted to make *papor* (a kind of crispy food) and pickles (*aachar*) at home and sell them in the nearby grocery. But my husband strictly stood against this offer and beat me a lot. I felt so ashamed to show my abused face to the neighbor women after that violence. This is why I cannot earn a single *paisa* (coin) for my children. Now that neighbor woman is running this business with other women and earning some money for her family.
>
> (Kulsum, a 29-year-old Muslim woman)

> My husband considers himself to be a pious man, but he does not say his prayers (*namaz*) regularly. But whenever I ask for permission to work, he does not allow me in the name of religion (*dharma*). One day I raised my

voice against him because of the poverty in our family, but he punched me and kicked my abdomen in front of my children and neighbors. I am afraid to say anything to him. If I do not listen to him, he will divorce me. I have no place to go with my four children.

(Momtaz, a 26-year-old Muslim woman)

For many women, working outside the home is not possible: first, because of their husbands' opposition (quote of Kulsum) and second, because of conservative patriarchal values paired with religious beliefs (quote of Momtaz), which emphasize the importance of household (*sangsar*) over individuality, especially women's individuality. Another reason why it is impossible for some women to work outside the home is men's perceptions of their roles as husbands and of social pressures concerning that role. In the *basti*, working women are perceived as indications of irresponsible, incapable husbands, and thus these husbands feel their "manhood" is threatened. In Bangladesh, a husband's responsibility to "take care of his family" has two meanings in this context: his shouldering economic responsibilities and his being the authoritative figure that controls his wife's behavior. Moreover, the limited options of work for working-class women, which are mostly low-paid and insecure jobs like domestic work and earth cutting work, dissuade women from working outside the home. The economic pros and cons of a woman's working outside home are calculated by the woman herself or in conjunction with her husband. As research has consistently shown, women contributing to household production does not mean that they control the fruits of their labor, which are often co-opted by the household's men (Whitehead, 1990). Similarly, Ursula Sharma (1986) argues, however much women contribute to production, without control over resources, neither their public nor private statuses will change.

Some researchers (McCloskey, 1996; Kaukinen, 2004) point out that each partner's economic and symbolic control over household resources is the key to understanding gender relations. While other researchers (Macmillan et al., 1999) claim that husbands perpetuate domestic violence against their wives because they have lost their instrumental and symbolic role as a breadwinner. If the wife in a family becomes the chief breadwinner and economically independent, her husband may resort to an available resource – namely violence against women to mitigate his inability, labor market difficulties, less or no economic power and frustrations. In the case of Bangladesh, Kabeer (2001) and Schuler et al. (1998) also state that the increased autonomy that results from women's greater economic self-reliance from micro-credit participation may often be able to precipitate greater intra-household conflict when seen as a challenge to male authority. But the analysis of the present study data leads me to argue that in the *basti*, husbands perpetuate domestic violence against their wives not only because of economic insolvency, but also because of patriarchal beliefs, customs and to show their masculine power, which is embedded in their minds and attitudes. I will describe this in the next chapter.

From the above discussion, it is evident that, depending on the context, those women who are facing obstacles from their husbands feel disempowered and a lack of agency on one hand; but on the other hand, their working opportunities outside their household work and income-generating activities provide light for transformations in the lives of some women and provide the basis for alternative discourses to counter the dominant discourses in the social structure.

Conclusion

In this chapter, I have discussed how some *basti* women work in the public domain to earn a livelihood for the family and have changed their everyday lives, achieved opportunities for improving their personal and families' economic security. The working *basti* women's self-esteem and bargaining power increase after becoming part of the income-generating workforce, which shows in such issues as their ability to be involved in family expenditure, saving pocket money for personal or children's expenses and in meeting family's recreational demands. But I also found that women's income-generating activities do not fully question or change the existing patriarchal power relations in households or values relating to femininity and masculinity. Almost all the women who work in the public domain with the consent of their husbands develop their own strategies once they have opened up some room for change. However, I argue that it is hard to change the existing gender roles and values at either the personal or collective levels, but women's participation in the workforce restructures women's own positions and perceptions to some extent.

Note

1 In Bangladesh, supernatural spiritual powers are denoted as *giin*, *bhut*, *batash*, *alga dosh* and *pori dhora*. These are the most common and dangerous spirits. Spirit possession and spirit exorcism could be seen as forms of resistance, a domain in which subordinated groups can escape and act in a way that is not possible in non-possessed states. The spirits are usually considered invisible and living around the community in an amorphous state.

4 Women's married life and domestic violence in the slum

Bastis by their very nature are contested sites. From morning to night, there are conflicts over space, resources like water, cooking place and even over shared toilets. As they are places for public conflict, it is not surprising that within them there is an acceptability of domestic violence. Although domestic violence occurs in all social classes, poor women experience more violent behavior than do the non-poor (Kalil and Danziger, 2000; Rodriguez et al., 2001; Tolman and Rosen, 2001). Hadi (2005, p. 187) found that in Bangladesh socio-economic conditions and the living standards of households were inversely associated with violence against women. Poverty and economic crisis might have forced the lower classes to behave violently where minor disagreements among spouses have tended to create violent situations. In Bangladesh, *basti* women belong to the lower socio-economic class and are entangled with poverty, the sphere of dominance by the male and sometimes by older women, and a lack of opportunity for income-generating work.

Even though domestic violence is common, not all women in the two *bastis* suffer from it. Quite many families live without such problems. But many women themselves discuss domestic violence openly in everyday gossip. In their talk about particular events of abuse, women simultaneously normalize and criticize the violence of husbands and the negative role of mothers-in-law. At the same time, women who are suffering from domestic violence sometimes fight back, abandon abusive spouses or seek help from their natal families. These different steps indicate the complexities of the lives, relationships and stories of women who clearly suffer from abuse, representing a different understanding of domestic violence against women. Much of my understanding of domestic violence against women in *bastis* is refracted through informal interaction with *basti* women. In this chapter, I will bring to the forefront the material and emotional ways that the women use to counter domestic violence. I will also base the analysis on some cases of domestic violence between husbands and wives and mothers- and daughters-in-law in order to trace the voice of *basti* women and to uncover how they are trying to establish their rights in their unfavorable position. To explore the changing views and experiences of *basti* women regarding domestic violence in their changed social settings, I have to find answers to the following questions from the Hindu and Muslim women of the *bastis*: How do *basti* women view and experience domestic violence in their marital lives? What kinds of changes have they seen when individuals have tried to seek help for domestic violence in the *basti*? How do women fight and resist domestic violence against them? If women have economic independence, why do they stay with violent husband and affines in a violent home?

The domestic violence against women is literally translated as *Nari Nirjaton* or *Nari-r proti shohingsata* in Bangla. However, these are not the terms that are used by the *basti* women. They use simple descriptive terms to indicate the acts of violence, humiliation and discrimination against them such as *maar-peet* (hit), *gala-gali kora* (uttering filthy language), *bhat-kapor deyna* (not giving maintenance), *arek-ta bie koreche* (multiple marriage), *alga khani khai* (bad character/ having an extra-marital relationship).

From the women's description about domestic violence against women in the *bastis*, I learned that husbands behave badly to their wives for various reasons, for example, sometimes husbands behave rudely because their meals are not ready on time, if there is a bit more salt in the curry, if the children disturb them while they are resting, and if the wives gossip for a long time with neighborhood women. These are very silly issues in day-to-day life, but husbands become angry and start to abuse their wives using filthy language. According to the *basti* women, these are very painful (*kosto*) and shameful (*lojja*) for a woman. But women most times try to tolerate their husbands' bad behavior (*kharap beboher*). Sometimes women cannot tolerate foul language (*kharap kotha*), and they also become angry and start to brawl with her husband. Most of the husbands cannot stand their wives' answering back. In the case of wives' altercation and misbehavior, the husbands become angrier and in some contexts the angry husbands throw kitchen utensils at their wives and sometimes begin to hit them.

It is a common belief that the nuclear family is an arena where there is a dyadic relationship, and a wife may also play a significant role in the power structure of the family. In Pirer Tila and Durga Bari *bastis* I found that in most of the cases, women struggle to maintain the routinized daily life (such as cooking, cleaning and caring) of the household even though they are living in a violent family environment. For the most part, women recognized the importance of fulfilling a myriad of responsibilities to their children, husband and household, whereas violent husbands have generally elevated their own personal requirements above all others and remained inflexible when it comes to them. The following citations from a focus group discussion elaborate the conjugal relationships of a nuclear family in the *basti*:

> Bilkis (around 23; a housewife): If I want to live in my husband's household (*swamir ghor*), I have to face both happiness and unhappiness. My husband seldom beats me, but slapping and punching are his regular practices of violent behavior to me. I try to bear all the sorrows deep in my heart. I have to tolerate it if I want to eat my husband's income (*swamir bhat*). Everybody will call me bad if I do not tolerate it.

86 *Experiencing and reacting to domestic violence*

> Kanon (about 25; a housewife): Although we are cobblers, after coming from the village, my husband has been working as an earth worker (*mati kata sromic*). He is a very rude man. Every night I have to massage his feet for a long time, and if I feel sleepy he kicks me like a ball. Then I cry, but he does not change his behavior. For about ten years I have had this kind of experience, but I cannot do anything. I have no right (*odhikar*) to attack my husband physically. If I do this everybody will call me a sinner (*papi*). My husband would also abandon me.

It becomes evident from the above narratives that housewives face domestic violence in the *bastis*. In their everyday lives they have to compromise and cope with their husband's violent behavior to maintain their marital bonds due to social-cultural code of the society. They have almost no say against their husbands' attitude because of their economic dependency. But in contrast to the housewives, I found a bit of a different attitude in the working women's narratives:

> Naseema (35 years old): I cook in a university student's dormitory and my husband is an earth worker, but he does not find work regularly. Most of the days, he stays at home and spends his time sleeping, gossiping in the nearby tea stall or playing cards with his friends. All the expenses of our household depend on my income. He does not like my income; rather sometimes he becomes very angry with me and uses bad language. I also quarrel with him, but I have to always surrender to his anger. But there is no good solution in front of me. I have to maintain my family life and this is the rule of society (*somaj-er niyom*).

From a general point of view, a husband who does not have an income nor has an irregular income should support his wife's income, which provides for the family; but from the above narrative, it is evident that Nasima's husband does not support her economic role in their family life. Indeed, in patriarchal societies if a man feels he does not have the supreme position of power in the family or if his role is threatened, he may defend himself by using violence toward the weak. Some other researchers (Honeycutt, Marshall, and Weston, 2001; Romero, Chavkin, Wise, and Smith, 2003) also argue that a man may show antipathy toward a woman's economic independence, and therefore take steps to interrupt her employment.

In *basti* life there is a lack of work, a lack of opportunity, poverty and unhealthy living conditions; the *basti* dwellers cannot fulfill any of their basic needs properly. Different types of tensions arise from poverty and vulnerability that create mismatches in marital lives (Farrington, 1986; Straus, 1994; Kurst-Swanger and Petcosky, 2003). Poverty-stricken women have to face many obstacles and burdens; they have to do their household chores, look after their children and work outside home doing laborious jobs. But men try to establish their wishes in their households and some think their wives are only female (*meye manush*) not human (*manush*). Brawls between couples and domestic violence against women are regular events in the *bastis*. Husbands beat (*maar-peet kore*), kick (*lathi dey*), slap (*chor mare*), punch (*ghushi dey*) and abuse their wives with foul language (*gala-gali kore*). Wives do not beat their husbands but quarrel with them using abusive language.

Moreover, most of the families have many children who do not get proper food and care from the poverty-stricken households. They play with mud and in dirty places and go to the sides of the roads to play. They want to eat extra food and snacks, so the women feel a mental burden (*kosto*), lose their tempers (*mejaj*) with their children and beat them. Most of the husbands prefer not to use contraceptives and don't care about their wives' contraception. In regular conjugal life, they do not want to take any responsibility related to their children (*baccha-kaccha*), pregnancy, childbirth or childrearing; all these are considered to be women's duties. In the *bastis*, the women vividly described their marital lives, their feelings of pain and their steps to save themselves from domestic violence. They gave reasons why *basti* women become the victims of the domestic violence that is endemic in *basti* life. The following narratives from a focus group discussion highlight the scenario:

> Rakiba (a 23-year-old Muslim woman): In the *basti* sometimes a husband and wife quarrel with each other as a result of bad comments made in the neighborhood. For example, one woman says to another woman's husband, 'you are such a good man but your wife does not properly take care of you and your household. Alas! You are so unlucky.' Then the husband treats his wife roughly and sometimes hits her.

> Zulekha (around 25-year-old Muslim woman): Sometimes a man also makes comments to another man about his wife and sometimes a woman to another woman. If a husband fails to run his family's daily expenses properly then other *basti* women may say to his wife, "your husband is not good, follow his activities closely, he probably has another wife somewhere or he has an extra-marital relationship. Then there is a problem (*jhamela*) in that family and the husband beats his wife."

> Suhasini (a 21-year-old Hindu woman): In the *basti*, husbands and wives both abuse each other verbally. Those husbands who work also have dirty greed for their wives' earning and demand money from their wives. Naturally most of the women protest about giving their earnings to their husbands. Then the husbands become violent and force their wives to give them the money or create obstacles in her work.

It is evident from the above narratives that the *basti* women are not only entangled in the vulnerability of poverty but sometimes also with the hostility (*hingsha*) of other unrelated persons in the neighborhood, gender inequality, contested relationship between spouses and domestic violence.

In Bangladeshi families, girls' bonds to their mothers are maintained and strengthened through daily sharing and close interaction at home. A mother's love for her child is considered the strongest of all loves and the most highly valued, so in everybody's mind there is a respectable place for the mother. In the study, the *basti* women said that there is a high prevalence of verbal abuse among the men toward their wives and frequently they involve their wives' mother when they scold their wives. In such situations the women feel very humiliated and nobody can tolerate someone saying bad things about their parents. Then the women also feel angry and they also utter abusive words (*kharap khota*) toward the men. When the women start uttering bad words, the men cannot tolerate it and the quarrel escalates and sometimes the men start to hit their wives.

Due to internal migration, in Pirer Tila and Durga Bari *bastis*, there is an increasing trend toward the nuclear family as a pattern of residence; however, I found six extended households in Pirer Tila. Living in an extended family is often difficult for a woman, especially when the members of the household do not share the same opinions and there is unequal treatment for younger or senior women. The woman's mother-in-law most of the time plays a significant role in the domain of authority in marital family. Researchers (Säävälä, 1997; Lamb, 2000, pp. 71–75; Aura, 2008, p. 86) found in the South Asian context, if a woman resides with her mother-in-law, it is very hard for her to have authority in the household, and this creates a contested relationship between the mother-in-law and the daughter-in-law; they fight to capture the son's/husband's attention and loyalty. In this case, most of the time, the marital bond of the husband and wife is contested by the parent-child bond of the mother and son. I found some unhappy lives in some extended households in the *bastis*. According to the respondents in some of these households, the mothers-in-law have a habit of quarreling. They often provoke conjugal problems. Amanot (a *basti* woman, around 25 years old) says that her life is very unhappy. She is an earth worker and labors very hard for the family, but her mother-in-law can't tolerate her. The mother-in-law is not working for the family, but she is always rebuking Amanot for working in public space. Sometimes when Amanot comes back home from work, she starts shouting to irritate her son. She tries to look for mismanagement in the household chores. As a result, Amanot's husband becomes irritated and angry and starts quarrel with Amanot and abuses her.

A similar picture is also seen in other parts of South Asia. In the Indian cities of Chennai and Hyderabad, it is evident that mothers-in-law often provoke their sons to act violently to their wives for different activities, such as keeping an untidy house, poor child care or for disobeying, disrespecting and immodest movements. The senior women in the marital family of a woman may also abuse young brides directly by frequent scolding, back-biting them to others, beatings, withholding food or giving them less and inferior food compared with other members of the household (Vatuk, 2006, p. 211).

Krishnan (2005) revealed the relationship between marital violence and the structural inequalities (gender, caste and class inequalities) in rural communities in Karnataka State, South India. She found that women's experiences of male violence were primarily located within the home and were part of their everyday lives. The women described different types of violence against them, from verbal abuse to beating and burning. In a number of interviews, women and men noted that beating a wife is justified if she has not followed her husband's orders. The researcher found that there are a number of causes leading to a husband beating his wife. These include doubts about her fidelity; if the dowry is felt to be insufficient; if his wife is earning and he is not; if he wants to be superior while she objects to his behavior or actions; if she refuses to give him money; and if other men expect him to use violence.

Similarly, gender-specific violence, specifically violence by husbands prevails across all strata of Nepali society, but the issue of domestic violence in Nepal mostly remains unrecognized, unreported and unchallenged (Deuba and Rana, 2001). SATHI (meaning "friend" in Nepali), a non-governmental organization that works toward ending domestic violence in Nepal, found in their survey of 1,250 Nepali women and girls that 93 percent reported experiencing mental or emotional abuse, 82 percent had been physically assaulted and 30 percent had been raped. According to Paudel (2007), domestic violence against women is an attitudinal problem of men toward women in Nepal. Men try to maintain their superior position over women and keep them as subservient as possible, but if the women do not respect and obey their sentiments, the men use violent behavior against them.

The process of responding and coping strategies of domestic violence in the *bastis*

With respect to responding domestic violence, all the respondents' narratives express the same phenomenon that in the *bastis* if a husband beats his wife or a husband and wife quarrel then most of the time, it is their neighbors who try to keep the peace. Sometimes some males do not want to listen and rationalize their position by stating in an angry voice, "If I beat my wife, why is that the business of others?" Indeed, due to the patriarchal structure, a husband thinks that he has the right to control his wife. He thinks that he gains this control through marriage, by giving shelter and maintenance to his wife. These cultural and sometimes religious privileges are thought to grant husbands the right to use some degree of physical violence, such as beating, scolding, not giving food and clothes, multiple marriages and so on. With these weapons, the husband establishes his will and enjoys the social and religiously structured wifely ideal.

Despite mentioning earlier that *basti* women have a good we-feeling, this does not make them immune from hostility or brawling. Some women point out that sometimes when a husband beats his wife, some neighbors enjoy (*tamasha dekha*) and get pleasure from it. But when a husband beats his wife severely or attacks his wife with a weapon (e.g., fire wood, spade, iron rod) or with a thick hard stick, their neighbors and elders (*murubbi*) have to take the initiative to stop the violent husband forcefully.

Many women in the *basti* get a good opportunity to keep contact with their natal family; there are many groceries where by paying a small amount of money they can talk with their natal family members by mobile phone. By calling to natal family members, women try to get relief from humiliation in their marital lives. A 23-year-old *basti* woman says, when her husband abuses her using filthy language, she feels very sad and she cries a lot. She doesn't find peace in her mind. If she talks with her mother over the mobile phone, she feels sad for her pain. After talking with her mother she again tries to cope with the humiliation.

But when the marital violence becomes regular and severe, then it is impossible for the neighbors to solve the problems. In these cases, those victims who have contact with their parents, in-laws, elder siblings and kin that live in the same city can appeal to them to solve the conjugal problem. Basically in most of the cases, the women's fathers and older brothers try to solve the conjugal problem. They have no alternative: if their daughters or sisters are separated or divorced it will create great problems, as they will become economic burdens and sources of disgrace for them. So they never want a divorce or separation of the women and may scold their daughters and sisters by talking the sides of the grooms and marital family members. From the women, I learned that the natal family members of women scold them for not having patience and for example say to them:

*Don't break the peace of the family. Look after the household properly. This is your own home.

*A woman enters her marital home wearing a red wedding *sari* and only comes outside of home forever after her death wearing a funeral cloth (*kafon-er-kapor*).

*If you do not listen to your husband then Allah will punish you.

In this study's ethnographic documents, there are cases where sometimes the women had done nothing wrong, but their parents and elder brothers silently accepted all the blame against their daughters and sisters and did not in any way criticize the wives' husbands and in-laws, rather they very politely requested that they forgive the bride's faults. Sometimes when it is totally unbearable and pathetic for the women, they do not say anything about a divorce or separation, rather they hope for a solution.

From the respondents in the Pirer Tila *basti*, I learned that no woman in the *basti* wants to break *sangsar* (family) for marital problem, even a woman who is a frequent victim of domestic violence tries hard to keep her marital bonds intact. According to the *basti* women, to break up a family is "the wish of bad people." Nabila Espanioly's (1997, pp. 587–589) writing about Muslim women in Palestinian communities in Israel also found the same situation. She has highlighted the fact that some forms of violence and spouse abuse are accepted socially. It is said that "men sometimes lose their temper – women have to be patient" or "a woman should not destroy her marriage just because her husband hit her." These ideas are widely accepted and expressed openly. Cultures differ in their construction of what defines abusive behavior, and thus, the experience of violence among women can differ substantially. For example, several studies (Heise, et al., 1999) have examined the concept of "wife disciplining" and have found physical chastisement or punishment of wives to be permissible by individuals in some parts of Latin America, Asia and Africa.

To show the vulnerability of a *basti* woman, I would like to use one morning's incidence. When I was sitting in the Afia's home in Pirer Tila *basti*, I heard a woman crying with her old father just beside her house. I asked Afia about the matter and wanted to know what was going on. Afia told me to go and see. I went with Afia and saw Tazmina (a Muslim woman of around 23, the mother of two daughters) was crying with her father. They were not embarrassed when they saw me because Tazmina had known me for some days. I asked Tazmina's father about the incidence. Then Tazmina's father (around 55 years, a day laborer living in another *basti* in Sylhet) said that for two or three years Tazmina's husband was not caring about family. He couldn't do anything. If he sought to know any cause then Tazmina's husband beat his daughter. Tazmina does not work because her husband does not allow her to work outside home. For two days she had been starving with her daughters. Now after getting the news, he came to give his daughter some money to buy rice.

I asked Tazmina's father about his future thinking about Tazmina's marital life. The following quotations illustrate more about the vulnerability of Tazmina:

I: What do you think about the future of this marriage? (I asked Tazmina's father)
TAZMINA'S FATHER: Allah! He himself knows well. I see a very dark future for this marriage bond. But we are very poor.... How can we feed these three persons? Where will they live? Who will look after these two daughters? I am old now, so how long can I bear this? Because of this we have asked our daughter to tolerate the violence as long as she can.
I: Why do you not take any legal action? Do you not have any information about legal action?
TAZMINA'S FATHER: Yes, we do. Sometimes we have decided to take legal action. But we fear what will happen after that if we take any legal action? Who will bear the expense of legal action? Who will save my daughter from stigma (*kolonko*)? Do you think my son-in-law becomes a good husband? So we feel ashamed to go to the courts. It is not so easy for poor people.

We can see that Tazmina is an example of a vulnerable woman in the patriarchal social structure of Bangladesh. She has no freedom in her life; she cannot work outside her home to earn her livelihood as her husband does not allow her to work. Although her husband does not look after the family properly, she is bound to endure it and has no courage to raise her voice. Her natal family is poor and lives in another *basti*; and his father is a day laborer. So it is also very hard for her old father to support her in overcoming her vulnerable situation; although sometimes he tries to support her and looks after her family. He is unhappy with his daughter's conjugal instability, but he feels ashamed to take legal action not only on economic grounds, but also because of personal, social and structural barriers. Therefore, to him, compromise is the only preferable way of solving the marital conflict.

When I ask the Hindu women about the process of solving domestic violence, they said that their natal family members rarely come to solve their conjugal problem because they are living too far from Sylhet city. They think that their parents have little or no right to solve their daughters' problems in their marital families. Actually, in Hindu society daughters are treated as objects, and if any object is sacrificed or given to anybody forever, no one has the right to demand it back. From their perspective, they are poor and don't have anything in their natal family. Before marriage, they were considered as burdens by their natal families, now again they don't want to create any problems in their natal families due to their marital conflicts. As they were born women, it is their fate to endure all the tortures in life. They consider that all the misfortunes in their lives have been written by *Bhagawan* (god), they have to bear them and they have to try themselves to solve their conjugal problems. Moreover, they point out as there is no provision for divorce in the Hindu religion, they want to stay with their husbands. They argue that they dislike the practice of divorce in Islam. According to them, it devalues the women's position in marital life. But some Hindu women mentioned that despite the fact that they face violence by their husbands in the *basti*, they are happy at least, due to migration, that they are free from conflicts with their in-laws. "Who wants to fall in danger? We don't want to fall. Now our husbands only torture us. If we lived with our other affines, they all would torture us," expressed by Nirupoma (a 26-year-old Hindu woman). So it is evident that migration brought more scope for the women to gain more opportunity to escape domestic violence by their affines.

I also got conservative and traditional ideas about women's duties and roles in marriage. Some women legitimize the violence against women by their husbands and in-laws. They use the verses of the Holy Quran to support women's suppression. As far as I can understand, religion is the strongest weapon that is frequently used in the patriarchal social structure to control the members of a society, especially women. So some Muslim women of Pirer Tila tend to view women's submissiveness to their husbands as their religious duty and the pillar of marital happiness. Here some women from Pirer Tila *basti* expressed limited ideas about women's role in the family:

> Fakrunnessa (40 years): In the *basti* some women do not listen to their husband's orders and advice. They do not respect their husbands. A wife should follow society's and religious rules and listen to her husband because a husband's position is higher than his wife's. When women earn money, they do not respect their husband. So husbands become angry and try to control their wives by scolding and sometimes by beating them, and according to religion they have the right to control their stubborn (*obbaddo*) wives.

Mariam Begum (around 32 years): Our guardians say, for a wife, the husband is the main person in the world, the husband is the pillar of her existence, the heaven lies under the feet of the husband (*swamir paa-er niche estrir behesto*). Many people say we should visit shrines (*mazar*) to search for earthly happiness, but for a woman it is not necessary to visit shrines; rather a shrine is inside her household, this is her husband, she can find all her happiness in her household. Her husband, in-laws and parents are the most respectable persons in a woman's life. A wife should even be ready to jump into fire to make her husband happy.

These women are not only talking in favor of the embedded patriarchal norms and values but also about the ideologies of Islam, which are sometimes misinterpreted in the society to create obstacle to women's rights. By their reference to religion, they are trying to strengthen the authority of males in society and the subordination of females. In my opinion, this type of dominant anti-female notion is the reverse of the notion of women empowerment and this inequity ideology always pushes women into weak "breakdown positions" (Sen, 1990) in households and society.

Women's views on divorce

In Bangladeshi social structure, in all religions, divorce or separation is considered as a problem in a woman's life. Society expects that a battered woman should try to stay married at any cost. Most of the time the person who has battered her is of little concern to most people, neither are the reasons behind the torture or how she is coping with the violence; rather everyone expects that she should somehow bear the violence and not get divorced. The natal family of women rarely supports divorce even in the most extreme cases of abuse. If a woman gets divorced, she would probably have to face bitter experiences regarding housing, economic support, work and custody of her children, and being a burden and disgrace to her natal kin.

According to religious teachings, there is no provision for divorce among Hindus in Bangladesh unlike in India, so Bangladeshi Hindu women have to deal with the customary practice leaning on mythological models. I asked the Hindu women whether they would want any changes in their marital lives if they faced severe domestic violence; I got their strict views about the maintaining of their marital life. Some of the quotations from a focus group discussion are given below:

Probasini (28 years): We cannot divorce our husbands and the husbands also cannot divorce us, because in our Hindu religion (*Sanaton dharma*) divorce is not permitted. According to our religion, after marriage it is considered that a husband and wife belong to each other, they are one body and one soul. But some men are very bad; they marry several times and do not take care for any of their families. A married woman is obliged to remain a wife the whole of her life and bound to keep her *tip* (red round mark in the forehead), *sindur* (red mark in the parting of the hair) and conch and iron bangles (*shakha and noa*), all these are symbols of the married status (*bibahito*), a married Hindu woman can never be free from her husband.

Rongmala (around 30 years): We never see divorce among the Hindus and it is not desirable for us, we do not want this divorce as our right. What type of human right (*odhikar*) is that? We don't understand it; we wish to follow our religion (*dharma*). *Rama* abandoned *Sita* and she did not dishonor or protest, she silently obeyed her husband's decision and orders. We are not *Sita*, but it is desirable among the Hindus that a Hindu woman should follow *Sita's* path.

I asked the Muslim women in the Pirer Tila slum the following questions: How do they see divorce? How do they judge a woman remarrying? Most of the women said that they do not like divorce (*talaq*), to them it is not a solution to marriage problem, it does not bring happiness for women and it is always a threat for the children's future. In Bangladeshi society, the children suffer most when a family experiences a separation or divorce. The women of the Pirer Tila said that in this *basti* they had observed some cases of divorce and they have also seen second, third and even fourth marriages of divorced men. They have seen the misfortune of the separated women after their husband's second marriage. According to them, some *basti* men have the bad habit of remarrying after their first marriage but now the situation has changed and now bad men have very secret extra-marital relationships without marrying a second time. But according to them, this type of behavior is impossible for a woman as her movements are always restricted before and after marriage, women are always trapped by a strict life, early marriage, pregnancy, childbirth, childrearing and household chores.

In the Pirer Tila, a divorce does not take place in written form. Most of the time males divorce their wives orally by saying three times "*Talaq* One," "*Talaq* Two" and "*Talaq* Three" in front of adult males and females. According to the women, the regular scenario is, when a husband and wife brawl with each other or a husband beats his wife, sometimes the husband says: "I shall give you Talaq, I shall not keep you in my house. Go back to your natal family with the children. I don't like you and I will give you Talaq and I will marry a good wife." To me this is the "weapon of the strong" in the patriarchal social structure – the male who keeps his weak and helpless wife obedient and in fear.

Most of the Muslim women I talked to in the *basti* considered that a Muslim woman should have an equal right to divorce her husband. In their account, if the husband is very short-tempered (*matha gorom*) and beats his wife frequently, if he beats or punishes his wife brutally, is characterless, wicked or lecherous, is a drug addict, has extra-marital relationships with other women, visits brothels and searches for street-based sex workers, does not work to meet the family's expenses and needs, then his wife should have the right to divorce him. From their explanations I understand that although women have the right to divorce their husbands in Muslim marriage and family law, most of the women do not know of this right in the *kabin* (marriage registration paper) for self-divorce or about the existing rules of Muslim family laws. When talking about divorce with the women, I got almost uniform views about divorce. According to them, for some women who are severely tortured by their husbands or in-laws, divorce is to some extent a necessary rescue. But for most married women who belong to the lower socio-economic class, divorce is not considered as a good option. It is very hard for a previously married woman (with or without children) to remarry after a divorce. According to the women, no male likes to marry a divorcee, a separated or a widowed woman because they are seen as "used."

In a focus group session, while I was talking about divorce, a young woman (Halima, 18 years old) asked me, "Where will the women go after getting divorce (*talak*)?" I could not give her any answer, so I was silent. After some time, she started to talk again with a sigh and told us about her situation:

> I don't have any *kabin* (marriage registration paper) for my marriage because my father and mother were very simple (*sida*) and foolish (*boka*), so to them a *kabin* was not an important document for married life. Marriage takes place by the wish of Allah and he makes the couple by taking bones from the husband's thorax so it is a decree of fate who will marry whom, nobody can select a spouse totally by herself/himself. So for some people it is totally useless and irreligious work to make marriage contracts/registrations (*kabin*), *Den Mahar* (bride price) fixing through argument or mutual discussion and thus giving the authority of divorce to women according to her desire. So I don't have anything to support me although I was forced to marry a divorced old man with two adult daughters.

I felt that Halima was insecure and vulnerable. As a result, finding no other strong basis for survival, she somehow tries to adjust to her vulnerability. This vulnerability can be seen in the way she referred to the informality of rights, voice, entitlements, services and opportunities in the context of institutional imperfections, structural barriers and socially embedded norms and values. Even now in Bangladeshi society, female survival without male protection and the economic resources is a highly problematic option. Most of the women try to cope with a violent environment and relationship because coping strategies reflect conscious and rational decision-making and responses to environmental and/or internal demands (Aldwin, 1994; Schuler et al., 2008, p. 333).

Wood and Salway (2000, p. 683) found in their research in the slums of Dhaka city, Bangladesh that threats to marital relationships are risky consequences for women and children. In the slum settings, many traditional rural codes and norms are weak, and family control over marriage choices has changed. As their familial and lineage ties are weak, women cannot protect themselves by calling on their relatives or other social resources. Women now contribute to their families' finances by working outside home, and they have altered their gender identities, but males still abide by the principles of masculinity. This creates disorganized and imbalanced relationships among the couples. Moreover, there is an increasing acceptability of remarriage, which creates high marital tension and the breakdown of marriages in urban poor settings, which exhibit intra-household gendered inequalities and violence.

Most respondents of the present study unanimously stated that in poverty-stricken families, no one in the natal families of a woman considers divorce or separation as a solution; rather the natal kin prefer that their daughters/sisters should stay in the husband's house tolerating misbehavior and violence. About women's remarriage, Sufia (40 years) says:

> I have seen some women remarrying after divorcing their first husbands. But their second marriages were not good. These marriages were not the harbinger of happiness for women. If a woman has children, they suffer most. When a woman enters into the house of her second husband with or without children, he treats them like dogs or cats, and the real father who does not take the responsibility for the children marries again and enjoys his new married life with a new young wife.

The above quotation supports the belief that a woman's second marriage is not appreciated in the *bastis* and that it is believed that such a marriage would lead to a lack of support for the children. In Bangladesh, family breakup is especially for women associated with the major features of stigma and vulnerability, because they lose their general standing of being good women and face a loss of family-based social protection. Thus the vulnerability of the divorced woman is reflected in her almost total loss of resource profile, with no entitlements or other moral claims to assets, goods and services from the rest of society. To my view, Bangladeshi women are expected to tolerate and endure abusive marriages and women tend to forgive and rationalize their husbands for minor abuse; they prefer to endure and stay because of stronger concerns for their children, social stigma and financial dependence. There is no literature for the processes Bangladeshi women use for coping with domestic violence against them. It is hoped that the results of this study will provide a better and more in-depth understanding and explanation of the coping processes and strategies chosen by Bangladeshi women.

Narratives of violence and different coping strategies

The women in the slums thought that if a husband was angry, it was the duty of his wife to placate him. On most nights the wives massage their husband's muscles, oil his soles and sleep with him. Normally, a wife makes her husband calm with her subservient behavior. If there is a brawl between husband and wife or a husband beats his wife severely, it does not create any pressure on the husband. By caring for the husbands' bodies with massages and sexual relationships, women make their bodies loved bodies, which soothes their husbands' anger and bring back sympathy and love for her. Sometimes husbands also show urges of love and sympathy for their wives and blur their experiences of violence with love. So after a brawl, after being hit, scolded and being in pain, women try to reconstruct their marital lives with love, sex and simple everyday household chores such as cooking, cleaning and looking after the children.

This section is made up of two specific case studies. I choose these case studies from the Pirer Tila *basti* because each case demonstrates some typical features of domestic violence, conflict and negotiation in the familial web. My aim is to show the lives of two families where women are working as wage laborers and maintaining their household's livelihood, however, they have lack of choice to have any life outside of marriage and family for the fear of more vulnerability. Because it is generally accepted that the most vulnerable group of women in Bangladesh are those without any adult male, sick or healthy, in their households (Rahman, 1991, p. 169).

Case 1 Renu and Parvin – blaming and fighting in the household

I found different types of domestic violence cases in the *basti* areas. One of the instances of violence and fighting was between a husband and his two co-wives, Renu and Parvin. While I was doing the fieldwork and talked with the co-wives, I found it to be a case manifesting many common qualities in cases of family violence. Most women in the slum referred to this family as a hell (*dozok*), because brawling (*jhogra*), fighting and beating wives (*bou mara*) are regular occurrences in this household. The husband punches his wives, slaps, kicks and beats them with sticks. By the same token, the wives also quarrel (*jhogra*) with their husband and use foul language. Added to this, the wives sometimes quarrel with each other and the husband often has to exercise his masculine power over them by beating and scolding, but both the wives are struggling to sustain their conjugal families with the husband. According to the *basti* women, the second wife (Renu) is more hot tempered than the first wife (Parvin); she scolds (*gala-gali*) her husband more and fights with the first co-wife (Parvin).

Renu (24 years, a mother of two children) and Parvin (25 years, a mother of three children) are co-wives (*sotin*) of a rickshaw puller, Nuru Miah. They reside in a 15-square-meter room divided by a cloth stand (*alna*) partition between two cheap wooden beds (*chouki*). They cook and eat separately, but their husband's eating place is not fixed, he eats according to the quality of food that they cook; if Renu cooks small fishes (*choto mach*) and Parvin cooks only pulses (*daal*), the husband eats with Renu. But most of the time he eats twice, each meal time from both sides. To most slum women, their conjugal life is very clumsy and shameful because the wives take turns to sleep with their husband in a small room. The slum women said with shameful voices, "they have no shame (*lojja*), they have lost it forever." When I asked them about their married life, several of them humorously said,

We feel shame ... suppose, when the husband sleeps with his second wife the first wife watches everything; she sometimes out of anger and hostility utters bad words. Most of the times, the children hear what is going on during the night and cry out with fear.

Some women expressed their anger about them, "they have totally destroyed the *basti's* environment."

To depict their everyday conjugal life, the women shared an interesting story of this household with me. They described, one day during a brawl, Nuru Miah cracked open Parvin's head by striking it with stick. At once, blood started oozing from the wound and Parvin fell unconscious. Some neighborhood women rushed quickly there, took her inside the house and immediately called a doctor from a nearby pharmacy. The doctor came and stitched up her forehead. The neighborhood women and men captured Nuru Miah and forced him to pay for the doctor's treatment fee as well as the cost of the medicine. When Parvin came back to consciousness, she decided to go to police station (*thana*) to file a case against Nuru Miah. Since she was sick, some women asked her not to go that day but wait till the next day. Because she seemed adamant, most of the neighbors firmly believed that this time she might go to the police. But they were astonished, as she did not go to the police rather the next morning she was talking normally to her husband, as if nothing had happened the previous night. In most cases their quarrels, which usually happen several times a month, are stopped by the intervention of the other *basti* dwellers.

Parvin and Renu also came to me, sat with the group of women and shared everything about their marital life. In Parvin's account, some years ago her husband worked as a seasonal agricultural laborer in Sunamganj and he lived there alone for three months. At that time, she resided in this slum and worked as a domestic helper at a nearby house. One day after completing her work, she returned home and found her two daughters aged six and four were sitting silently in front of the entrance of the door. Parvin did not understand what was going on so she asked them whether they had not eaten their food. She then pulled away the curtain of the door and was astonished to find her husband with a woman sitting close to him and scratching his head. Parvin's husband very calmly introduced the woman as his new wife. Parvin was so shocked by this disclosure that the only response she could give was to start crying out loudly. Her female neighbors rushed into the room and tried to pacify her. But this did not bring any change in her husband's attitude. He told Parvin if she wanted to stay with him, she could share the house with her children, otherwise she could go. According to Parvin:

My husband knows well that I have nobody there because my father died when I was only five years old and my mother died just after my marriage. I have two elder brothers but they did not keep contact with me. That night I stayed with my daughters at a neighbor's house. Some women advised me not to leave my house (*sangsar*) because it would not bring any benefit to me, rather Renu will alone establish her rights forever and my husband would divorce me. At first I did not understand what they meant, but then I understood their logic and moreover as I had no alternative options so I started living as a co-wife (*sotiner sangsar*) and spent every day of my life fighting and bargaining.

While Parvin was describing her husband's second marriage story and feeling sorry for herself, her *sotin* (co-wife) Renu was sitting on the ground with her sucking child. She became angry and said that it was true that her natal family did not arrange her marriage. Before marriage Renu did not know that the man was married and had two children. If she had known it, she would not have done it because she was also married. Renu spent only two years with her first husband. It was the harvest season; along with her first husband she also came from Comilla to work in Sunamganj, Sylhet. Nuru Miah made her fascinated (*tabiz korec*). Every day, he gave her some small gifts, such as pickles (*aachar*), lipstick, ribbon, hairpin and earrings. She became charmed by his behavior and fell in love with him. After three months of this relationship, she fled with Nuru Miah and married him in a mosque with the help of one of his friends. According to Renu that was a great blunder. When she came to this *basti*, she found that Nuru had a family, but at that time it was impossible for Renu to leave this man because nobody in her natal family would accept her back.

These two narratives produced a contested image of co-wives (*sotin*) in the family and gender relations. Both the wives had given details of their personal lives without hesitation, sometimes trying to accuse their husband and sometimes they condemned each other. During the conversation with Renu when she called Parvin, her children and Nuru Miah "swine," Parvin immediately objected and started to quarrel with Renu. The neighborhood women and I tried to stop them and after a while we succeeded. Then Parvin said that Renu was not a good woman because after discovering that Nuru Miah had a wife and two daughters, she (Renu) did not leave the house; rather she started to fight with her (Parvin) and strengthened her (Renu) position by fascinating Nuru Miah. According to Parvin, "Renu is a woman of loose character who left her first husband and got married to my husband. No good woman in Bangladesh would do these types of illicit activities." Since Parvin said that she was suffering a lot, I then asked Parvin, "Why don't you leave your husband?"

Parvin was silent for a while, she only said, "Why should I go and where would I go? Rather Renu should leave my husband." And then she started to cry. One of the neighborhood women came up to her and took her inside her house. Parvin's two elder daughters also started crying with their mother. I felt quite uneasy about the whole situation and remained silent for a while. The women tried to convince me that this is quite usual in Renu and Parvin's lives. After that I wanted to talk with the women about other issues, but Renu again came near to me and remonstrated angrily, "*Apa*, are you overwhelmed with sorrow for Parvin? Do you not hear me? Do you think I am the main culprit?" I smiled at her and showed my eagerness to hear her counter statements. Renu informed me:

I am working as a domestic helper and earn my livelihood, but Parvin does not and for the last two years she has been sitting idly and consuming all her husband's income with her three daughters (after Renu's marriage, Parvin again gave birth to a daughter). Now Parvin is pregnant again for the fourth time as a part of her wicked scheme to cause confusion in the family and to get me (Renu) out. Parvin and her two older daughters frequently disturb me and sometimes they steal money and sneak food from my cooking pot.

Then I asked Renu, "Since you fight every day and you earn a livelihood by yourself, why do you not leave this family or your husband?" Renu said:

> Where would I go? I have no way to go back to my previous life. And why should I leave him and give my place to this ugly woman? I did not do anything wrong (*ami kono dosh kori nai*); I did not come into this family with any children. I loved him and left my previous husband. I cannot break my *sangsar* (household/family) again. I can't make mistakes all the time … I am not the burden to this family. Parvin is now not working, she is the burden; she should go…. All the time she gives birth to daughters. But I have given my husband two sons…. And I have also taken the responsibility and expense of using contraceptives. All the mistakes have been made by my husband … he hid the fact from me that he was married. He should think about what he should do…. Will he keep me or Parvin? As long as it is possible, I will try to live here…. This is my family (*sangsar*)…. The rest is known by Allah.

In this example, the triad relationship of the husband with his two co-wives (*sotin*) is complex. The relationship between Renu, Parvin and their husband is conflicting, competitive and contradictory. It can be best explained by the William Roseberry's (1994) concept of "field of power." In fields of power, each field is a social site in which actors occupying "positions" endowed with different amounts and types of "capital" (economic, cultural and/or symbolic). They struggle against one another to improve their positions within the field (i.e., to obtain more capital) or to change the field's rules or its boundaries. Renu and Parvin are in power relations to control the household and their relationships with their husband. Renu uses different types of capital and techniques to improve her position or to obtain more capital on the household power level. She is working outside the home as a domestic worker and earns money (economic capital) for her and her two children's needs. She does not fully depend on her husband's income, rather she feeds her husband to gain his love and support. Moreover, Renu has two sons, which give her a strong position in the patrilineal culture of Bangladeshi society (cultural and/or symbolic capital). She is aware of her husband's demands and desires, so she uses contraceptives to avoid multiple pregnancies and tries to keep her body fit.

Renu blames her husband for the disorganization of their family life, but she does not want to leave her husband as she has no other options. Sometimes she talks in favor of him and sometimes she scolds (*gala-gali*) him with foul language (*kharap kotha*). Researchers in South Asian context have revealed that a woman may manifest independent ideas about her family and surroundings depending on her context, lifecycle, class, caste, religion, education, occupation and economic well-being (Säävälä, 1997; Tenhunen, 1997; Aura, 2008). Similarly, I find that as Renu feels too insecure to leave her husband, what she says about her relationship to her husband is totally context specific, sometimes she acts as a subservient wife and as the ideal model of patriarchy, and sometimes she uses bitter and filthy language about the same husband. Her vulnerable situation makes her agency totally ambivalent.

Parvin also uses different strategies; she totally depends on her husband's income and adapts the policy to depend on him as the senior wife. She always claims that Renu is a bad woman and expresses doubt about her marriage to her husband, which puts Renu and his two sons in a vulnerable position in the locality. On one hand by what she says and expresses, she tries to legitimate her marital position, and on the other hand, she is a vulnerable woman who has been cheated by her husband and tries to extract sympathy from others in the *basti*. She chooses to operate within the parameters of the code of conduct in the patriarchal social structure without directly challenging its embedded cultural discourses.

This is a marked example of a triadic relationship between a husband and his two co-wives, where in every situation the relationship is contested in the triad. In this co-wife family, the husband is the supreme boss in the patriarchal power structure and the two co-wives are continuously struggling to strengthen their positions with the husband. In this case, it is striking that although there is a hostile relationship between the two co-wives, the husband enjoys the supremacy of masculinity in the patriarchal and gender unequal social structure.

Case 2 Zakia – a blow against patriarchy

Zakia is a 25-year-old woman; she has been living in this *basti* for the last five years and works as a casual unskilled laborer (earth worker). She is responsible for all her family's expenses with her excessive hard work. Her husband is a good-for-nothing; he does not do any work. Zakia earns while the man enjoys the food with great pleasure. When Zakia and other people tell him to work, he claims that he does not feel well and that he has no strength in his body so he is not able to do manual work. Sometimes he behaves abnormally and tells everybody that he is possessed by a *giin* (supernatural power). To prove this, he lies in the toilet and smears his whole body with human excreta. Sometimes he lies on the mud near a small open space of the slum. All the slum dwellers consider him to be an irritating person and a madman (*pagol*). Occasionally, when he is in good mood, he searches for bindweed (*kolmi saak*) and the arum creeper (*kochur loti*) and sells these in the market. After selling them, he does not give what he earns to Zakia to spend on the family or bring anything for his small daughter. He spends all the money on different kinds of food for himself. When Zakia does not find work, she does not eat, but at night her husband beats her and forces her to borrow money or food for him.

Zakia told me that previously her husband often physically assaulted her so some of the well-wishers (women in this slum) advised her to behave rudely to him. She took their point and from then on whenever her husband came to beat her, she also chased him with a stick and attempted to beat him; consequently, the husband no longer beats her. Zakia shared many interesting events and experiences of her marital life. She took me inside her house to describe the events of her conjugal life. Some slum women and children also joined me. She offered me a stool (*mora*) to sit and placed some biscuits on the plate in front of me. She asked me to take a biscuit from the plate; I delightfully accepted her hospitality and asked the other women and children to share with me. After the snacks she started to describe how she took steps to control her violent husband and saved herself from the violence in an animated manner:

> One day when my husband started to beat me, I also started to beat him with a stick. During our fighting, my husband's *lungi* (men's waistcloth) became loose. Many children and adults in the *basti* had watched this fight and when his loose *lungi* slipped off the lower part of the body, he became very much embarrassed. Everybody laughed at him and made jokes about him. That day I felt so much peace in my mind when I realized that at least I have some courage to stand up to a man and silently thanked all those who had advised me to do this.

Zakia told me that one day she bought a small *Pungas* fish. Her husband was very happy to see the fish and politely requested her to cook it nicely. She also cooked a fish curry with tomatoes and served him this before them. But when he started eating he found a piece of a nail in the curry. At once he started shouting and insulting Zakia using foul language. First, she tried to calm him down and politely requested him to stop. She told him that this was not her fault because maybe the piece of nail had fallen into the curry from outside because here they all do their cooking outside. But he did not try to understand anything rather he took the *boti* (a long knife with a short haft) to kill Zakia. She was very tired that day because of her hard labor, but she did not lose her courage and ran from the room and went into the lane outside. Her husband also ran behind her with the *boti*. All the men, women and children who were standing there started shouting with fear. She felt so angry and humiliated that she took her earth cutting big sharp spade (*kodal*), which she kept outside the door, and stood in front of her husband. As a result, her husband was afraid and shouted to make her stop. He threw the *boti* down. According to Zakia, "I wanted to teach him a lesson again in front of many people." People also started to scold him and warned him to stop violent activities in the slum. After that Zakia felt that she was not alone. Although many men assault their wives in this *basti*, nobody was encouraging her husband's violent behavior toward her. Zakia became more courageous and suddenly kicked her husband in the scrotum (*gota*); he fell to the ground in pain. Everybody who was watching the quarrel laughed at him. From then, it became a spicy subject of gossiping among the slum dwellers.

As Zakia earns her livelihood but was always having scuffles with her husband, I asked her why she keeps on sharing her conjugal life with that man. Her answer upholds the argument that in spite of all these occurrences she still belongs to her husband, as she illustrated in the following way:

> I have no place to go; my parents are not alive in this world. My brothers also do not keep in contact with me. They are poor and leading very miserable lives. I have nothing in my in-laws' house too. Even though my husband is a stupid man and has nothing, you know he also works as a protector for me in the slum. If he did not, maybe many bad men would try to molest me.... Moreover, I want to see how long it would be possible to sustain a relationship with him through quarreling and fighting and I do not want to let him marry again. But if he flees leaving us alone in this *basti*, this is up to him. Because he knows well that he is fully dependent on me, but I am not on him.

Although Zakia struggles with her husband and in different way she mitigates violence against herself in the patriarchal social structure, the extent of women's vulnerability in the wider society is also highlighted here in the above statement. She believes in her lot and feels strong because she is the breadwinner for herself, her daughter and even for her husband. But she believes without a husband, she would not be able to take on the challenge to lead a husbandless life. From Zakia's example, we can see that the women who openly question cultural gender-based aberrations and provide alternatives for themselves, maybe cannot bring change to the established structures. They can only try to establish their rights for survival and to control violence against them. According to Ortner (1994),

> Change comes about when traditional strategies, which assume traditional patterns of relations (e.g. between chiefs and commoners, or between men and women), are deployed in relation to novel phenomena ... which do not respond to those strategies in traditional ways.
>
> (p. 399)

But Ortner emphasizes that change does not easily take place in most societies because people do not only live within a system, they embody it and are bound to it. So it may take two or three generations to change the structures and meanings of deeply embedded practices.

Zakia is protesting against the culture, but she cannot totally break down the norms; she does not leave her unemployed and violent husband only because as a married woman she needs him as symbol of protection and relatedness in the patriarchal social structure. So in the case of Zakia, again some questions are: How does Zakia form this resistance to protect herself from torture? Why does she feel relief after open aggression? For answers to these questions, I can consider Scott's (1990) idea of hidden transcripts. Scott characterizes individuals' backstage activities as a hidden transcript. Scott's central argument is that those people who are weak and discriminated against in society search for ways to resist the oppression, exploitation and discrimination through formulating and using their own hidden transcript. The hidden transcript is used, expressed and discussed in safe contexts such as in a group or a friendship "beyond the direct observation of the power holder" (Scott, 1990, p. 4).

Zakia gained her resistance capacity through hidden transcripts but her resistance, which is directed at her husband, is now not hidden, it takes an overt form of resistance. Zakia gained the idea of hidden resistance power from the group of slum women's separate sphere and collectivity, where she has friendship and networks. For a woman to beat her husband is considered a transgression by Islamic religion and culture. Her open resistance and aggression are against the Islamic religion, culture and the patriarchal social structure of the society, but Zakia does not feel she has committed a sin (*paap*) after beating her husband. From Zakia's example, I get the impression that if women (considered to be the weaker sex) stand up to men (considered to be the stronger sex) and show that they too can be aggressive, long-established practices of patriarchal violence against women will to some extent be reduced.

Conclusion

In this chapter, I have showed how *basti* women in their everyday lives are fighting, coping and taking a position against domestic violence in their families and communities and how some women are adopting alternative discourses against the dominant discourses in their battles in everyday life.

The *basti* women generally use the term *kharap beboher* to refer to psychological violence. Women also use the word *kosto* (pain/difficulties) that encompasses both psychological and physical violence. I found that some women in their daily lives experience psychological violence from their husbands, that is foul language (*kharap khota*) and misbehavior (*kharap beboher*) and they feel *kosto* (pain) when they are humiliated by the "rough behavior" and "foul language." But in general these women also use *kosto* to describe the difficulties in their lives such as poverty, poor living conditions, ill health, problems with the husband and children, and unemployment.

With one's angry gesture and verbal behavior, one tries to make the other obey one's rules, orders and ideas of appropriate behavior. As such, one is using power over the other. From this perspective, physical violence is an attempt to impose the desires and priorities of one person upon the other (Lahti, 2001, p. 183). The women perceived physical violence to be both *bou mara* (wife-beating) and *jhagra-maar-peet* (fights-beating). In their accounts, it breaks the silence of the woman, uncovers her private life to unrelated persons and disgraces (*oshomman*) her position in married life as a *bou* (wife), *maa* (mother), daughter-in-law (*cheler bou*), and *bhabi* (sister-in-law). It is also evident from the ethnographic data that to some women *wife-beating* is justified under some circumstances as they consider that in patriarchy the male is always superior to the female because they have mobility and masculine power in society. Moreover, religiously (both in Islam and Hinduism) males are treated and considered as individuals with more authority.

In patriarchal cultures, the male body is normatively linked with a good physique and violence. The fact that stereotypical heroic masculinity is often related with violent bodily demonstration the purpose of this is not to use the body in actual violence but to use it as an instrument of threats (Bourgois, 1996; Dobash and Dobash, 1998). For men, violence is rooted in a net of physicality, experience and male culture such that it is more easily used and more readily available as a weapon (Dobash and Dobash, 1998, p. 164).

It is often said that women's subordinate position in society or in the household reflects their lack of participation in economic activities. So the dominant hypothesis regarding women's empowerment is that if women are involved in economic activities, this will lead to or at least facilitate their empowerment. But it is evident from this study that although many women in the *bastis* run the home as the main breadwinner and have gained economic freedom and physical mobility in the public domain, most of them cannot exercise power over practices linked to society's structures and bring about changes because they are tied to feminine subordination in the patriarchal power relations deeply embedded in social-cultural and religious beliefs.

From the present study, it is also evident that divorced women, widows and childless women are generally held in low regard in Bangladeshi society; their positions are always inferior and sometimes stigmatized. Moreover, in families, most of the women simply choose to stay within the parameters of their cultural and religious code of conduct because if they raise their voice against deprivation, inequality and violence, it would most probably not establish their rights; rather they would find themselves in vulnerable situations. Even in the case of domestic violence by husbands or other affines (especially mothers-in-law), the *basti* women in this study try to cope the best they can because support from their natal relatives is limited and restrained, despite Bangladesh being a kin-based society. After the marriage of their daughters, in most cases, natal relatives feel that they are free from duty toward their daughters, and it is desired that young women should try to adjust to their husbands and other affinal relatives. So in cases of domestic violence, the natal relatives of women do not want a separation or divorce to take place; instead they want the women to somehow tolerate and adjust to the situations.

In the next chapter, I will focus on how women tolerate and informally try to solve long-lasting domestic violence against them and finally break the barriers and appeal to a formal institution for legal support. What happens when abused women come to the formal institutional arena? Do they manage to solve the problems of domestic violence?

5 Unveiling domestic violence from the privacy of home

This chapter focuses on how the daily lives of women in their marital homes can be disrupted by domestic violence by their husbands and in-laws. This makes their homes places of violence and fear by destroying the ideal pattern of a home. I looked for the causes of domestic violence against women from the clients of the counseling center to detect loopholes that could lead to women's subordination in their struggle to establish their rights. I will start my discussion by looking at the concept of home in the context of Bangladeshi society, and I will then describe the case studies of some women who have broken the silence of their home and brought their private lives into the public domain and uncovered the real causes for domestic violence.

The concepts of home and house are closely linked with each other. According to John Burnett (1985, p. 3), houses are physical structures of dwelling, and homes are social, economic and cultural institutions. Although home and house are interconnected to each other, because houses are altered into homes by the act of inhabiting, in almost every culture, the notion of a home is related to emotional and cultural values. To those people, a home is regarded as the private arena where they feel that they are separated from the public arena, and it is the domestic space that keeps people comfortable and closely tied with some specific persons. As Johnston and Valentine (1995, p. 100) write, "a home is considered as a stable and intimate hearth, a site of preservation and security, and a location of emotional and physical well-being, and loving and caring social relations." Very simply, homes are identified as places of respite and retreat and their territories are the locus of intimate relationships and families (Lahti, 2001, p. 145).

In Bangladesh, the physical structure of a home depends on the space and economic condition of individuals, but the overall construction patterns of Bangladeshi homes for poor people are simple and straightforward. Besides the physical structure, a home consists of objects, furniture, atmosphere, dwellers and the routines of domestic tasks, which are also simple but make the home secured, a warm, smooth and peaceful place and gives its people feelings of intimacy, security and belonging. It is generally perceived in families that the inside domain of the home is a woman's domain where she leads her daily life with belongingness; women organize homes, care for them, arrange them, manage them, enjoy them and are responsible for them. Most women in Bangladeshi society generally spend most of their time in the home or around it. Even for those women who work outside the home, domestic work is one of their main duties where the males make a negligible contribution.

Even though many changes have taken place in South Asian society, however, socially and culturally, women are still expected to bear responsibilities for domestic work and are treated as *grhini* (female housekeeper). It is expected that women should manage all the domestic work; whereas, men are considered to do work outside the home. In this context, Sharma (1986) states, traditionally it is considered that, "Housework is part of the female role and that efficiency as a housewife is an important measure of success as a woman" (p. 64). Lahti (2001, p. 146) mentions that the domestic setting determines social relations, symbolic systems, divisions of labor and intimacies of everyday life. In his study of a Kabyle house, Bourdieu (1990) highlights the fact that the house is the primary locus for the identification of culturally and socially meaningful systems of classification. In this context, he argues that by one's daily practices within the domestic arena, one acquires a tacit understanding, which embodies the understanding of social relations and local worldviews. According to him, the organization of the Kabyle house reflects the structural principles of gender, age, status and cosmology.

These private, intimate and gender-specific structured characteristics of homes pose confusion and problems when we consider a home as a place of domestic violence against women. In the Bangladeshi social structure, any disharmony in the familial relationship between husband and wife and with other family members by and large is considered private. Moreover, young women are always under the pressure of submissiveness, so when women face violent behavior from their husbands and other family members in their marital homes, they try to hide it to maintain social order in the home's harmonious relationships. Some studies (Jahan, 1994; Schuler et al., 1998; Hadi, 2000; Naved et al., 2002; Ali, 2002; Koenig et al., 2003; Ameen, 2005; Naved and Persson, 2005; Rashid, 2007) have indicated that married women in Bangladeshi society face more physical and psychological violence in their marital homes from their husbands and in-law's than from strangers in public. But most of the time, women tolerate the violence against them and try to protect their husbands' honor inside the shell of the privacy of home. Women also maintain this secrecy and isolation for the sake of the children and themselves. In Bangladeshi society, most women avoid reporting violence against them to the police or other agencies. Basically, when women face frequent domestic violence, they try to mitigate it or solve it with the help of their natal family members, and most of the time, both women and their natal family members want to keep the marital relationship intact, as they fear social stigma. In one sense, domestic violence against women disconcerts the preserved notion of a home; and in another sense, people try to organize these disorganizations of home and re-establish the disrupted relationships by tolerating the violent incidents.

I have selected six cases from the clients of the counseling center to explore the reasons why their natal and marital families and homes have been made insecure for them and put the women into vulnerable positions as a result. Through these cases I will provide accounts not only of the domestic violence they faced, but also of their feminine lives, their marriages and their relationships with their husbands and in-laws. The objective of these cases is to understand in a comprehensive and holistic way the life journey of Bangladeshi women who face domestic violence. To highlight their vulnerability, I will deal with their cases under different sub-headings, which in turn will provide a better understanding of the emergence and practice of domestic violence. Moreover, in some cases, I shall focus on the women's kin's narratives to express their views and ideas related to domestic violence. Some of the questions that I have addressed in this chapter include: Why do women become the victims of domestic violence by their husbands and in-laws and why do they try to bear this violent behavior for a long time? Do the victims seek informal support to solve the situation? Why do some victims choose to come for formal support at the counseling center and what do they usually demand?

Dowry and domestic violence: makes the women helpless

The issue of a dowry is a significant cause of domestic violence and this practice portrays women's inferior status and position and vulnerability in a patriarchal society like Bangladesh.

Moni is a Muslim woman of around 20. Her village of origin is Kapnakandi, in Jayantiapur, Sylhet. She had been schooled up to the fifth grade and is a housewife. Her husband is 25 years old and illiterate. He worked for a year as a laborer in Dubai, but now for the last four years he has been running a small grocery shop (*mudi dokan/vushimal-er-dokan*) in his village. Moni in her six years of married life has a four-year-old son. After marriage, Moni lived in an extended family with a mother-in-law, a brother-in-law and a sister-in-law.

Moni's parents are illiterate. Her father is a poor farmer and mother is a housewife, but in the harvesting season she works as a day laborer in different economically well-off households in the village. Moni has three brothers and six sisters. Moni is the second oldest child. According to Moni, her natal family is a large family, so the amount of crops that they produce cannot fulfill their yearly demands for rice. She claims her father is a simple man (*sida manush*) and such a big family is a great burden (*boro boja*) for him.

Moni got married in 2004 with a *Den Mahar* (bride price) of Taka 100,001. Her husband is her paternal cross cousin (*fufato bhai*). Because they were acquainted with each other, before and during the marriage arrangements, her parents did not ask her opinion. Her father was happy about this marriage proposal because his sister was taking his daughter to be her daughter-in-law. And Moni was also fascinated because she would be going to her aunt's family as a wife. As Moni is the eldest daughter of her father, it was the first wedding in their home. Her father happily arranged the wedding feast; he fed 60–70 persons and spent a lot of money on food. But her affines did not arrange any wedding feast. Even after the marriage ceremony when Moni's father and her uncle brought her from the marital home, they served only sweets (*misti*) and *sorbot* (a type of drink-water mixed with lemon juice and sugar) to them. They only spent a small amount of money on the marriage. They didn't give her any bride presents. They promised her father that they would give her *sari*, a pair of gold earrings and a gold necklace, but on the wedding day they did not bring anything. After the marriage arrangement, Moni's father was forced by her mother-in-law to provide them with all the household items and Taka 1,500 for their prestige in their village. Moreover, the main condition of the marriage was to send the groom to Dubai with all expenses paid.

When I asked Moni's father about the conditional marriage, he told me that he agreed to her conditions only for his daughter's happiness. At that time, he thought his daughter would be happy forever in a relative's home. He requested his sister not to ask for any other marriage gifts, but after the marriage date had been fixed, she tried to force him to provide other gifts. So he was forced to provide all the household items to hide his shame in the locality; because in the meantime everybody knew that his daughter's marriage to his sister's son had been arranged. He claimed that they are poor, but they have *izzat* (honor). He feared at that time for his daughter's *izzat* (honor) in her affinal home. Moreover, he thought if his sister broke the proposal it would destroy his daughter's reputation and her future possibilities of marriage. His other unmarried daughters would also be affected by this dishonor. He did not imagine that they would torture his daughter so inhumanly, and he did not understand his sister's ugly motive. So he was forced to fulfill all the demands of his younger sister. After the marriage, within six months, his elder son spent Taka 200,000 to take Moni's husband to Dubai; and consequently his son had become a beggar (*pother fakir*).

Later, he showed me a list of household items from the counseling center's registration file. This list was prepared by the marriage registrar at the time of marriage along with kabin, although they did not mention the main condition of the marriage, that is, to arrange and foot all the expenses of sending the groom to a foreign country after marriage. Only the list of clothes and household materials is given below.

There are several factors here that disadvantage Moni: first of all, her father had limited resources to support her natal family. Her birth order of being the eldest daughter of her parent's five unmarried daughters put her in an unfavorable situation because of the cultural expectations governing eldest daughters' early marriage in Bangladeshi families. Another disadvantaging fact is that Moni's marriage was arranged to her paternal cross cousin (father's younger sister's son), who was unemployed, had no income and no agricultural plot. But her father expected this conditional marriage proposal without considering Moni's conjugal future; as he trusted that the strength of their kinship bonds would make everything all right. Moni's father did not think about his capacity to meet the marriage conditions he had agreed to, rather he only thought of his daughter's happiness. He thought that his daughter would go to her relative's house as a bride and the alliance would be stronger. Furthermore, he was going to help the future prospects of his sister's son, not those of an outsider. From his statements,

Table 5.1 Happy wedding gifts of Moni Begum

Furniture and bedding	Number	Kitchen utensils	Number
Palong (bed)	01	Deg dekchi (cooking pot)	04
Mitsef (cupboard)	01	Korai (cooking pan)	02
Alna (clothes hanger)	01	Kurchun (flat spoon)	01
Chair	04	Beri (hot cooking pot holder)	01
Table	01	Chorta (betel nut cutter)	01
NamazerChouki (prayer bed)	01	Paan daan (betel leaf keeping pot)	01
RazaiBed (high mattress for bed)	01	Taua (frying pan)	01
Balish (pillow)	02	Belun (hand bread making roller)	01
Bichanar Chador (bed sheet)	01	Chunga (a funnel for burning fire in the mud stove)	01
Moshari (bed net)	01	Pitol-er-chamoch (spoon made of brass)	01
Haricane (kerosene lamp)	01	Torcarir chamoch (curry spoon)	01
		Cup-pirich (cup and saucer)	One set
		Tray (tea serving tray)	01
Clothing and others	**Number**	Bodna (water pot for toilet)	01
Sifon Sari (synthetic sari for bride)	01	Balti (bucket)	01
Ghori (watch for groom)	01	Ketli (Kettle)	01
Sonar Naktul (gold nosepin for bride)	01	Pakha (hand fan)	01
Zuta (groom's shoe)	01	Pitol-er-kolosh (pitcher made of brass)	01
Shirt for groom	02	Tin-er-kolosh (aluminum pitcher)	01
Gengi (upper under garment for groom)	02	Sora (lid)	02
Zangi (lower under garment for groom)	01	Jug	01
Muja (socks for groom)	01	Baltir mog (mug for bucket)	01
Lungi (lower part dress for groom)	02	Paanir glass (water glass)	06
Panjabi (kind of loose shirt for groom)	01	Kupi (tiny kerosene lamp)	01
Chata (umbrella for groom)			
The Holy Quran	01		
Zainamaj (mat for prayer)	01		
Cash: TK.1500 (for groom)	01		

Source: Counseling Center Register File.

it also seems that like other dowry cases in Bangladeshi society (Jahan, 1994; Ameen, 2007): he was also pressured before and after the wedding proposal had been settled to pay a dowry to the groom and his family.

Moni claimed that her husband was a very bad man and he did not keep any contact with her when he was abroad. He was angry with her and never bought anything for her. He neglected her in the discussions of family affairs. He dishonored her as an unwanted person in the family and beat her brutally on every part of her body with whatever came to hand. She demonstrated how inhumanly her husband beat her: "He grabbed my hair with his fist and then kicked me in my abdomen, buttocks and chest. He slapped me on my cheeks and ears and punched me roughly." Sometimes Moni's husband beat her with the wooden handle of a blunt spade, home bread-making roller, firewood, stick and umbrella. She said there were many black marks all over her body and her husband's torture was unbearable. When asked to explain how she tolerated the violence of her husband Moni stated, "When I can't tolerate his torture and screamed, he pressed my mouth and neck with his hands. He pressed so hard that I felt my breathing might stop forever, my teeth would break and I would die."

It is Moni's conviction that the reason was her husband and in-law's abused her with foul language and beat her like an animal because they wanted her to get them more money. Moni's father arranged everything and spent a huge amount of money to send Moni's husband to Dubai, but he (Moni's husband) did not work properly there and had problems with the manager of the company and was sacked. After losing his job, he again started to bother Moni's brother to arrange another job for him, but Moni's brother failed to arrange a new job for him. Finally, because he could not get a job, Moni's husband quarreled with his brother-in-law and returned to Sylhet, Bangladesh. After his return, Moni's marital family fell on economic hardship and they started to torture Moni to bring money from her father for her husband's grocery business. When the torture became too excessive and unbearable, Moni could not tolerate it anymore and she went to her natal home to get money. Her parents felt shocked about the marital violence she had to endure and cried at her misfortune. They saw the injuries and black marks on their daughter's body and feared for her future married life. To bring their daughter peace, her father sold an old big tree and gave Moni Taka 10,000 to give her husband. But Moni's affinal family members were not happy with it, after some months they again demanded Taka 5,000 to establish the grocery business. Moni's husband and mother-in-law again started their brutality to ensure they got the money. Moni's brother-in-law and sister-in-law also joined them in torturing her psychologically with their foul language to make her weak and vulnerable.

It can be seen from the Moni's case that marriage alliances between relatives in the Muslim society in the local setting sometimes do not play any significant role in determining whether or not a woman is subjected to domestic violence. While marriages between relatives are expected to establish mutual understanding and strong alliance, it is also considered that a close-kin marriage is a good solution because the women have known their husbands and their mothers-in-law since childhood and are affectionate to them (Säävälä, 2001, p. 105), but in some cases the reverse is true, as Moni's case shows.

To visualize her helpless state, Moni said that after all the violent attacks, she did not go out to get treatment because it is indecent for a young woman in a village to visit a doctor alone. She also emphasized that it is also very shameful for a woman to reveal private matters outside the home and to show her body to an unrelated male. A good woman tries to endure all types of pain and domestic violence in the marital home. In her husband's hamlet, everybody knew about these incidences and if sometimes women who were her neighbors came to rescue her from the torture, her mother-in-law was very harsh with them and roughly said to them that it was their private matter.

Moni's father and other relatives took an initiative to stop their violence toward her before coming to this counseling center, but they did not change. Sometimes her parents did not let her to go back to her marital home. But she felt that her natal house was living in poverty because of her marriage and how long they could endure this problem because sometimes her father also became irritated with her because he had five more unmarried daughters and three sons. Her father was also become irritated to look after Moni and her son.

I then asked Moni why she had come to the counseling center. She explained, one day her husband beat her with the handle of the blunt spade on her back near her shoulder. Immediately blood started ooze. She became faint and some women neighbors rescued her and took her to one of their homes. There they took care of her wound with herbal medicine. She stayed in that home with her child; in the meantime, they called her father by mobile phone to take her from her marital home. In the morning when her father came to take her back to the natal home, her mother-in-law and husband were very rude to him and her husband raised his hand to hit her father. Her father slapped him on his cheek. Her mother-in-law spat on the ground and abused her father with foul language. The neighbors tried to control the quarrel but could not. Her husband and mother-in-law accused her of being a wanton woman as she had stayed one night outside the marital home.

That day, her husband gave her "Three *Talaq*" (oral divorce in the Muslim religion). She cried a lot and came back to natal home. Now she wanted again to go back to her husband's home, so she was looking for help from the counseling center to rearrange their marriage. She said, "I did not get married to come back in my natal home. I do not want a divorce. People will say that I am bad; they will not see the violence." When I asked why she wanted to go back to her husband's house, Moni pointed out that she wanted to go back to her husband's home because she felt she had no support to stay forever to her natal home where there were too many "mouths to feed." This was no lifelong welcoming environment for her and her son. She highlighted the fact that despite being battered, she wanted to go back to her marital home for her *izzat* (honor) and support. She thought that she would be stigmatized by society at large if she did not have a husband and father for a child. She also criticized her society's norms that allowed a man to become bad and violent as a husband but ostracized a woman if she left a violent husband. She was acutely aware of her status as a poor, barely educated, unsupported, battered and already divorced woman, but she did not want the dissolution of her marriage and to face the uncertainty of the future and the certainty of social stigma that is associated with divorce.

In Moni's case, she wanted to present herself to the person around her as someone who embodies the ideals of patriarchal ideologies. In my discussions with her, I got the impression that she just came to the counseling center to resolve her divorce case and to again go back to her marital home. Though she did not think she would have a domestic violence-free life in her marital home, she was more in fear of the ideologies of her patriarchal society.

Driven from husband's house – no place of her own

In this section, I will sketch another prominent cause of domestic violence against women in Bangladeshi society. In the next two cases of Nahida and Chaya, I will describe how some husbands' extra-marital relationships reinforce domestic violence and the vulnerability of women in their conjugal lives.

The first story is about a teenage girl, who presents herself as an example of domestic violence. Nahida is a 16-year-old Muslim woman from Chatak in Sylhet district. She can only write her name and she is a housewife. Her husband's name is Sunab Ali, a 53-year-old man from Bishawnath in Sylhet district. The man can also only sign his name. He had worked as a laborer in Dubai for ten years. According to what Nahida knows it is his first marriage. In their three years of married life, they have had an 18-month-old daughter. Nahida lived in her husband's house only for eight or nine months.

According to Nahida's statement, the economic condition of her natal family has always been deplorable. From childhood, she had observed and experienced severe poverty, starvation, her father's ill health and death without treatment, her mother's sickness and a monotonous life with a heavy burden of work, sufferings and diseases. Her natal family has no material resources, other than a small plot of homestead land. Their condition is so bad that if their mother dies, they will have to beg on the streets to survive.

Nahida got married in 2007 through a registered kabin with Taka 150,000. Although at the time of marriage she was just 14 years old, her marriage negotiator (*ghotok*) claimed she was 18. Describing what she recalled of the marriage arrangement, Nahida said, like other arranged marriages in the village, her marriage proposal came from a *ghotok* (marriage negotiator) from another village to her elder paternal uncle (*jetha*). At first her mother was reluctant to consider this marriage proposal because the groom was much older than Nahida. Even though the groom was older than her mother, most of her relatives from her father's side and some neighbors put pressure on her mother to agree to the proposal because the groom was rich in their eyes. Moreover, the groom had made no demand for a dowry, and it was thought he would able to help the impoverished family after the marriage. Nahida did not want to marry this old man and cried a lot, but she did not get any sympathy from anybody. Her mother and maternal uncle (*mama*) beat her brutally and her paternal aunt (*fufu*) came with a *boti* (knife with a short haft) to threaten her because they had already given their approval to the *ghotok* (marriage negotiator) and some neighbors knew about their decision. The marriage involved their *izzat* (honor) and they could not tolerate her disobedience. Her mother forced her to agree to this lucrative proposal and threatened she would kill herself by taking poison if she (Nahida) did not agree to the marriage. Everybody tried to make her understand that it is not uncommon in the rural society of Bangladesh for women to have husbands who were much older than them. Finally, because of their insistence, Nahida found no other way but to accept this forced marriage.

Nahida's natal family's deplorable economic situation had pushed her to marry at this early age. Because of extreme poverty, her mother found it expedient to make an alliance for her daughter with a well-to-do groom to get help in the future in the form of cash and kind. She ignored the mismatch between the ages of the bride and groom. Apart from this economic factor, I find two factors that played a decisive role in Nahida's marriage. First, because of patriarchy, generally in Bangladeshi society, a family without an older male guardian is always seen to be vulnerable and weak. And second, as it is a kin-based society, the relatives always play decisive roles in marriage negotiations or other social occasions. In Nahida's case, we see that both factors worked positively.

When I asked Nahida about her conjugal problems and whether or not she received any support from her relatives or neighbors, Nahida explained her conjugal problem and misfortune that put her into a vulnerable situation. She said, one morning four months after her wedding, her husband told her that he would not be home for some days as he had some important work in another place. He gave her some money and ordered her to stay at home. After her husband's departure, some of her husband's relatives informed her about her husband's illicit relationship with his own older maternal aunt (*apon boro mami*). They informed her that many years ago her husband's older maternal uncle (*mama*) had lost both his legs and hearing ability in a road accident and from that time Nahida's husband had had an illicit affair with his aunt. After hearing about all these sinful activities (*pap kaj*) of her husband, Nahida cried a lot and talked with her mother over mobile phone. She asked her mother to take her back home, but her mother said that she was also helpless because she feared what society would say. She only cried a lot and advised her to be patient.

However, after ten days when Nahida's husband returned home, she asked him about his affair, so he then knew that Nahida had been informed about everything by her neighbors. As a result, he became angry and first he scolded his neighbors and beat Nahida roughly with his umbrella. The next morning, Nahida fled from her husband's home. She had some money with her, which helped a lot to return to her natal home. When her mother saw her, she did not like it but feared for her misfortune and insecurity. She talked with Nahida's paternal uncle and aunt. They rebuked them and suggested that they keep silent for some days. After two months, Nahida's mother found out that Nahida was pregnant. Then her mother along with Nahida's maternal uncle (*mama*) went to her husband's house and met him. They told him about her pregnancy, but the man shouted with rage and ignored his responsibility and produced divorce papers (*Talak nama*).

At the end of our conversation, Nahida said that she did not get any support from the community; rather everybody blamed her for leaving her husband's house (*swamir ghor*) and she had been stigmatized. The child was not accepted by society because she had no father, and some people considered her to be a bastard (*jaroj*). So for the legitimacy of the child, she now wanted to file a legal case against that man. I again asked her, "Why did you not come earlier to this counseling center when you realized that you were pregnant after the divorce?" Then she remained quiet for some time and said, "My mother and relatives were afraid of my husband, and we did not know about this counseling center. We know that advocates take a lot of money to file a legal case; we do not have any money."

After this conversation, I left the counseling center for that day because the advocates had already sent a letter to Nahida's husband, but he did not come that day for *shalish* (mediation) and did not send any massage to the advocates. So the *shalish* was postponed for that day and the advocates proposed a new date to them, and they again got ready to send another letter to Nahida's husband for a *shalish* for both parties.

Nahida's story tells us that, although Nahida has been married for three years and had a child, she herself was a child. She is helpless and vulnerable. Society now blames her for all her activities and claims that she is responsible for her bad luck. But according to the law, her natal family members, relatives and husband are responsible for a child marriage. The Child Marriage Restraint Act, 1929, Section 5 as amended in 1984, states that

> Whoever performs, conducts or directs any child marriage shall be punishable with simple imprisonment which may extend to one month, or with fine which may extend to 1,000 Taka or to both, unless he proves that he had reason to believe that the marriage was not a child marriage. For the purpose of the Act "child" according to Section 2, means a person who, if male is under 21 years of age, and if female is less than 18 years of age. Therefore, any person entering into marriage with someone under the stipulated age is guilty of child marriage.
>
> (Quoted in Chowdhury, 1993)

The irony is that the sections do not make a marriage void if the law is contravened but merely makes it punishable. So, from the Bangladeshi perspective, husbands are not criminally liable for sexual intercourse with a wife who is 16 years or above without her consent. Even when the husband and wife are separated, sexual assault by the husband may qualify as a sexual offence, but not rape. As Section 376 of the Penal Code states:

Whoever commits rape shall be punished with imprisonment for life or with imprisonment of either description for a term which may extend to ten years, and shall also be liable to fine, unless the woman raped is his own wife and is not under 12 years of age [now 16 years by the Women and Children Repression Prevention (Amendment) Act, 2003], in which case he shall be punished with imprisonment of either description for a term which may extend to two years, or with fine, or with both.

In the cultural context, sexual relationship between spouses is considered justified even if the wife is unwilling. As in many cultures, women are socialized to accept physical and mental abuse as part of a husband's marital prerogatives (Counts, 1990; Olavarrieta and Sotelo, 1996). In Bangladesh, women are taught to be obedient to their husbands, and the husbands are socialized to exercise their right to dominate their spouses, including their sexuality (Hadi, 2000, p. 790).

In Nahida's case, we can see that from her marriage arrangements, any existing law related to women's marriage acts did not work for her. In contrast to Nahida's case, Chaya Rani's case presents a different type of unfaithful husband where the husband has married several times and maintained extra-marital relationship with street-based sex workers. According to the Hindu religion, Chaya Rani has a marital bond with her husband forever.

Chaya Rani was a 28-year-old married Hindu woman with three children, two daughters aged ten and five and a son aged seven. She had a soft face and gloomy eyes, which were full of sorrow. She came from a slum of Sylhet city. She was illiterate and only could sign her name. She then worked as a domestic helper in various houses near the slum and earned only TK1,400–1,500. After her first menstruation, she married an illiterate carpenter, Nitai Bamo, and she was his second wife. Nitai was then about 40 years old. They both are from a scheduled caste.

Chaya Rani's natal family lived in a *basti* in Sylhet city. She was the fourth child of her parents who had six children. Her father was a carpenter and her mother a housewife. Her father's economic condition was very deplorable because he was old and sick; he did not work and sometimes could not work because of his ill health. Chaya Rani's two marriageable sisters were still unmarried.

Because of poverty and insecurity, Chaya's father was forced to arrange her marriage to the previously married Nitai. They knew that Nitai's first wife was a lunatic and was living with her natal family and he would not bring her back. Moreover, they were told that he did not have any children. But later after the wedding when Chaya went to her marital family, she found Nitai had two daughters aged three and one. At that point she had no way back, so at the tender age of 14, she had to accept these two girls as her daughters and started to look after them. After some years of marriage, she gave birth to her first child, a daughter. But her mother-in-law and husband were very angry with her and rebuked her a lot for this misfortune of not giving birth to a son. She was then at her father's house, so after the child's birth they did not bring her back to their house for more than six months. Later, Chaya's father took her back to her husband's house with the child.

After two years, Chaya again became pregnant. This time Chaya gave birth to a son. This time her mother-in-law and husband were happy and they brought back her to their home. But Nitai started a different game; he started to search for street-based sex workers. Chaya knew everything and protested about this, but Nitai started to beat her. Chaya found her life was totally unbearable there, but she was forced to stay. In the meantime, for the third time, Nitai got married again, to a 30-year-old woman with a dowry. With this marriage, he obtained a good sizeable sum of money for his business. And from then, Chaya had been living with her parents. Now Chaya wanted maintenance costs for her children with the help of the counseling center.

Troubles with a love marriage

In Bangladesh, women's love marriages are considered to be "individualistic" choices that work against the "common and accepted" good and holistic idea of family and kin. Love marriages are challenges to patrilineage, which becomes established through a woman's father or elder brother. These individuals may disown the woman, while at the same time, the groom's family may not accept the woman. Women entering love marriages are more or less deprived of their "relationality" and "belongingness" and as their marriages are not approved by their natal and marital families, they immediately become vulnerable in the patriarchal social structure. In the case of Golapi, these factors led to her becoming vulnerable, and her father could not accept her because of the social stigma and dishonor she had brought to the family.

Golapi was only a 15-year-old Hindu teenage girl. She was from Fenchugonj, Sylhet. She studied up to seventh grade. Golapi married a three-wheeler driver in a love marriage and she became a housewife. She did not know her husband's address and anything about his personal life. When I met with Golapi in the counseling center, it was a rainy day and the whole sky was overcast with black clouds. The day was gloomy and monotonous, the roads were dirty with muddy water and most of the people in the court arena were irritated because it had been raining for several days. I was sitting silently in an old simple wooden chair in the counseling center's client serving room. The coordinator was in his room talking with somebody on his mobile phone. The advocates were not present yet because of the inclement weather. The assistant was writing up some old cases in her room in the record keeping notebook. The peon went to the court's canteen to bring tea for everybody. At that lazy time, Golapi entered with an old bearded man in the client serving room of the counseling center. Her cotton *sari* was wet with rain-water, and water was dropping from her curly wet hair and her *sindur tip* (red vermilion mark on the forehead) was faded. After entering the counseling center, she talked in a low voice to the bearded old man and asked me to whom she should talk. I suggested her to go to the female assistant room pointing her out with my finger.

She entered the room slowly and the old man sat on the chair in the client serving room.

When she described her love marriage and vulnerable situation, Golapi was sorrowful and several times she burst into tears. She said she married a Hindu man of a different caste, named Sumon. Her husband is *Mala* (a scheduled caste, who earned their livelihood by singing) and she is a Nath (weaver). She met him at a girlfriend's (*bandhobi*) elder sister's wedding ceremony. He came there as a friend of the groom. They liked each other and before departure the man gave her a small piece of paper where he had written his name and mobile number. Golapi became so fascinated that she started to call him, stealing money from her natal home to pay for the calls. One of her girlfriends (*bandhobi*) had a mobile phone. Golapi gave her money and talked with him. She was in a listless state of mind and day-by-day she was becoming mad for his companionship. Golapi said he should marry her. He also told her to prepare for the marriage and proposed that they elope.

According to Golapi, she didn't think about any obstacles or any mishaps that might befall her, her parent's affection and the stigma (*kolonko*) that this would cause for her natal family. She did not think about her parent's sad and shameful faces. She only thought about herself, about the new married life, which was beckoning her. So one day she eloped with Sumon. Golapi recalled how she managed to elope with her fiancé. She described how the previous night, she wore her mother's gold chain and stole money from her father's pocket. Sumon brought a black veil (*kalo borkha*) for her to disguise her identity. In the morning, she asked for permission from her mother to go to her girlfriend's house. But she did not go there and on the way she wore that black veil and fled with him.

According to Golapi, she did not understand at that time that it would be a great blunder for her. She said after coming to Sylhet city, they got married in the temple (*mondir*). Then they went to Sumon's sublet rented room. Life was very happy and full of hope and love and she totally forgot the affection of her parents. After one month, she rang her father's mobile, and with an angry voice her father told her that her mother was very sick and maybe she would die because of her behavior; so they did not want to have anything to do with her forever. He ordered her not to disturb them anymore. As far as they were concerned, they did not have any daughter. She was the stigma (*kolonko*) for the family. Two months passed without incident, then Golapi found she was pregnant. She told her husband, but he did not show any expression of happiness. He told her in a calm voice that it was too early to have a child because he could not afford to support one. Golapi did not understand and told him, that a child is a gift from *vagawan* (god) and they should be happy. But he did not become happy. Some days passed without anything happening. But Sumon tried to avoid her; he started to stay away for long periods of time.

One day, she quarreled with him and cried a lot. She asked him why he was avoiding the issue of her pregnancy and not coming home. He slapped her and said that he had lots of work to do. She was hurt by his ugly behavior because he had never slapped her before or abused her using foul language. Then after some days she asked him again to take her to Sumon's village to his natal family as he was not living with them. He said he would take her within one month. After the sixth month of her pregnancy, one morning she woke up and found that Sumon was not in the room. Three days passed, but he did not come back to the house. She had no money and no food. She told everything to her landlady. The landlady said her that she made a great mistake because they did not know anything about Sumon as he was a new tenant. The landlady rang Golapi's father and asked him to take her home, but her father refused. The landlady also rang Sumon's mobile several times, but the number was not reachable. Golapi stayed with the lady for a day and then she sent her with the landlady's father to the counseling center for legal help and shelter.

After hearing her sorrowful story, in the course of my conversation with Golapi, I asked her for some evidence which will help to prove she was indeed married to Sumon. But she replied that she did not have anything to prove that she had been married and she even did not have any photo of her husband. She regretted her situation and said with a sad voice that she believed him so much that she didn't doubt anything he had said or keep any record of their relationship. I asked her, "Do you think it will be possible to find Sumon without a photo and address? How will you prove your marriage? How will the personnel of the counseling center find him?" She was silent and then she started weeping. I took her father's mobile number and asked the assistant to write it in the counseling center's register notebook. The old man asked if he could leave and asked us not to involve his daughter and himself in this problem. He gave their permanent address in Sylhet city and told us that they only helped her because she was a wretched woman, but they didn't want to get involved with her case because they feared the complexity of the law.

After reading the written statement, the coordinator came to the room and sat with us. He asked the old man to help them with this wretched girl. He asked with the girl's father over the mobile phone to help them, but the father told him that he could give some money but he could not take the girl to home because *samaj* (society in the locality) would exile his family because of the stigmatized girl and her illegitimate child. I asked the coordinator about possible shelter for the victim girl. He replied that they didn't have any shelters. So he rang the government shelter home and sent her there. As she was pregnant that was the only place for her to live. The coordinator mentioned that after the child was born, Golapi would face many problems and she would be insulted by people. It is obviously very hard to overcome her stigma (*kolonko*) in this society. The norms of the society are very hard, which was why Golapi's father also did not want to take her home. But considering the girl's situation, the counseling center would try as much as possible and send her to the government shelter home.

From Golapi's case, it can be seen that although NGOs and government social welfare service and rehabilitation programs are trying to help wretched women, but it is very hard for them to carve out independent paths or think differently for them.

A drug addicted husband and disorganized conjugal life

Like many developing countries of the world, drug addiction is escalating in Bangladesh (Department of Narcotic Control, 1995).[1] It has marched into every section of society in both urban and rural life and severely upsets all spheres of life and is recognized and considered as one of the most damaging national health and social problems. Most of the drug addicts are young adults, and the number is growing with time (Morshed, 1996). Multiple drug use is common among the drug addicts. Cannabis (*gaja*), morphine derivatives such as heroin (diacetylmorphine), pethidine (meperidine), codeine (3-methylmorphine), etc. are the most preferred drugs/substances used by the drug addicts. Moreover, the sexual life of addicts is in a vulnerable state as they are likely to participate in risky sex practices. It is usual for addicts to have unprotected sex with multiple partners, which ultimately results in their suffering from sexually transmitted diseases, and even from HIV infection (Begum, 1991; Islam et al., 2000). In this section, Nurjahan's case will illustrate the vulnerability of a wife whose husband is a drug addict.

Nurjahan is a 22-year-old woman with two small children. Her mother had become blind and was in poor health throughout her childhood. She had three years of formal education and poverty forced her to stop study. Besides, her family needed her to work helping in their household and also in the informal sector. Her family was always very poor because her father's income was insufficient to run a family of six persons; moreover, her father was frequently in poor health because of chronic diarrhea. She came to Sylhet city for the first time from Netrakona with her natal family when she was 10 and started working in the informal sector with her father making pickles and *pitha* (small sweet cake). They have been living in different slums in Sylhet city from that time till now. In order to earn a decent living, her father did various types of work, but he couldn't improve the economic condition.

When she was 17, she married a family acquaintance. After the marriage, she realized that her husband was violent and a drug addict, who constantly suspected her of having extramarital relationships and subjected her to horrific physical torture that included beatings with wood, a *beloon* (bread-making roller) and anything that he could get his hands on. She had been thrown out of the house along with her children on several occasions, yet she tolerated his inhuman behavior. Nurjahan said her father arranged her marriage hurriedly with the man because he came to her natal home several times a month to see her. Her mother understood that he was interested in her and suggested that her father propose a relationship to the man. Nurjahan also liked the man then and when her father proposed to the man, he gladly accepted the proposal. The marriage took place without a dowry. So Nurjahan's parents were happy that they had not been put under any financial pressure.

The couple was living in a slum of Sylhet city. Nurjahan's husband used to take *ganja* (cannabis) and did not work regularly. Nurjahan became scared and told her parents everything, but they asked her to tolerate it. They did not talk with the husband about it because they were afraid that he would beat Nurjahan and divorce her. After a month of marriage, the man started to torture Nurjahan. First, he used to rebuke her and insult her using foul language. Then he wanted spending money from her as she was working as a domestic worker in the nearby houses of rich people. Most of the time she couldn't give any money because she earned very little and she had to spend all the money on the rent and food. Then he started beating her and starting selling their belongings to get money for drugs. Nurjahan could not protect herself from his violence. He beat her severely and she screamed out loud with pain. On hearing the commotion, the neighborhood women came to save her from her drug addict husband. But Nurjahan did not get escape from the torture because her father was too afraid of his violent behavior and his filthy attitude. One day, the man went to her natal home to rape her younger sister. Her mother shouted to save her and the wretched girl managed to escape from the room. It brought great shame on the family, so Nurjahan's natal family left that slum. Moreover, Nurjahan told me, "What could I do? Where could I go? My natal family's condition was not good. How could my parents protect me?"

I then asked Nurjahan why she has come to this counseling center now. She said she could not tolerate her husband's violence anymore. She asked how long it was possible for a woman to tolerate domestic violence (*ottachar*). She described her husband as a heroin addict who had totally lost his human characteristics and behaved like a monster. He does not have the sense to evaluate good or bad. Frequently, he threw her and the children out of home and beat them mercilessly. On several occasions, he had come with a knife and *boti* (heavy knife with a short haft) to cut them. Not so long ago, he threw her baby boy to the ground and kicked him in an attempt to get money from her. One day, he tried to strangle their young daughter. The police had had to jail him several times for hijacking. He was a bother to her; she was afraid of him and could not bear his torture. When the torment first started happening, she did not think about losing her life, but now she feared for her children's safety. Moreover, she had started to earn money and become the family's breadwinner after the marriage. Her husband never took any responsibility for the family. For most of the year, she lives in her natal home with her children. But when she is there, it is very hard for her to escape from his violent hand. He went there and tried to beat them and demanded money. So she thinks it would be better for her to give him a divorce. Then the relationship will end forever and the drug addict husband would not be able to disturb her anymore. She had come to the counseling center to get advice on how she could free herself from the violence by getting a divorce.

It is seen from the above case that sometimes marriage with family acquaintances do not help to maintain marital relationships. Nurjahan got married without a dowry, which made the whole family happy, but the family did not know that the man was a drug addict. As he was an acquainted person, they did not try to find out anything about his private life. Moreover, from the description of Nurjahan's case, we can see that despite being battered, she stayed for a long time with her addicted and violent husband because she had no support due to her appalling poverty. Finally, she began to fear him too much because of his *heroin* addiction and his trying to murder their children. So finding no other way, she has decided to end the conjugal relationship in a legal way. She wanted to rely on the law and get protection from a legal agency.

The supremacy of the mother-in-law in married life

Taslima is from the village of Chatak in Sylhet district. Her father is a small businessman. Taslima studied up to ninth grade in a *Madrasha* (religious education school for Muslim children), but following the normal way of most Bangladeshi village adolescent girl, she got married when she was only 16 years old. It was an arranged marriage and her husband was a 25-year-old small businessman. Taslima's father was pressured by his relatives to arrange her marriage as the girl was growing older. At Taslima's wedding, her father gave her gifts according to his ability. From the groom's family, they did not want anything, but her father provided all the household furniture and kitchen utensils for his daughter's peace. After her marriage, Taslima came to live with her affinal family with great hope and many dreams in her heart.

But from the very beginning, the relationship between Taslima and her mother-in-law was contested. According to Taslima, there was no obvious reason for her mother-in-law's hostile attitude toward her, but soon after she moved in, her mother-in-law started to abuse her in many ways. Taslima stated that her mother-in-law did not like to see her idle. She had to do all the household chores from morning to night, but her mother-in-law always complained that her work was not neat. If she wanted to go to her natal family, her mother-in-law did not give her permission and became furious with her. Taslima tried to ignore all this misbehavior and kept all the sorrow in her heart. Sometimes her sisters-in-law came to the house, and they also joined their mother in mistreating her. She could not even talk properly to her husband. If she tried to talk in the daytime to her husband, she was abused by her mother-in-law for being a woman of "ill-character."

Taslima then silently lived for nine months with her affines. Day-by-day the violence of her mother-in-law became so severe that she could not tolerate it. She became sick and feared everybody in her marital house. Her mother-in-law thought this silence was due to her weakness and thought her abuse was just. Then she became pregnant. But her mother-in-law was still very unkind to her. Her parents came to see her and forcibly took her with them. This time Taslima told everything to her parents. They felt sorry for her but did not say anything to her mother-in-law and husband. Taslima gave birth to a daughter; her mother-in-law was angry and didn't even come to see the newborn daughter. Then she went back to her marital family with her father. But her mother-in-law did not stop her violence toward her. She could not tolerate it anymore and again went back to her natal family. Taslima did not know why just after her marriage her mother-in-law was always after her. She tolerated several different episodes of her mother-in-law's beating and misbehavior.

I again asked her, "Do you want to go back to your marital family?" Taslima replied that she asked for her husband to live in a separate house, but he refused because it would shame him. Her husband was always silent about his mother's misbehavior (*kharap beboher*) and violence (*maar-peet*). Moreover, she does not have any way to go back to her husband because just one month ago he got married again to his *khalato bon* (mother's sister's daughter) and sent her a divorce letter. According to Taslima, this marriage had destroyed her whole life. Her family members are now all insulted by what had happened, so she wants to file a case against her ex-husband and his mother.

Lastly I asked her, "What will you do in the future?" Taslima replied, "I shall start my studies again. My parents will look after me as until I am a graduate. I shall be a school teacher in future." Although Taslima claimed that she would start her studies again and try to become empowered, we should keep in mind that in the Bangladeshi social context it is always hard for a rural divorced girl to overcome such harsh vulnerability. But in her case what strikes me is that despite her limited scope and vulnerability, she raised her voice with the help of her parents and gained courage to stand up against domestic violence.

Taslima's case depicts the vulnerability of married women to the dominance of a mother-in-law in conjugal life, and these contested relationships are very common in South Asian societies (Säävälä, 1997; Nazneen, 1998; Aura, 2008). Wilson-Williams et al. (2008, p. 1188) highlighted the fact that in Gangadhar village, which is located in the Konkan coast of Maharashtra state, all the Indian women state that violence may be perpetrated by either a husband or a mother-in-law. Even when a mother-in-law is not directly involved in a beating, some women say that her influence is strong. Mothers-in-law play an important role in determining the appropriateness of a wife's behavior and guiding their son's disciplinary actions, sometimes in ways that are perceived by women to be malevolent.

Analysis of the case studies

In summarizing the commonalities and differences between the cases presented in this chapter, I find many important and notable issues, which are common to Bangladeshi society. There are several factors, interacting and reinforcing each other, which contribute to domestic violence against women. Very briefly, the important factors are: the practice of gender inequality and discrimination, which are buttressed by social and religious beliefs in favor of patriarchy; family structure; prevalent social norms and values for the upbringing and socialization of girls and the centrality of marriage in the women's lives that are linked to women's fluid positions in the realm of kinship: women's lack of empowerment and resources; and misconception, malpractice and vagueness of the laws for women.

An analysis of the cases above indicates that there are some similarities and differences between them. The first issue is early age at marriage. If they marry young, women are more prone to unhappiness and consequent abuse because young women are not mature enough to make the right choices for marital adjustment. Due to this custom of early marriage, households and families are tempted to marry off their daughters not necessarily to the most suitable man and family but to the first man who comes with a marriage proposal. In the cases of Moni, Nahida, Chaya, Taslima and Nurjahan, their natal families initiated their early marriages without thinking about their future lives. Puberty is considered to be the best time for marriage for girls in order to maintain their chastity. Moreover, girls have little choice over their age at marriage, because their marriage is typically arranged or orchestrated by their parents and relatives. It is also hard to stop the chain of events from a marriage proposal to the ceremony when things have been put in motion. Once the sharing of substances between the persons and families start it becomes very hard to stop it because it visibly and invisibly compromises their *izzat* (honor) in the locality. It is also mentionable that brides and their families are vulnerable in Bangladeshi society. If a woman's wedding arrangements are interrupted or cancelled then she becomes stigmatized (*kolonkito*) and considered inauspicious (*opoya*) in the family, households and neighborhood. As a result, if the groom and his family make the marriage arrangements complicated by demanding a larger dowry, the bride's family do their best to adjust – to wait, to console or to pay more all for their daughter's happy future life. They somehow compromise and try to prevent the threatened disaster of cancelling the wedding. Moni's case is a typical example of this state of affairs.

Early marriages are also cause for concern because of the potential adverse consequences for women's physical, mental and emotional development and well-being. First, early marriage is often associated with early age at the birth of a woman's first child often before physical growth and development is complete, which may have adverse health consequences for both the woman and child. Some of the cases presented above bring up this issue. Second, marriage is typically a barrier to education, since women are often expected to leave school in order to devote their time to the care of their new home or to childbearing and childcare. In this chapter almost all the subjects have had a minimal level of education, which makes them vulnerable all their lives to disempowerment for self-independency. Education is important for an individual because the accumulated knowledge of one's culture is primarily transmitted through its educational institutions, which facilitates the continuous process of adaptation in life through tolerance and mental skill. It broadens a person's outlook. A poor education reinforces a sense of low esteem and increases a woman's dependency on her husband and natal family.

The relationship between husband and wife may be influenced by the husband-wife age gap. In Bangladesh, more than 30 percent of young brides marry men who are at least 10 years older than them (World Development Report, 2012, p. 170). In particular, women who marry at an early age and who marry much older man may be less capable of asserting themselves and establishing their position in the household. As a result, they may have less power, status, agency and autonomy within the household. Also, the superior status of the husband is established on a solid base if an extensive age difference exists. However, this is not considered to be an impediment by a young bride's parents as age is recognized as a status indicator in Bangladeshi society. In the case of Nahida, her husband was nearly 20 years older than her; this creates fear, subordination, powerlessness and psychological imbalance between the spouses. As a result, she faced violence throughout her marital life.

During my conversations with the women, it became evident that the structure of the domestic unit exerts a deep and persistent influence on a woman's life. The structure of the co-residing family may be extended or nuclear. Along with changes in the structure or the domestic unit, the pattern of relationships of its members also changes. In nuclear family households, there are three types of relationships: husband-wife, parent-child and sibling relations. However, the spectrum of relations in the extended families is more complex. There are the husband-wife, parent-child, sibling relations and relations with the in-laws, like mother-in-law and daughter-in-law, father-in-law and daughter-in-law and similarly relations with other in-laws. Therefore, in an extended family a person has to make more adjustments with different sets of relations than in the nuclear family. In the three-generational stem family, especially the wife has to make more adjustments. If she is unable to adjust to any of these sets, tensions may arise which may lead to strained relations between husband, wife and parents-in-law. Similarly, in the case of nuclear family, adjustment problems may arise between the couple from mismatched expectations. Culturally, rural Bangladeshi society is more extended family oriented, while the slum dwellers mostly live in nuclear family units. The data of the study revealed that nuclear family structure has not protected the slum women from domestic violence.

Domestic violence, especially wife abuse, is not always a classic male-female conflict. The presence of female in-laws or the presence of a co-wife in a family, no matter if they co-reside or live nearby, may make the family dynamics especially different. Moreover, seeking individual happiness, freedom, power and possession at the cost of honor (*shomman*), happiness (*shukh*), right (*odhikar*) and will (*iccha*) of other family members is not seen as an appropriate action and behavior in Bangladeshi society. So, most of the time young girls and women are bound to sacrifice their own desires for the sake of others. As a result, even when they are tortured, devalued and punished, their predicaments easily remain unnoticeable and unreported. In the cases of Moni, Chaya and Taslima, it was found that their mothers-in-law and sisters-in-law were the main actors who instigated violence against them due to dowry demands, the birth of a girl child, maladjustment, greed and general hostility. All of them had to deal with the state of total powerlessness in their extended marital home and become victims.

In the case of love marriages, no dowry is given, the marriages are rarely performed publicly and the couple's family usually does not arrange the wedding ceremony. Moreover, love marriages confuse and lead to mismatches in the social order and as well as challenging kinship structures, class position, lineage hierarchy (*bongsho*), caste and religion. According to Osella and Osella (2000), it is always a girl's decision whether she will take the risk and move forward into a romantic relationship. In the case of Golapi, this was the case, too. She took her own decision to sustain this romantic relationship and broke her caste position by marrying a man from to a lower caste. Consequently, she lost her natal family's protection when she was cheated by her husband and fell into a vulnerable and stigmatized situation with an unaccepted pregnancy.

In the cases of Nahida and Chaya, I find that a husband's extra-marital relationships may gradually grow stronger during a marriage. In the case of Chaya, her husband first cheated at her and then he married again; moreover, he had the habit of visiting sex workers. In the context of Bangladeshi culture, Nahida's husband engaged in an illicit but also incest relationship (*zena*) with his own maternal uncle's wife (*mami*), which is religiously condemned as a sin (*pap kaj*). Extra-marital relationships of husbands make their wives' marital lives vulnerable, raise the risk of domestic violence and change the relationship between the husbands and wives. The case of Chaya depicts her vulnerability and sad life with different co-wives; which is also supported by her mother-in-law and other in-laws by their greed to have more and more dowries.

In this chapter, I show that women's unequal position in the family, lack of power, authority and opportunity, and economic insecurity in both natal and marital homes capture the diverse dimensions of vulnerability for women. As I have found in the cases of Moni, Nahida, Chaya and Nurjahan, economic hardship in their natal families makes them vulnerable. As a result, when they face domestic violence, they have to bear it for a long time and find no way to escape.

Conclusion

The most important finding of this chapter is that most victims have waited for a long time after the onset of violence before seeking outside help; in Bangladesh, the importance of marital home and vulnerability in a woman's life does not give her opportunity to raise her voice. According to WHO (2010) in Dhaka, Bangladesh, only 1 percent of women in the urban area and 2 percent of women in the rural areas sought outside help when they found themselves victims of domestic violence. In a quest for reasons why women who are victims of violence do not seek help, it was found in urban Dhaka that more than 50 percent of them felt embarrassed or ashamed, 20 percent felt fear of consequences and more than 60 percent considered violence to be normal or not serious. I found that slum women feel shame and fear that they would be blamed for their plight and do not urgently seek outside help to stop their abuse. Moreover, reporting to police and going to seek legal help from the legal institutions are not common practices in Bangladeshi society and even less among the women in the lower socio-economic class. So they try to resolve domestic violence through various informal tactics. Basically, the victims of domestic violence most of the time seek recourse from their natal family members and relatives because this informal help may not damage the family fabric, but may be able to address the problems that they encounter in their lives as a victim. If a victim cannot bear the inhuman torture for a long time, she breaks her silence with the help of her natal family members, neighbors and village elders (*murubbi*) and comes to the formal legal system with them. In exceptional cases, women from lower socio-economic class may seek help from a formal agency by themselves.

In analyzing the cases, it can be seen that some victims want help to return to their marital family and wish to stay with their abusive husbands and in-laws, or want *Den Mahar* (dower) and maintenance costs for their children, or at least to stop the violence. According to them, it is their bad luck that their husbands and in-laws are abusive and they can do nothing about it. Sometimes, victims did not seek help even when they were seriously injured. They only protested when the violence had been persistent. When I looked for the reasons for such delays I found that the women were constrained by various factors: patriarchal ideologies and family structure, economic constraints, shame and fear of blame, emotional attachment, having children, and lack of information and skills to engage with the institutional actors.

In the close knit traditional patriarchal social structure, where people live very close to each other and kinship bonds are strong, this "personal problem" or "private matter" is known by their relatives and many people in the neighborhood. In this case, some neighborhood women and natal family members and relatives come and try to offer advice on how a woman should behave to handle these problems or calm her husband and in-laws down. Common advice such as, "don't shout or say anything," "obey your husband and in-laws," "try to adjust to your husband and in-laws" only worsen a woman's feelings of inadequacy, subordination, lack of power and adds further support to the idea that this is indeed her fault. "Blaming the victim" is an attitude that legitimizes men's superiority. The victims (women) are to blame and must accept responsibility for what is happening. This practice keeps the woman busy looking for problems and shortcomings within herself, and she does not have the courage or scope to look for sources of help. Blaming the victim is also an obstacle to the solidarity of women and a barrier to the development of support systems for women.

One of drawbacks of taking up action in cases of long-lasting domestic violence is that women are often dependent on their husbands or in-laws financially, emotionally and socially. So leaving home, uncovering a "private issue" of domestic violence and seeking informal and formal help to mitigate or stop the violence or filing for a divorce are often considered by woman as shameful, personal failure, disrespectful and problematic for her natal family. All these facts deter victim women from coming to counseling centers for formal legal support at the onset of violence. Moreover, most of the women and their natal family members do not have any intention of sending the abuser to prison or subjecting them to other kinds of legal punishment, because they fear that the abusers may feel dishonored and when they are released from prison they may become even more violent. Schuler et al. (2008, p. 337) also came to similar conclusions in their study on Bangladeshi rural women. My argument is that in the Bangladeshi context gender, class, economic inequality, religion and place of residence are critical for contextualizing women's sufferings in general and domestic violence in particular.

Note

1 "National drug demand reduction strategy: a working paper." Department of Narcotic Control: Dhaka, Bangladesh, 1995.

6 Legal battles at the counseling center
What do the women get?

The problem of domestic violence against women has been acknowledged by international and national development agencies as well as the government of Bangladesh. Many organizations[1] and the Bangladesh Ministry of Social Welfare are working to combat domestic violence. Third-sector organizations have tried to stop the trafficking in women and children and they provide legal counseling and training in community awareness against domestic violence (Ashrafun and Säävälä, 2014; Chowdhury, 2011; Ameen, 2005; Jahan, 1994).

The law has a potential for fostering social transformation through establishing human rights. In every society, the law serves as a strong weapon and resource for the weak and oppressed. After several months of my fieldwork in the counseling center, I found that some victim women of domestic violence broke their silence and came to the public arena to seek help with their natal family members or other relatives. The counseling center's facilitators helped them get acquired with victim-friendly legal provisions by modifying the traditional *shalish* (mediation) practices. But when the facilitators were unable to solve the marital problems and domestic violence against women, they were able to provide legal advice including the costs of a legal suit, when necessary. The facilitators dealt with the police and/or doctors to get incident injury reports of domestic violence from them if needed or to bring the oppressor to court.

Disputes within the family and cases of domestic violence in Bangladesh have traditionally been resolved either among kinsmen or in village samaj by *shalish*. In Bangladesh, *shalish* (mediation) is still an informal form of community mediation. The Union Councils[2] have only limited arbitrary power in matters of marriage and divorce following the Muslim Family Law Ordinance of 1961. However, informal *shalish* is a very common practice in Bangladesh. A *shalish* committee typically consists of elderly, honorable and influential members of a community. The elected Union Council chairman and other members also participate in these *shalishes*. To enforce its resolution, a *shalish* committee uses monetary fines and social boycotting of the offender's family. This traditional *shalish* has no formal accountability in the modern state and thus may be used to aid the weaker members (mostly women and the poor) of society. Basically, in traditional *shalish* processes, women are not allowed to be present during the arbitration. They are usually represented by their male relatives.

Therefore, this alternative dispute resolution system (ADR) may favor men more than women. It is simple and avoids the complexities of the formal process; it is less time consuming and less expensive. It is founded on locally based principles and values, participatory and empowering. It seeks to restore community ties and relationship and helps to resolve disputes in a non-discriminatory, simple manner.

ADR was developed in the USA in the 1970s and 1980s, particularly as a court reform project (Cohen, 2006; Nader and Grande, 2002) to provide an alternative way of reconciling civil disagreements. ADR refers to dispute resolution mechanisms such as negotiation, mediation, arbitration, conciliation, early neutral evaluation and mini-trial mediation (Cohen, 2006). It is a social innovation developed for resolving disputes with the aim of enabling disagreeing parties to reach agreement without lengthy and costly litigation. The US-style ADR includes the involvement of a neutral third party, a mediator, who facilitates the resolution process, although she or he does not impose a resolution on the parties.

ADR has traveled from the USA to other parts of the world and has been adopted as a common component of development projects intended to modernize and rationalize state judicial systems, for example, by USAID and the World Bank (Capulong, 2012; Cohen, 2006; Maru, 2010). Nader and Grande (2002) view the effects of the US-based ADR as so penetrating that they speak of a "global ADR revolution" in the justice field. When the original model has been adopted in vastly different socio-economic and developmental contexts, it has, however, not remained unchanged: "Mediation changes as it travels; its instantiation anywhere is subject to local variation and invention as it makes contact with state and customary law, politics, and social struggles" (Cohen, 2006; Nader and Grande, 2002).

Although ADR as a distinct social innovation was developed in the USA only a few decades ago, forms of community mediation as an informal social process of delivering justice has long historical roots. It has been present in some form in all societies prior to the introduction of formal legal institutions. In South Asia, village elders or *samaj/panchayats* have traditionally acted as mediators or arbiters in the place of formal legal bodies (Sharma, 2004). Introducing the US-style ADR in South Asia has been an innovation in the sense that it occupies a space between the judiciary and civil society. In India, ADR has been an institutionalized part of the legal system since the Arbitration and Conciliation Act of 1996 and even prior to that, based on other acts (Sharma, 2004). In Bangladesh, where the formal legal system has been built on the same colonial legacy as in India, ADR does not yet have a similar level of institutionalization. Following the model provided by the Canadian, American and Indian judicial systems, ADR has been tried out in some Bangladeshi courts as an alternative to formal legal procedures (Kamal, 2004) because the legal system of Bangladesh is extremely formal, complex, time consuming and financially draining. Conversely, the level of community awareness of legal rights and how these might be enforced is extremely limited particularly for the women, less literate and disadvantaged.

The BLAST is one of the prominent legal services organizations in Bangladesh, and it provides access to legal aid across the spectrum, from the frontlines of the formal justice system to the apex court. BLAST's mission is to make the legal system accessible to the poor and the disadvantaged. It envisions a society based on the rule of law in which every individual, particularly the poor, women, children, people with disabilities and tribal people can have access to justice, and so their human rights will be respected and protected. It also provides legal aid, advice and representation across a range of areas, including civil, criminal, family, labor and land laws, as well as on constitutional rights and remedies, providing access to judicial remedies alongside ADR wherever appropriate.

BLAST was established in 1993 as a free legal services organization and is currently operating in 19 districts across the country. It works through its staff lawyers at headquarters and in each district unit. BLAST is governed by a Board of Trustees comprised of eminent jurists, lawyers and human rights advocates. Besides its own core staff lawyers at headquarters and at each district unit, BLAST has an enlisted panel of about 2,300 lawyers across the country who provide legal redress to clients on a pro bono basis, with a nominal honorarium. It is also well represented by lawyers pursing its cases in the High Court Division and Appellate Division of the Supreme Court of Bangladesh.

The board mandate of the Trust, following its vision of ensuring an equitable, fair and accessible legal system, consists of providing legal assistance and advice for the poor, women, disadvantaged and vulnerable people by promoting mediation or *shalish*. BLAST facilitates ADR through mediation for family, land, financial, petty crime and laborer matters. The majority of individuals who come to BLAST seeking help prefer to resolve their conflicts through mediation rather than litigation due to the reduced costs and time involved, and the relative effectiveness in terms of sustainability of the outcomes. But those disputes that cannot be resolved through mediation can be filed as decree execution cases in the courts. It also undertakes rights awareness campaigns, establishes effective networks and provides training with different stakeholders such as Upazila members, NGO representatives, students and workers of various factories.

In a quest to establish women's rights within the frame of the social and legal environment, this developmental NGO, BLAST has started focusing on the law and women's rights related issues. This NGO plays a vital role in Bangladesh by practicing informal *shalish* to keep the traditional methods in the legal system to make it easy and approachable to the people of the disadvantage classes, as most of them do not understand legal procedures and are afraid to go to court because they fear complexity, expenses and prestige. So this NGO through informal *shalishes* tries to give an opportunity to the poor women to have their voices heard with the help of their natal family members, relatives, acquainted persons and advocates. In these *shalishes*, women are not only allowed to be present, but they have the right to talk and express their traumatic feelings about their oppression to violence and its resolution. They also get enough time to think about their decisions. Although the NGO officers have no statutory responsibility for abused women, they try to work closely with the problems, to consider the severity of the cases and the positions of women. In the case of domestic violence, the NGO officers serve notices to the husbands and their natal family members and kin to appear at the center for mediation when a written complaint is made by their wives. In most cases, mediation takes place informally with several sittings; either the husband takes back his wife or signs a bond to abide by the agreement, he divorces her, she divorces him (if she has the right to divorce by herself in her marriage registration papers) or he gives her *den mahar* (dower) money and settles the custody of the children. In cases where the husband and his natal family members do not appear for the mediations, the counseling center remind them several times before having the police issue warrants against the husband and other oppressors of his natal family to appear at the counseling center. If the parties do not settle the dispute through mediation, the advocates of the counseling center take the case to the court and handle the case free of charge.

The uneven development of law is evident in the legal system of Bangladesh. That is why in spite of several statutes intended to protect women, for example, the restrictions on child marriage and polygamy or prohibiting dowries, the law does not in practice benefit many women in Bangladesh. The weakness of the law lies in the fact that both substantive and procedural law is not gender-neutral. The laws governing women's private lives are discriminatory. They not only discriminate against women of the same community against men, for example, women have either delegated their rights of divorce or that the court has to be satisfied on their behalf that their husbands should release them from their marriage contracts; they also discriminate between women from different communities, for example, a Hindu woman does not have the right to divorce in Bangladesh as a Muslim woman.

The legal solutions that have been made available at various times have also been constrained by a number of practical factors: the weak economic position of the women affected (and that of women in general), the reluctance of the police to become involved in marital disputes, the difficulty of enforcing and sometimes obtaining injunctions, the problems of providing protection against husbands seeking revenge, a lack of alternative accommodation and assisting agencies (doctors, social services department) who have tended to emphasis reconciliation and compromise rather than separation, divorce or empowerment. The emphasis on mediation or arbitration by legal aid workers and professionals as well as the clients themselves reflect the lack of the formal legal system's ability to remedy a wrong satisfactorily. However, mediation is not always the best solution either. Moreover, the only gender violence that receives prime public concern is stranger violence, for example, rapes, or murders and kidnapping. Although, the Government of the People's Republic of Bangladesh, is committed to uphold the rights of women and eliminate discrimination against women and both the Constitution of Bangladesh and several special laws guarantee equal rights and protection of women against violence inside the private and public domains. However, these laws are not strong enough to protect women in the patriarchal social structure.

Through encounters with family law, domestic violence and mediation in contemporary Bangladesh, this chapter examines how marriage is reflected and shaped through law and, conversely, provides an ethnographic portrait of everyday law as depicted through the governance of marriage. I also point out how women in socially vulnerable groups make use of an ADR process in a collaborative project between a judicial body and a counseling center (third-sector agent) in Sylhet, Bangladesh. I will seek an understanding of how informal mediation affects the bargaining position of the battered women. This is followed by some interlinked questions: can such socially innovative mediation alleviate their situation and does it lead to sustainable solutions? Do women get a chance to express their views in the legal arena and obtain justice to establish their rights? In this regard, here I focus on some examples of *shalish* (mediation), which I obtained from participation observation.

The mediations (*shalishes*) of domestic violence at the counseling center

Description of marital disharmony serves as a "trouble cases" in the cultural frameworks in the South Asian region (Basu, 2015). When a woman goes for legal help, it is not appreciated in this region. Because conceptualizing women as "the dominated" and men as "the dominators" encourages us to view men as agents, as "having" and wielding power, and women as passive recipients of men's acts, violent or otherwise (Boddy, 1998). The most evident socio-cultural factor affecting the practice of mediation is the social legitimacy of the violence perpetrated by husbands and in-laws against young wives. The narration of Lipa's experiences of domestic violence and the mediation of her case through the NGO highlight the dynamic of domestic violence among women in lower socio-economic class and the process of mediation.

Can multiple *shalishes* stop domestic violence?

In the counseling center, I participated in Lipa's mediation for domestic violence and marital maladjustment with her husband and in-laws. To me, this example of mediation is significant in the changing social context of Bangladesh because it highlights how migration brings tremendous change to the lives of the lower socio-economic classes in urban slums and allows them to participate in urban formal legal organizations instead of depending on the traditional practices of rural settings. Lipa is a 22-year-old housewife; she is an illiterate woman. She was born in a slum of Sylhet city. Her parents migrated from Netrokona to Sylhet city 25 years ago. Lipa got married when she was 19 to Shamsul Islam (29 years old), an illiterate three-wheeler driver. After marriage, Lipa moved to live with her marital family members in another slum of Sylhet city.

When Lipa was sitting silently with her two-year-old daughter in the client serving room of the counseling center, I heard about her marital problems. According to Lipa, her husband is a very bad man, he beats (*maar-peet*) her frequently. He always scolds her using bad language (*kharap kotha*). For two months, Lipa's husband had been having extra-marital relationships with other women and had not provided food (*bhat*) for them. Describing her vulnerability in her affinal home, she said her mother-in-law also always abused her using foul language and blamed her for her husband's extra-marital relationship. If her husband did not come back home at night, her mother-in-law would abuse her and claim she was a worthless wife. Her mother-in-law never said anything bad to her son because he gave her a small amount of money. Her father-in-law was also a very bad man, according to Lipa; he had two wives and two families. Some days, he stayed there with his senior wife, and some days with his other family. On a few occasions, her father-in-law had slapped (*chor*) her because of his son's extra-marital relationships. One day he rebuked his son in front of her, so her husband became very angry and hit her with a thick stick. Everybody in her marital family saw this torture, but nobody came to save her or stop her husband. Lipa felt much shame (*lojja*) and pain (*kosto*).

When I talked with Lipa at the counseling center, Lipa's mother and elder sister were also with her. They were very angry about Lipa's husband's behavior. They could not keep silent and started talking with me about Lipa's violent affines. Lipa's sister told us about the violent behavior and extra-marital relationships. Lipa was now in a vulnerable situation. She had been living for six months with her old parents, and his in-laws had not enquired about Lipa and her daughter. As Lipa's mother was a very poor woman who worked as a domestic helper, it was not possible for her to look after them for a long time.

Previously, just after one year of marriage, Lipa's husband had kicked (*lathi mara*) her in her abdomen when she had been two months' pregnant. She had immediately miscarried and went unconscious, but Lipa's affines had not even called a doctor. When they did not manage to bring Lipa to her senses, Lipa's sister-in-law had called her parents on her mobile phone. After having received the bad news, they had rushed to Lipa's home and called a doctor, but Lipa's husband and mother-in-law requested so they say nothing about the violence to the doctor. Because of their request, they hid the true nature of the incident from the doctor by lying and saying that Lipa had fallen near to a tube-well when she was bathing. Lipa's elder sister and mother had borne all the expenses for her treatment and had taken her to their home, and Lipa had lived with them for two months. Then her mother-in-law had come to take her back. However, even after this serious incident, Lipa's husband had kept on beating and disparaging her. As a result, she had lost her mental balance.

Lipa's mother told me that her son-in-law (*jamai/daman*) beat her daughter's legs with a bread-making roller (*beloon*) and now Lipa could not walk properly. He pulled Lipa's long tufts of hair and tore it out, and now she has frequent and severe headaches. He made her a body without a soul (*jento laash*), and this time, she won't let her go back to that family. Lipa's mother informed me that they had previously come to the counseling center twice to solve the conjugal problem, but nothing had happened. Lipa's husband did not correct his behavior and bad habits. Lipa's husband promised the advocates of the counseling center that he would become a good man and leave all his bad habits behind, but he did not. His parents also swore to protect their daughter-in-law (Lipa), but they did not do so. In fact, they continued to torture her. Now Lipa was very sick and behaving like a mad (*pagol*) woman, and they couldn't see any hope for the future.

I then asked the female advocate about the mediation of Lipa's case. She said that another advocate had dealt with Lipa's previous mediation. She had reached a solution by making the man and his parents swear in front of relatives on both sides not to torture Lipa and sent her back to her affinal home. But again the man acted violently to her and now Lipa has become very sick. The victim's family came here again to solve their problem and in the *shalish*, the advocates of the counseling center had made a compromise between two families. This was the third time the victim's family was coming with an appeal for a divorce, dower and maintenance costs for the child. The advocate felt sorry for the poor girl, but she could not make any decision by herself. After sometime, the other party would come and the advocates of both parties would arrange a mediation to make a decision.

Within half an hour, Lipa's husband along with his parents and maternal uncle (*mama*) came to the counseling center. They sat in front of us and the advocate asked me to talk with them. I wanted to know about the marital disputes from Lipa's husband's side. Lipa's husband told me that he always tried to behave properly to Lipa, but she was always suspicious of him. She always complained about his extra-marital relationships, but he didn't have any kind of amicable relationship. Lipa did not believe him and quarreled (*jhagra*) with him, so he became furious. The man claimed that his parents did not torture Lipa, but his mother-in-law and sister-in-law were telling lies and instigated Lipa to complain about them at the counseling center, and they always tried to harass them and destroy their normal family life.

Lipa's husband basically claimed that he was faultless (*dosh*) and he blamed his wife (Lipa) for all the problems. He tried to establish the fact that because he was a man he couldn't tolerate any questioning and arguments, so there were quarrels between them, and he hit Lipa as any normal man would act.

Lipa's father-in-law also ignored the issue of fights with Lipa, and told me that they liked their daughter-in-law, and they happily accepted her as their elder son's wife. They tried to keep their *natni* (granddaughter) and *bou* (daughter-in-law) with them, but Lipa's elder sister and mother always poked their noses into their private affairs and frequently took Lipa from their home and did not let her come back for several months. If they went to bring Lipa back, they were insulted (*opoman*) in many ways. He totally ignored his son's violent acts toward Lipa and accused Lipa together with her sister and mother of everything.

When Lipa's father-in-law accused Lipa's natal family members, Lipa's elder sister became angry and jumped from her chair and said to us loudly that Lipa's father-in-law was a liar. He was also not a man of character and he married twice, so he is supporting his son. His son kicked her sister in early pregnancy, and Lipa could have died. She admitted that it was their fault that they foolishly did not keep any evidence of this violent act and told a lie to the doctor. The affines of Lipa tortured her and made her sick and she was now near death's door.

Lipa's mother-in-law stood up from her chair and told Lipa's elder sister to shut her mouth. Then the advocates of both side requested them to stop their arguing and follow the rules of the *shalish*. They stopped and the advocates started *shalish*. The advocate of Lipa's side asked for her decision and wish. Lipa replied in a low voice that she doesn't want to go back to her affinal home because her affines always promised in the counseling center that they would not beat her and not insult her with foul language, but they did not keep their promise. According to Lipa, they were "hypocrites" and she started to cry. At once Lipa's mother cried out in a loud voice, "Oh, dear! Dear me! I do not want to let my daughter die at their hands." Lipa's elder sister also started to cry with her old mother. They became furious and pointed to Lipa's husband and said, "One day he will kill Lipa. We will not let her go; we do not want her dead body."

The advocates on both sides became embarrassed and asked them to become calm. Then from Lipa's husband side, the male advocate, said in the *shalish* that this time again they (Lipa and her husband) could rearrange their conjugal life because they were not alone. They have a two-year-old daughter, and she needs her father. Moreover, Lipa's husband wants to take her back and the father-in-law and mother-in-law have the same desire. So the affines of Lipa wanted to have another chance. A woman's life without a husband is very hard, so Lipa should consider this again and give them a chance to make good their word. The advocates are always beside her, and if the next time Lipa's husband makes any mistake or acts violently against her, they will not give him another chance and they would initiate litigation proceedings.

Lipa's advocate tried to get her to understand that she had to think about her daughter's future. She told her that as a Muslim woman, it would be easy to get divorced whenever she wished, but then she couldn't go back to her conjugal life whenever she wished. She told her that she should not concentrate on other peoples' emotions because she was living with the man and she had feelings for her husband and for the family. Bangladeshi women like to live in families (*sangsar*); it is a well-known characteristic of a Bangladeshi woman. Lipa's mother may find work for her, but how long could she look after both of them. Her elder sister had a family of her own and she was not independent. Her husband may not let Lipa live with them and women do not live with their brothers-in-law's families in Bangladeshi society. So the advocate recommended to Lipa to go back and give another chance to her husband and parents-in-law.

After the advocate's argument, Lipa again firmly said that she did not want to go back to her husband and in-laws. But the two advocates did not stop trying to convince her, and they finally succeeded. Lipa was forced to agree to go back to her husband. When she agreed, her mother felt sad and told her that this time she feared for her life. Then the two advocates harshly said to Lipa's mother to stop forcing to Lipa to break her marital relationship because according to them, in Bangladesh society it is very hard for a young woman to live without a husband. The society does not encourage this practice and the advocates have over the years seen the sufferings of divorced women. The advocates requested Lipa's old mother not to be afraid and let her to go back to her husband.

From the above account it can be seen that Lipa had two mediations (*shalish*) without any success. It is obvious that despite severe violence, Lipa and her natal kin did not report any incident to the police. Although Lipa came twice to the counseling center, her case was completed in one simple meeting; the mediators expected that the *shalish* would deter her husband and in-law's from being abusive. But the mediation probably would not work, because the perpetrators did not consider this case as a matter of great importance. They took their violence lightly and only promised the lawyers that they would not commit any violence against Lipa. The lawyers also noticed Lipa's physical and psychological condition was bad, but they did not try to take legal action nor arranged psychological or medical help for Lipa despite her deplorable condition. Lipa and her natal family members assumed that the husband should be ashamed and threatened by the counseling center, but it did not work because after several months the perpetrators would no longer be afraid, and they would know that there wasn't anyone to monitor the case.

In this *shalish*, that was the third in this marital dispute, it was again obvious that the perpetrator's family tried to justify their violence. This time Lipa wanted a divorce from her violent husband, but the advocates did not give any importance to her desires and somehow they forced her to give her consent by scaring her with the uncertainties that would befall the future of her two-year-old daughter and the perils of a divorced life. They also did not consider Lipa's mother and elder sister's fears. Although according to Islamic rules, a woman who has been subjected to family violence has the right to seek a divorce, this may be a hollow solution for her because divorce does not guarantee that she would be protected from violence, and some women who are subjected to such violence may not be able to marry again and their child/children's future would become uncertain for different reasons, such as a lack of proper care and shelter, economic insecurity and a vulnerable position in the family and household.

Who benefits from a divorce – a husband or a wife?

In Bangladesh and elsewhere in South Asia, domestic violence tends to involve both kin groups and not only the perpetrator and the victim. However, due to the structural asymmetry in most South Asian kinship systems between wife-givers and wife-takers, the wife's kin is the underdog that tries to succumb to the demands of the husband's kin and to derive prestige from fulfilling this virtuous, subordinate role. The mediation practiced by the NGO is kin-based. Kin groups come to seek resolution for the marital problems of their members together, as a collective. The problems are understood as being part of wider kin relations. That is why it is considered essential and natural for relatives to be present at the mediations. When domestic violence is involved, it is evident that in some cases the aggressors are also other affines than the husband, for example, the mother-in-law, sister-in-law or father-in-law. A daughter-in-law is a member of the affinal kin group and thus mediation cannot be described as successful unless the in-laws are prepared to accept her back, even in situations where the young couple lives separately from the affines.

This narration is about a divorce. In South Asian region, a divorced or separated woman does not have any clearly defined place in the culture. She is no longer a wife, a virgin (future wife) or a widow (a married woman with a deceased husband). In this case, my aim is to highlight how divorce may be seen in some circumstances to generate loss for the victim women in their practical lives.

The second example of Joyfull's mediation case is different from Lipa's mediation case, where Lipa failed to free herself from the violent husband and in-laws. Joyfull was able to free herself from domestic violence by her affines. Joyfull is an 18-year-old housewife, and she is from a village of Biswanath, Sylhet. She was married to 26-year-old Ali Noor of Osmaninagar, Sylhet. They both could only sign their names. Ali Noor was a farmer, but he had no land of his own; he worked on the land of his elder sister and other people. He also sold his homestead land to his elder sister and now he lives in the corner of his sister's homestead land in a small hut. In the rainy season, when there is less agricultural work, Ali Noor becomes unemployed and his brothers and sister help him with money to eke out his livelihood.

Joyfull is from a very poor family. She does not know anything about her father because he married another woman and left Sylhet with his second wife just before Joyfull's birth. Her mother did not marry a second time and did not keep any relationship with her husband. After her separation, she lived with Joyfull in her father's (Joyfull's grandfather) homestead land in a thatched hut. She does different works to eke out a livelihood; sometimes she works as casual day laborer, sometimes as a domestic helper and sometimes she sews *kantha* (winter quilt) for other people. Although Joyfull is the only daughter, her family have always struggled against dire poverty and difficulties (*kosto*). They have nothing of their own, no land or assets. Two years previously, in 2009, Joyfull married Ali Noor in a registered *kabin*; her dower was 20,000 TK. When she married, she was only 16 years old, but her age was recorded as 18 years in the *kabin* for reasons of legality. Ali Noor and his mother chose Joyfull, and they did not want a dowry for the marriage. So Joyfull's mother and *khala* (mother's sister) did not make any delay and arranged the marriage as early as possible.

In the counseling center, while Joyfull was describing her sufferings and incidences of domestic violence in the affinal home with me, she said that she had only eight months of happy conjugal life with her husband and then the problems between them started because Joyfull's sister-in-law interfered with every aspect of their family life, and she started to torture her by using foul language (*kharap kotha*) and hitting her. Joyfull told me her sister-in-law works in an insurance company as a motivation worker. She used to be able to spend a few hours each day at work while Joyfull looked after her four children. She looked after them very well, but her sister-in-law was not pleased with that. She frequently scolded (*boka*) Joyfull using foul language. She also accused Joyfull of being a bad cook and doing untidy domestic chores. It became her daily routine to torture Joyfull and to give her pain in different ways.

Joyfull's sister-in-law also encouraged Joyfull's husband and mother-in-law to torture her. In the beginning, she tried to tolerate her sister-in-law's torture, but this made her sister-in-law strong because she thought that Joyfull was silent due to fear. Joyfull's sister-in-law also started to brawl with Joyfull's aunt who lived in the same hamlet of the village. She did not let Joyfull go to her aunt's house. Then Joyfull also became furious and abused her sister-in-law using foul language. She could not tolerate it and started to hit Joyfull with a thick stick. She pulled her (Joyfull) hair and kicked her in the chest. Joyfull also kicked her in her lower abdomen. Joyfull's aunt came and rescued her. When Joyfull's husband came back home, his sister ordered him to divorce Joyfull and remarry. She handed a big stick to Joyfull's husband and he beat Joyfull brutally. That night, Joyfull stayed in her aunt's home, and the next morning she went to her mother's house. After one month, her husband and mother-in-law took her back home from there.

According to Joyfull, her sister-in-law is a very bad woman. When she came back in her affinal home, her sister-in-law started to abuse her with foul language. Joyfull said her sister-in-law said, "Beggar woman's daughter came back again." In her statement, Joyfull characterized herself as a modest person because at that time she remained silent and tried to keep her patience. After some months, Joyfull became pregnant and wanted permission from her mother-in-law to go to her mother's house. When she wanted permission, Joyfull's sister-in-law became angry to hear this and did not want to let her to go. She roughly said to Joyfull, if she created any problems in their family life then she would not let her enter their house. Joyfull was also so shocked by her rough and irritated behavior that she could not control herself and told her that she did not care about her permission because she was not living in her house. The quarrel escalated and Joyfull's sister-in-law slapped her; then Joyfull slapped her back. When Joyfull's husband came back, he beat her. Then again her aunt came and saved her. On that day, she went to the Chief Judicial Court with her aunt and filed a case (*mamla*) against them. Joyfull's mother came to take her from the affinal village and without her husband's permission, Joyfull left with her mother for her natal home.

When Joyfull filed a litigation case, her husband, mother-in-law and brother-in-law came to her natal home and swore at Joyfull's mother that they would never torture her. With this assurance, they took her to the court and requested her to withdraw the litigation through mutual understanding. Joyfull and her mother believed them and withdrew the litigation and Joyfull went back with them. Joyfull's sister-in-law stopped her violent behavior for some months after this, but she then again started her old habits just a few months before Joyfull gave birth. Joyfull became sick again, and again her mother took her from the affinal home.

In her natal home, Joyfull gave birth to a son. Her mother-in-law was happy and she came to Joyfull's natal home to take them. Joyfull claimed that she again happily started her *sangsar* (household life). But her sister-in-law was envious of her and could not tolerate Joyfull's happy life in her husband's home (*swamir ghor*). She again started to irritate her and started to use bad language. She was angry with Joyfull for going to court and threatened her because she had dishonored the family.

According to Joyfull, quarreling again became their regular practice. She described one violence episode thus: One day her sister-in-law slapped her on the ear, so she also slapped her sister-in-law. Her sister-in-law cried out and kicked her. At that moment, Joyfull's husband came and joined his sister hitting Joyfull. Joyfull argued that it was not possible to fight two people, so she was injured and vomited a lot. Her maternal aunt called the local police to rescue her. At last, the police rescued her and brought her to her mother's house; from then on she and her child have been living with her mother.

After hearing Joyfull's case from her conversation, I noticed Joyfull's husband, affines and local union council member entering the counseling center. The coordinator then came with two advocates to arrange the *shalish*. The coordinator asked me to join them and give my opinion. The *shalish* began and we all started talking to both parties.

When Joyfull's advocate asked her about her decision, she said that she did not want to go back to her husband's sister's house. Although her husband had no homestead land of his own, she wished to live with him in another place. She said that she would work with him to maintain the family. If her husband did not consider this could be done for her, it was totally impossible to go back to her husband. In the *shalish*, the advocate narrated Joyfull's desire to Ali Noor and asked him about his opinion. Ali Noor was unwilling to live separately and said that as he did not have any land so living separately would be very hard for him. But if the *murubbi* (elder people) and the advocates ordered him, he would try to do that.

I talked with Ali Noor about their conjugal life and wanted to hear his opinion about future reconciliation. Ali Noor said Joyfull was a sulky woman, and he said, "Her head is always hot." He always asked her shut her mouth and to be silent, but Joyfull never heard to him. He accused Joyfull of arrogance and said that she also did not listen to his mother. She had several times beaten his elder sister and her children. She also showed her shoe to his elder sister's husband. She did not respect anybody in his house. Joyfull's aunt always poked her nose in every matter in their conjugal life, and on the instigation of her *khala* she filed a case against them. She had brought the local police to their home, and now everybody in their village laughs at him. She destroyed their *izzat* (honor) in the village. It is not possible for him to listen what Joyfull says because it is not good to behave rudely to one's own elder sister only because of his wife and destroy their relationship.

In the course of the conversation in the *shalish*, Joyfull's aunt said that Ali Noor's sister was not good and that she does not like Joyfull so she wants to break their *ghor* (family). Maybe she would arrange for her brother's remarriage to her sister-in-law (*nonod*). When during the *shalish* Joyfull's aunt accused Joyfull's sister-in-law (Abirun) of the cause of the violence and maladjustment between couples, Abirun jumped from her chair and started quarreling with her. She said,

> We are all are bad and you are all good. People know well that you are the main culprits. Everybody knows that Joyfull did not learn from her mother

how to respect elder people. We brought a bad woman as our *bou* (wife). In our hamlet, everybody knows that you are also a bad *bou* (wife).

Then Joyfull shouted at her sister-in-law and said,

> Allah will punish you. Allah knows well that you are a bad woman. You get me out of home (*ghor*); Allah will also get you out of your home. You take my husband from me; Allah will take your husband from you.

Joyfull's mother started to cry loudly and continuously hit her forehead. Then the coordinator and the advocates tried to stop the quarrel. I held on to Joyfull's hand and asked her not to quarrel. Joyfull cried out and said that she didn't want to break up her family, but her sister-in-law did not give her any peace. She wanted to arrange Ali Noor's second marriage to her sister-in-law, and she was trying to motivate him to do this. After hearing Joyfull's statement, the local union council member said that, as Joyfull wanted to live in a separate house and did not want to leave her husband, he could let them have a small plot of land near his house for some months. The couple could make a hut and live there until the reunion of the family. He said although in Islam divorce is permitted when there are irreconcilable differences between spouses, divorce is not good; it makes Allah displeased. Instantly, everybody praised him for his generosity and hoped for a happy ending of the *shalish*.

The coordinator asked the assistant to write the solution in the register book. But Abirun (the sister-in-law) whispered something by Ali Noor's ear. Joyfull became angry and asked her sister-in-law, "Are you giving some bad motivation to your brother?" The sister-in-law at once replied to Joyfull, "A market woman can never be a wife (*bazaar-er meye kokhono ghorer bou hoina*)." Then Joyfull said, "She always calls me a market woman. I want a divorce. I don't want to go back and live with these low-born people."

They began to quarrel again and destroyed the soothing environment of the *shalish*. Then all the advocates and the coordinator tried to stop it, and the coordinator apologized for their incapacity to reach reconciliation. He said that the *shalish* couldn't solve the case because Ali Noor was totally dependent on his sister and brothers. He had also no wish to stay with his wife and son and Joyfull also did not want to respect the decision of the *shalish*. As a result, it was better to call the *kazi* (marriage/divorce registrar) to write the divorce paper (*talak nama*) and end the relationship. After that the kazi came and prepared the divorce paper. Then again Joyfull's mother started to cry loudly holding the kid to her chest. Joyfull's mother-in-law ran to touch the baby, but Joyfull pushed away her hands and did not allow her to touch the baby. After the divorce, I saw Ali Noor stand up and look down at the floor. I asked him about his feelings and future steps. Ali Noor was unhappy about the way things had gone and thought that Joyfull was responsible for the divorce. And he related his relatives' decision about paying child maintenance.

Joyfull's case is an example of a victim who tries to protect her right to get legal justice. She went to the Chief Judicial Court and filed a case against her husband and his elder sister, but she was motivated by her husband and in-laws to withdraw the case. Actually, due to extended family and the family oriented social structure in Bangladesh, women ideally perceive their happiness as taking care of the happiness of other family members. Thus, going to a legal system to get a remedy for domestic violence is often socially undesirable. In the case of Joyfull, she was blamed even when she withdrew the case and went back again to her husband's house. Although Joyfull had a nuclear family of her own, as her husband had no homestead land and resided with his elder sister in her homestead land, he (Ali Noor) was always submissive to his sister. As a result, the sister-in-law (Abirun) always behaved rudely to Joyfull and tried to rule Joyfull's life according to what she desired. Joyfull was at first submissive to her, but when she came out from the cocoon of the artful attitude of a bride (*bou*) and protested about Abirun's misbehavior, Abirun could not tolerate it. So a conflict broke out, and Joyfull and Abirun started to quarrel with each other.

As Ali Noor was economically dependent on his natal family, he also started to torture Joyfull rather than protect her, which jeopardized Joyfull's conjugal relationship. So during a fight with her sister-in-law and husband, Joyfull was injured and felt ill. Meanwhile, Abirun (Joyfull's sister-in-law) was trying to convince Joyfull's husband Ali Noor to remarry her own younger sister-in-law to have control over his marital relationships. Ali Noor and Joyfull have a son, but this fact did not play any significant role in stopping the violence against Joyfull and did not establish durable conjugal relations between the couple. Moreover, Joyfull's husband and sister-in-law did not like her maternal aunt helping her to improve her situation, especially concerning the violence toward her.

So in the *shalish* we saw Ali Noor and Joyfull's sister-in-law involved in a brawl with her maternal aunt with the two warring factions accusing the other of wrongdoing. During the *shalish*, Joyfull first reluctantly agreed to go back to her husband's house as she wanted to continue her married life for the sake of her child in a separate house on a neighbor's homestead land. Moreover, she wanted to keep the family together. Finally, the couple got divorced. This was an uncertain solution for Joyfull and her son. Because Ali Noor was dependent on his elder sister and natal family, it might be also impossible for him to pay the dower (*den mahar*) and the child maintenance cost regularly without their help and approval. Moreover, Ali Noor might marry again, so he may be forced to stop the child maintenance payments as they would be an extra burden on his state. As Joyfull was also young, she may marry again to other man, so it is obvious that the child's future could be problematic. It should also be noted that in future, the counseling center would not further investigate the case and monitor the child's situation, so although the *shalish* initiated the divorce and freed Joyfull from the violent relationship and home, it did not guarantee that she got her legal rights.

Do *shalishes* ensure maintenance cost for a wife and children?

In the third example of mediation, I will present a case of domestic violence that is different from the cases of Lipa and Joyfull. In the case of Neharun Begum, I found that the counseling center has arranged a fourth arbitration for the maintenance cost of Neharun Begum (around 34 years old, a Muslim woman) and her five daughters, but I heard from the advocates that the polygamous husband does not regularly provide the maintenance costs to his children according to the agreement with the counseling center. So Neharun came again with her natal family members to seek help from the advocates to get her children's maintenance cost by pressuring her husband.

In the *shalish* when I asked Neharun's husband, Lal Mia (a 40-year-old Muslim man) about the reason for his irregularity in providing the maintenance costs, he said that he was a farmer and also involved with small agricultural business. Now he has to maintain two families. He had asked Neharun to stay with him in his own house. But after his second marriage, she quarreled (*jhogra*) with him and the co-wife (*sotin*) and left his house with her children. Several times he went to her natal house to bring her back, but she became angry (*rag*) with him and refused to come back. After that for some days he was reluctant to try to bring her back and busy with his work. At that time, along with her father and brothers, she went to the counseling center and issued a letter against him. He felt dishonored in his locality, because his first wife was against him, but he respected the letter of the counseling center and came here on the date he had been given. In the *shalish* according to the decision of the advocates and local *murrubi* (respected elder people in the locality), he built a tin-shade hut for Neharun in her father's *vita* (homestead land) and now every month he is giving them TK1,000 for maintenance costs. But sometimes he has problems (*jhamela-te-pore jai*) and he could not give them their monthly money. Neharun couldn't tolerate this and came to the counseling center to arrange a *shalish*.

About his second marriage, his excuse was he could not find any opportunity to get permission from her first wife because he did not know about the law. He claimed that he had a problem and was forced to marry a second time. Moreover, he does not have any sons. He thought that Neharun could not have given him a son, but he needed to maintain his family's lineage so he did nothing wrong.

While I was talking with Lal Mia, Neharun was sitting in a chair near to us. She broke into our conversation and started to quarrel with Lal Mia. She complained to Lal Mia about his frequent irregularity in paying his children's maintenance costs and not taking any responsibility for his adolescent elder daughter's marriage arrangements. The small quarrel between Neharun and Lal Mia started to grow bigger. We sometimes heard the quarrel as they raised their voices. The advocates tried to stop them and asked Neharun about her decision. Neharun replied that she wanted the family maintenance every month and a financial contribution toward the marriage arrangements of their oldest daughter.

The advocate suggested that Lal Mia should begin to make regular family maintenance payments. Lal Mia asked the advocate to wait for some months because he had having economic difficulties. Neharun did not want to hear any excuse, she started to quarrel again. Then Lal Mia replied in an angry voice,

> You are disturbing me too much. Maybe I will die because of your pressure. I can only provide what I have. Don't put me under any more pressure. If you are not satisfied with this, you can divorce (*Talak*) me.

Resource theory stresses that the unequal status of power between spouses influences the propensity toward violence (Anderson, 1997). Basically, the most powerful partner tends to abuse the least powerful partner, and if the female has the less resources and power, she has the greatest risk of abuse. According to Bina Agarwal (1997), not owning a house or land visibly indicates a woman's fallback position, which leaves her in vulnerable situation when she faces domestic violence by her husband and in-laws. To Agarwal, women who own a house or land would have an immediate escape option. A house is significantly important in this respect since it can provide a ready roof over the head. Agarwal (ibid.) has mentioned that employment alone cannot protect women because many women are unpaid workers on family farms or have insufficient income to rent a place. Moreover, it is often difficult for women to rent a house not only because of economic insufficiency but also due to social barriers. To Agarwal (1994), a woman who owns a home or land has a reduced risk of domestic violence as her possessions provide her with a safe shelter and economic security.

After that Lal Mia stopped and Neharun started crying. The advocates seemed tired of the case because everything was not under their control. Finally, they told Lal Mia to give some money to Neharun and pay her maintenance costs regularly every month. Lal Mia gave TK 500 to the advocate and left the counseling center. Then the advocates asked Neharun not to lose her patience because if her husband divorced her in the future, she may fall into severe situation with her five daughters. Neharun cried a lot about her misfortune and vulnerability and took the money from the advocates. Still weeping, she left the counseling center with her younger brother.

After Neharun's departure from the counseling center, one of the advocates described the weakness of Neharun's case to me. He said that they were trying to help the poor and vulnerable women, but for a long time it had been hard to protect them. Neharun's husband married for a second time without her permission as he did not take any written permission from the Union Council. When she came here for the first time, the advocates told Neharun to file a suit, but her father and other respected elder people in the locality would not allow her to do it because of the five daughters. In Bangladeshi society, everybody knows that it is very hard for a woman to raise her daughters without a father's assistance and that separated women face difficulties in arranging their daughters' marriages. In Neharun's case this was absolutely correct, so considering her vulnerability, the counseling center refrained from taking any legal action and normally arranged a *shalish*. But now Lal Mia was not giving her monthly maintenance costs. The counseling center could now file a suit for dower and maintenance, but this would not bring a fruitful solution because the man was economically insolvent.

How does a convicted husband escape?

The fourth example of a mediation case is about domestic violence and the maintenance payments of a Hindu woman. Nirmola's *shalish* represents the vulnerable condition of a Hindu woman in the realm of Hindu laws in Bangladeshi society. Nirmola (a 25-year-old Hindu woman), along with her two small daughters, was living in her poor natal family in a village in Sylhet. Her husband and mother-in-law did not like her and always put pressures on her to bring a dowry from her natal family. But when they were married, her father provided a dowry despite his poor economic condition. So according Nirmola, it was impossible for her father to provide dowries. As a result, they always abused her inhumanly and tried to kill her. Nirmola could not tolerate their torture and feared after an attempt to murder her, so she left her husband's house with her two daughters for a year. For one year, she had been fighting for the maintenance of her two daughters. To resolve her case, the counseling center arranged four *shalishes* (mediation) for Nirmola. At the first *shalish*, the advocates asked her to go back to her husband's house; but she refused because she was too afraid of her husband and his family and thought they might kill her at any time. The advocates of Nirmola's side did not push her to go back to her affinal home and managed to arrange maintenance costs for the wretched family. Her husband paid the maintenance for two months, but then he stopped. Now without informing Nirmola, her husband left Bangladesh. He had then been living in Malaysia for five months and did not have any contact with Nirmola. It was the fourth *shalish* in the counseling center with Nirmola's in-laws for the maintenance costs.

From the mediation, I knew that Nirmola's husband had left the country without informing the advocates of the counseling center. According to the advocates, he disregarded the law and made a mistake. In the mediation, Nirmola's father-in-law was present and tried to give various excuses to the advocates to escape any blame. Nirmola's advocate was not convinced and pointed out the domestic violence against Nirmola. It was a case of attempted murder. The advocate had evidence from the doctor that the Nirmola's affines had wanted to kill her by poisoning her food. Nirmola and her parents did not file a case rather they just relied on the formal mediation procedure. They feared for the future of the two children and did not proceed with litigation.

In the mediation, Nirmola's father-in-law denied that any of his family had attempted to murder her. He claimed that they did not do it. They did not poison her food and did not know who did this sinful act (*pap kaj*). His son was always dutiful to Nirmola and their children. This case was just harassment of the family. According to him, Nirmola's parents made up the details of these events with Nirmola in an attempt to destroy the honor of his family. His family had never been implicated in a court before, but because of this wrong marital alliance they had lost their face in the village.

After listening to Nirmola's father-in-law's statement, Nirmola's advocate again confronted him with the attempted to murder allegation, because when it happened, Nirmola was living with them and on that day she did not cook the curry. That day her husband and mother-in-law were well behaved toward her and the mother-in-law gave her food in a separate bowl. After eating the poisoned food Nirmola started to vomit and was taken to hospital where she was admitted with the help of the neighbors. The doctor of the government medical center washed out her digestive system and certified that she had ingested poison in her food. She was lucky that she was alive and the doctor helped her to come to the counseling center by putting pressure on her poor father. In order to get her maintenance payments, her lawyer frequently brought up the evidence of failed attempt to murder. Her father-in-law admitted that the doctor had found poison in her digestive tract, but again he claimed that there was no proof that they mixed the poison in her food. According to Nirmola's father-in-law, Nirmola sometimes quarreled with her mother-in-law and husband so she guessed that they had tried to poison her. As the mediation came to an end, Nirmola's father-in-law gave some money to the advocate for the maintenance costs and assured him that from the next month his son would send the maintenance payments regularly.

Conclusion

The examples of the four *shalishes* point to the numerous problems in the legal system in Bangladesh concerning women's issues in general and domestic violence in particular. The criminal laws and personal laws, taken together, are insufficient to solve women's problems when we take societal reality into account.

In BLAST, I interviewed six advocates who engaged in ADR processes. After speaking with them separately, it seems to me that they have a rigid and fixed mindset in defining what is "good" and what is "bad" for women according to the patriarchal structure of society. They are not trained sufficiently to help victims of domestic violence on a case-by-case basis. The advocates have not been sensitivity-trained to reflect on gender asymmetries or to question their own values and conceptions of a woman's position in the family. They were rarely conscious of the need to find out how the female victims themselves saw their situation and instead concentrated on finding a way to convince the woman to return to her affinal family and on creating goodwill in the affines so that they would stop maltreating the young wife. The advocates took for granted the culturally hegemonic view of the wife-takers as the ones entitled to make demands on the young wife and her kin. They help them by providing informal *shalish*, legal advice and mental support. But they do so by following their own ways of thinking without finding out what would be best for the victims. The advocates also thought that the victims were unable to make rational decisions because they were women and situated in a vulnerable position. They thought that educated people and lawyers could help them decide. The class difference and power asymmetry between the advocates and their clients was not seen as an impediment by the layers themselves, but it evidently created difficulties for the clients' ability to communicate their own interest. So in some of the cases depicted earlier, it is seen that the women were suppressed, unable to make their own decisions and to express their own views. To me, this attitude might be problematic in providing justice and free agency for victim women. Sometimes, *shalish* does not play a significant role in stopping violence because there is no follow-up to the outcome of the *shalish*, which leads to a high proportion of the cases returning again for mediation. As a result, victim families lose hope of getting justice and drop the case and the oppressors automatically escape from their duties or punishment. Moreover, there is no long-term supervision available in the counseling center for victim women after the *shalishes* to make sure that they getting regular maintenance for their children or receiving proper treatment from their previously violent husband or in-laws. In a number of the ten mediations examined, the women's voices were suppressed and they were unable to make their point of view heard. The patronizing and at times even chauvinist tone that was evident in some advocates during the interviews and in the mediations may be problematic from the perspective of delivering justice and securing social agency for female victims of the lower socio-economic class.

This NGO is very limited in its resources and availability of services to clients. The facilitators are not always well trained in dealing with victims and offenders well; they simply know the laws, but they do not give any importance to human psychology, do not know about criminology and do not provide counseling to the abused women when needed. They also lack sufficient planning, organization and a standard operating procedure to follow since they use personal discretion to deal with cases. Above all, this NGO tries to satisfy foreign donors, which mean that administrative issues easily become more important than the interests of their target population. The NGO has to fulfill the administrative targets set by the donor agencies. They act on a short-term funding based agenda, not on a holistic long-term sustainable one.

Notes

1 Ain-O-Shalish Kendro, Bangladesh National Lawyers' Association, Women for Women, BLAST.
2 The Union Council is the only level of local government that is elected in Bangladesh. A Union Council is comprised of several members and headed by a chairman and each council represents 10–15 villages.

7 Conclusions

In this study, I observe and experience and describe as accurately as I can, how Bangladeshi women negotiate their lives with domestic violence in their marital lives and curve out the limited space for emancipation in the changing structure of Bangladesh. I was inspired to carry out this study by the highlights and banner news from the daily newspapers and the writings of the scholars about the widespread events of domestic violence against women in Bangladesh. In the light of the news and studies, I saw a need to sketch out an in-depth representation of domestic violence against economically and educationally backward women in Bangladeshi society. A significant number of studies (Bates et al., 2004; Naved et al., 2005; William et al., 2011; UNICEF, 2011) have shown that in Bangladesh young women from impoverished households face domestic violence more commonly than in economically better-off households. But most of these studies are based on analysis of register and survey data or secondary sources. Although survey data helps to draw generalizations, it leaves the experience and coping strategies vis-à-vis domestic violence against women understudied (Renzetti et al., 1993, p. 3; Liamputtong, 2007). I have relied on qualitative data and methods that I consider as the main strength of this study because it helps me to uncover the situation of the young wives in the impoverished families in a meaningful context. I am not comparing my study with quantitative studies based on survey data and statistical analyses. The findings of this research may not be applicable to wider populations or generalized to the same extent as quantitative studies, but my ethnography has portrayed an in-depth description of the life of the impoverished women as a part of the local social, cultural and economic setting in a globalized economy of a developing country.

Like in other South Asian countries, a Bangladeshi woman starts her marital life through a romantic journey with dreams, blessings and greetings; individual characteristics such as religion, class and caste do not create any obstacle to the dreams of a bride for an inauguration of a new family (*notun sangsar*) or home full of love, peace and hope. But domestic violence against women often breaks the ideals of a dream home and makes women's lives vulnerable. Actually, domestic violence against women is a culturally, socially and religiously embedded practice; it never takes place in a social, historical or material vacuum. In Bangladesh, the female body, socialization, conceptions of self and pain, relationship with natal and marital family, and lack of power and autonomy are all intertwined in a complex and multilayered social system now in a state of flux. In many stages, the government of Bangladesh has made changes in laws in favor of women's emancipation, safety and empowerment of women. The government has committed itself to lessening and stopping violence against women. But the practice, which is deeply rooted in the practices and beliefs of society, cannot be simply stopped by laws, declarations of the United Nations, women activists and feminist writings. If the nation really wants social change, it must engage diligently, sensitively and knowledgeably with the individuals, cultural and religious practices that sustain this activity.

As imposed by the process of globalization, urbanization, migration and neoliberal policies, Bangladesh has experienced drastic changes in its socio-cultural and economic structures. After independence, economic liberalization in Bangladesh has led to the emergence of a number of export-oriented industries of which the manufacture of ready-made garments is the most prominent. The industry currently employs around 1.5 million workers, the overwhelming majority of whom are women (Kabeer and Mahmud, 2004). Women from all social classes from both rural and urban areas are enjoying the fruits of globalization and the taste of a changed lifestyle. Vast networks of feminist professionals and activists, or citizens who are committed to women's issues, along with the government are at work today to establish women's rights to have the position of full-fledged citizens and to uproot gender inequality (Feldman, 2010; White, 1992; Kabeer, 2000). Over the last two decades, an increasing number of women from poor and lower-middle-class backgrounds have been involved in income-generating activities and found opportunities for physical mobility; women have started to negotiate within patriarchal bargains (Kabeer, 2000, p. 60). However, paradoxically, Naila Kabeer (ibid.) stated that these various changes indicated the deterioration of both women's status as women and the "patriarchal contract" (men's obligations toward women). Moreover, the rise of dowry practice plays a significant role in the fragility of marriage relations with an increase in the divorce rate, polygamy, abandonment and separation (Kabeer, 2000; Rozario, 1992, 2001). So within this changing socio-economic structure, the poor and lower-middle-class women are considered as liabilities in their natal families because they are an expense to maintain and to marry off, and consequently, they face unequal treatment from early childhood. In their marital families, they go through asymmetrical gender relations, economic devaluation and discrimination.

In this connection, I have tried to uncover the meaning, causes, coping strategies, resistance as well as the effect of domestic violence in the lives of impoverished women in Bangladeshi society. I also presented how these women break their barriers and come to the legal arena to establish their rights. In this study, I have questioned women's agency and the struggle to problematize the position of women in gender relations, social, cultural, religious and the legal arena. I have shown how women in the lower socio-economic class are vulnerable because of the prevailing family and social structure and are exposed to domestic violence.

This study began with the deceptively straightforward question: why and how do some women become the victims of domestic violence in the changing socio-economic setting of Bangladesh? It critically seeks to trace domestic violence against impoverished women in Bangladeshi society by paying keen attention to the different factors of inequality and subordination of women in their everyday lives. I have portrayed the position of womanhood in the lower socio-economic class in its social and cultural milieu. More specifically, I have shown the position of girls in lower socio-economic families and how the socialization of a girl is marked by tradition to make her a woman. I have studied how these women perceive and practice the stereotypical notion of gender relations, kinship and the marriage system in the patrilineal and patriarchal social structure. Hence I have focused on how women are entangled with the dominant structural practice of the society. By the same token, I have also shown how some women become subjects, and their actions in practice, contest the dominant structure.

Martha C. Nussbaum (2000, pp. 5–6) has said that women in developing nations suffer pervasively from acute capability failure. To her, human capabilities are what people are actually able to do and to be – in a way informed by an intuitive idea of a life that is worthy of the dignity of a human being. In this study, I find that women's participation in income-generating work in the slum to some extent has changed their everyday lives, and they opened up opportunities for adopting strategies by personal and practical ways to gain economic security and freedom. Regarding the importance of employment, Nussbaum (1995, p. 54) emphasizes that employment outside the home and receiving an independent income is a means for women to improve their self-respect and the perceived societal value of women. Nussbaum (1995) continues: "[…] it represents a means of escape from male control over female labor. It represents a means of economic independence. […] it serves to increase women's bargaining power and autonomy within the household and within society more broadly" (p. 54). But she concludes that employment is a necessary but not sufficient condition for women's position and influence in society. This is true because women might, for example, gain access both to employment and an independent income, but if the working conditions are poor, the actual situation for women has not qualitatively improved. Further Nussbaum (2000) argues that women in much of the world lack support for various fundamental functions of a human life, and these unequal social and political circumstances give women unequal human capabilities.

As I found that many *basti* women are engaged in income-generating activities and enjoying some freedom of physical mobility in the public domain of the urban area, I have expanded my discussion on whether *basti* women in their everyday lives face domestic violence toward them and it is clear that no *basti* woman is leading a violence-free life. Moreover, *basti* life is entangled with poverty, unemployment and lack of descent life facilities. As a result, *basti* women belong to the extreme position of gender inequality that Nussbaum (2000) also discusses thus: "Gender inequality is strongly correlated with poverty; when poverty combines with gender inequality, the result is acute failure of central human capabilities" (p. 3). The ethnographic material of this study explored how *basti* women in their everyday lives are fighting, coping and curving a position against domestic violence in their family and community. I maintain that although many women in the *basti* run the home as the sole breadwinner and gain economic freedom and access to mobility in the "public" domain, most of them cannot exercise power over the practice of the society's structures and to bring about changes because patriarchal domination is deeply embedded in social-cultural and religious belief and may always ultimately be manifested in the form of physical violence.

The authority of a husband is culturally and religiously permitted and legitimated so that he can control his wife by verbal or mild physical abuse (e.g., a slap) but a wife cannot. The ethnographic accounts on the tolerance of violence toward them express the same phenomenon: "I have to bear all the torture of husband if I want to eat husband's income" or "Everybody will say I am bad if I hit my husband or leave my husband's family due to violence." Similar findings are also prevalent in other studies (Bates et al., 2004; William et al., 2011; UNICEF, 2011). The study shows that if open confrontation becomes common (women engaging in violence, retorting by using foul language or hitting back), then the weaker ones (the women) will always finally lose. Using foul language may ease the psychological tension in a woman as an individual and give her strength, but as a wider development, it would most probably lead not to less, but more domestic violence. I could find no women in the slums who would support severe domestic violence toward women. In the women's accounts, severe violence is beating wives with a stick, kicking or punching during pregnancy, injuring them and not providing food, clothing and shelter to wives and children. Although the slum women collectively do not accept severe domestic violence against women and in their everyday life they share their conjugal problems with each other, they do not get usually involved in domestic disputes before something serious is happening.

Focusing on domestic violence, I examined why and how women tolerated and tried to solve informally domestic violence perpetrated against them by their husbands and other in-laws for a long time and why some women break the barriers and come to formal legal institutions to seek help. The documents in the study suggested that dowry demands, husbands' extra-marital relationships and their multiple marriages, drug addiction and contested relationships with other affines (mother-in-law, sister-in-law) play a significant role in domestic violence. For many women, reporting domestic violence, punishment of affines or divorce is not necessarily what they are seeking. What they are trying to do is protect their marital bonds and end the abuse. Because marriage is perceived as an institution that gives a woman her status, privileges and, through her children, social security and honor for the future, most women do not want the perpetrators of violence to be punished. It is clear that many women do not have access to resources or are not acculturated for demanding their rights or do not find the opportunity to protest against domestic violence by their affines. In the counseling center, I found some female victims who were willing to go back to their violent homes even after being granted a divorce.

Many women are vulnerable to extremes in the social structure of Bangladesh. Silva (1995, p. 15) suggests that a vulnerable person is an individual who experiences "diminished autonomy due to physiological/psychological factors or status inequalities." Based on Silva's definition, Moore and Miller (1999, p. 1034) contend that vulnerable individuals are people who "lack the ability to make personal life choices, to make personal decisions, to maintain independence, and to self-determine." I find that in the impoverished households from the natal home women face gender inequality due to poverty and a lack of resources, skills, opportunities and structural barriers, which ensnares them in vulnerability and throughout their lives, they find it extremely difficult to emancipate themselves from this vulnerable situation. According to de Beauvoir (1952), the social construction of women has created a "second sex" in which women do not even regard themselves as a locus of dignity, as a self. Instead, they regard themselves as "other," and like men, reserve the notion of self-hood for men. Nussbaum (2000, p. i, 4) said that in the third world this lack of support is frequently caused because they are women, and in every sector of life opportunities, they face greater obstacles and inequalities. So they are more vulnerable to physical violence and sexual abuse than men or women of the middle and upper classes.

It is obvious from the study that women's vulnerability is related to household insecurity, which incarcerates the difficulties, experiences and incidents of women's lives that expose them to violence. To me the term "insecurity" is the best to employ here to focus on the vulnerability of the poor young women's lives, which is caused by certain insecurities, such as food insecurity, shelter insecurity, job insecurity and physical insecurity. In the chapters of the study, I have shown how insecurity related to having a shelter forms an obstacle to poor women standing against domestic violence. In the patrilineal and patrilocal residence based South Asian societies, after marriage, women lose their right to live permanently in their natal home. After marriage, a woman is considered as a guest in her natal home and her marital home becomes her permanent home. Moreover, as I looked at the impoverished slum women's lives, I could not find a single woman who had a secured shelter where she could live permanently.

From the study, it appears that food insecurity and shelter insecurity in the impoverished households frequently create conditions that encourage domestic violence against young wives and constrain victim women's abilities to receive help informally from their natal relatives and legally from the formal institutions. Martha C. Nussbaum (2011, p. 2) found poor parents (or siblings, if the parents have died) are often unwilling to take back a married daughter/sister in the household by breaking marriage relationships through divorce, abandonment or separation. Because for the impoverished households, accepting back daughters/sisters who have been married off means receiving extra mouth/mouths to feed and a new set of anxieties. The study pointed out that the parents or elder brothers usually rebuke the victim women and advise them to adjust in the violent affinal home. This attitude does not only reflect economic poverty and shelter insecurity; it also results in the deep embedded notions of ideal femininity and the proper husband-wife relationship deriving from religiously and culturally sanctioned ideals.

152 Conclusions

In the context of Bangladesh, the study reflects that in the poor households, material constraints include poverty or material deprivation caused by loss of agricultural land and employment due to the changing socio-economic structure, migration from rural to urban areas, death or serious illness of the primary earning member in the family, natural calamities, such as river erosion, drought, flood, tornado, etc. In short, any shock of these above-mentioned causes push a household to the edge of economic adversity and place the members in degrading situations. Households belonging to the lower socio-economic class are routinely exposed to such shocks. I have shown in this study how impoverished young women's life courses are structured by such events that not only impoverish them materially, but also deprive them of life-altering choices. Examples of social-cultural and religious constraints include norms related to early marriage, the practice of purdah, dowry practices, unequal treatment between sons and daughters in the natal family, not having one's own permanent shelter, not getting property from one's father or not having property rights, a father's lack of land, obstacles to women working outside home, a preference for sons, social stigma related with marital separation or divorce. The analysis of the women's lives from the two slums and the counseling center helped me to understand how all these constraints as a whole mute the voice and limit the agency of young women both within their natal and marital homes.

The issue of women's rights as human rights has traveled from the international arena where they were first formulated to offer new leverage to local activists (Ferree and Tripp, 2006). Domestic violence has moved from the privacy of the home into the light of the political and social arenas in Bangladesh. The issue has shifted focus from a particular man or woman relationship to the societal institutions or dominant ideology such as gender inequality, the varying constraints under which women and men live, the material, social and the legal options that they access or mobilize. From the 1980s and 1990s, Bangladesh has seen an escalation in the growth and role of NGOs. These NGOs have played a vibrant role in social and political mobilization in the country alongside the government for democratic nation-building. These NGOs are providing services for the development of peoples' lives, especially concentrating on poor women and children (Chowdhury, 2011).

The study reveals that in Sylhet district, women are now becoming encouraged to come out to the public domain and seek help from legal formal institutions and NGOs. It was promising to find that these young women from the impoverished class are not only passive victims of domestic violence. They are now trying to express their demands and establish their agency and stop the violence against them. But this study shows that when a victim woman raises her voice against domestic violence in the mediations in the counseling center, she is certainly not challenging to the structures of the social system in which she lives. Rather I find most of the women are simply trying to improve their personal situation as a wife or daughter-in-law in their marital home. They do not want to file a case against the perpetrators of crimes against them for fear of breaking their marital bonds, insecurity, fear of more violence and social stigma. In this sense, their agency is not consciously intended to bring about social change by rejecting the status quo and the gendered relations of power. However, the efforts of the victim women to stand up against domestic violence in the counseling center has formed a sound basis for women's emancipation from violence and establishing human rights in the long run.

There is no doubt that poor victim women are slowly but steadily raising their muted voices and protesting against domestic violence. However, it has also become especially clear that in order to compete for equal footing and the establishment of their rights, women need to acquire appropriate skills, improve their life situations and develop enough self-confidence. But increasing women's bargaining power can also risk increasing the likelihood of violence (Bates et al., 2004; William et al., 2011). Therefore, specific mitigation measures may be needed. When violence does occur, victims need timely and effective assistance ranging from the police and judiciary to health and social services. Service providers – the police and judiciary, health and social services – need to target women explicitly, and additionally, the service providers should get proper training. Targeting women also requires bringing services closer to women to deal with time and mobility constraints – for example, by providing community paralegals and mobile legal aid clinics that enable women to use the justice system. In many contexts, bringing services closer to women can be combined with increasing the awareness of service delivery organizations, particularly management, about gender issues.

Still, there are numerous problems with the legal systems in Bangladesh concerning women's issues in general and domestic violence in particular. The criminal laws and family laws, taken together, are insufficient and weak to solve women's problems when taking into account women's position and the prevalent structural barriers. I realized that the weakness of laws allows violent husbands and in-laws to find a way to escape compliance with them. In my opinion, the law alone is not capable of bringing social change and has less power to change peoples' behaviors in gender relations and social practices for establishing human rights. Generally, in the societies, people fear the law, legal procedures and punishment, but fear is not enough to uproot violence, immorality and injustice against women. If domestic violence against women is to be stopped, strong law enforcement and state intervention are required. People should be informed and educated about the laws in an informal way and cultured to practice the establishment of human rights to ensure meaningful everyday lives for all citizens. In this research, I have tried to add new viewpoints to the concept of domestic violence against women in the context of Bangladesh. I hope the professional community will benefit from being made aware of the gaps in this field that this research has identified and know that more can be uncovered about these gaps by future studies.

References

Abdullah, T. (1974). *Village Women as I Saw Them*. Dhaka: Ford Foundation.

Abdullah, T. and Zeidenstein, S. A. (1982). *Village Women of Bangladesh: Prospects for Change*. Oxford: Pergamon Press, Vol. 4, Women in Development Series.

Aekplakorn, W. and Kongsakon, Ronnachai. (2007). "Intimate Partner Violence among Women in Slum Communities in Bangkok, Thailand." *Singapore Medical Journal*, 48 (8), 763–768.

Afsar, R. (1994). "Internal migration and women: An insight into causes, consequences and policy implications." *Bangladesh Development Studies*, 22 (2), 217–243.

Afsar, R. (1999). "Is migration transferring rural poverty to urban areas? An analysis of longitudinal survey data of Dhaka city." Paper presented at the workshop: Changes and Determinants of Urban Poverty. Dhaka: Grameen Trust, Grameen Bank.

Afsar, R. (2000). *Rural Urban Migration in Bangladesh: Causes, Consequences and Challenges*. University Press Limited, Dhaka.

Afsar, R. (2003). "Internal migration and the development nexus: the case of Bangladesh." Paper presented at the Regional Conference on Migration, Development and Pro-Poor Policy Choices in Asia. Dhaka, Bangladesh.

Agarwal, Bina, Jane Humphries and Ingrid Robeyns. (2003). "Exploring the Challenges of Amartya Sen's Work and Ideas: An Introduction," *Feminist Economics* 9 (2–3), 3–12.

Agarwal, Bina. (1994). *A field of one's own – Gender and land rights in South Asia*. Cambridge: Cambridge University Press.

Agarwal, Bina. (1997). "Bargaining and gender relations: Within and beyond the household." *Feminist Economics*, 3(1), 1–51.

Agnes, Flavia. (1998). "Violence against Women: Review of Recent Enactments." In S. Mukhopadhyay (Ed.), *The Nature of Justice*. New Delhi: Manohar.

Agnes, Flavia. (2002). "Transgressing Boundaries of Gender and Identity." *Economic and Political Weekly*, Vol. 37, No. 36 (September 7–13), 3695–3698.

Ahearn, L. M. (2001). "Language and Agency." *Annual Review of Anthropology*, 30, 109–137.

Ahmad, F. A., Riaz, P. B. and Stewart, D. E. (2004). "Patriarchal beliefs and perceptions of abuse among South Asian Immigrant Women." *Violence Against Women*, 10, 262–282.

Ahmed, S. M. (2005). "Intimate Partner Violence against Women: Experiences from a Woman-focused Development Programme in Matlab, Bangladesh." *Journal of Health, Population and Nutrition*, 23 (1), 95–101.

Ahmed, S. U. and Motahar, H. A. (1999). Introduction. In S. U. Ahmed (Ed.), *Sylhet: History and Heritage*. Bangladesh Itihas Samiti (Bangladesh History Association), Bangladesh.

References

Ahmed-Ghosh, H. (2004). "Chattels of Society: Domestic Violence in India," *Violence Against Women*, 10 (1), 94–118.

Akanda, L. and Shamim, I. (1984). *Women and Violence: A Comparative Study of Rural and Urban Violence on Women in Bangladesh*. Women's Issue 1. Dhaka: Women for Women.

Alam, M. S., Shamsuddin, S. D., Rashid, M. S. and Hossain, M. D. (1999). "Sylhet and its evolving geographical environment." In S. U. Ahmed (Ed.), *Sylhet: History and Heritage*. Bangladesh Itihas Samiti (Bangladesh History Association), Bangladesh.

Aldwin, C. M. (1994). *Stress, coping, and development: An integrative perspective*. New York: The Guilford Press.

Ali, S. (2002). *Violence against women in Bangladesh, 2001*. Dhaka: Bangladesh National Women Lawyers Association.

Ali, T. S. and Bustamante-Gavino, I. (2007). "Prevalence of and reasons for domestic violence among women from low socioeconomic communities of Karachi." *Eastern Mediterranean Health Journal*, Vol. 13, 1417–1426.

Allen, C. (1988). *The Hold Life Has: Coca and Cultural Identity in an Andean Community*. Washington, DC: Smithsonian Institution Press.

Allen, C. M. and Straus, M. A. (1980). "Resources, power and husband-wife violence." In M. A. Straus, and G. T. Hotaling (Eds.), *The social causes of husband-wife violence*. Minneapolis: University of Minnesota Press.

Ameen, N. (1997). *Keeping a Wife at the End of a Stick: Law and Wife Abuse in Bangladesh*. An unpublished Ph.D. thesis. Essex: University of East London.

Ameen, N. (2005). *Wife Abuse in Bangladesh – An Unrecognised Offence*. The University Press Limited. Dhaka.

Amnesty International. (2001). *Broken bodies, shattered minds: Torture and ill- treatment of women*. London: Amnesty International Publications.

Anam, S., Kabir, R. and Rai, P. (1997). *Staying Alive: Urban Poor in Bangladesh*. Dhaka: United Nations Children's Fund.

Anderson, K. L. (1997). "Gender, Status and Domestic Violence: An integration of feminist and family violence approaches." *Journal of Marriage and the Family*, 59, 655–669.

Angrosino, M. V. and Mays de Perez, K. A. (2000). "Rethinking observation. From method to context." In Norman K. Denzin, and Yvonna S. Lincoln (Eds.), *Handbook of Qualitative Research*. Thousand Oaks, CA: Sage Publications, Inc.

Arce, A. and N. Long. (2000). *Anthropology, development and modernities: Exploring discourses, counter-tendencies and violence*. London: Routledge.

Archer, M. S. (2000). *Being Human: The Problem of Agency*. Cambridge: Cambridge University Press.

Arefeen, H. K. S. (1982). "Muslim Stratification Patterns in Bangladesh: An Attempt to Build a Theory." *Journal of Social Studies*, 16.

Arens, J. and Beurden, J. V. (1977). *Jhagrapur: Poor Peasants and Women in a Village in Bangladesh*. Amsterdam: Third World Publications.

Arjan de Haan. (2003). "Calcutta's Labour Migrants: Encounters with Modernity." *Contributions to Indian Sociology*, 37, 189.

Ashrafun, L. and Saavala, M. (2014). "Domestic Violence Made Public: A Case Study of the Use of Alternative Dispute Resolution among Underprivileged Women in Bangladesh." *Contemporary South Asia*, 22 (2), 189–202.

Ashrafun, L. and Uddin, M. J. (2010). "Fertility Practices: A Qualitative Study of a Slum in Sylhet, Bangladesh." *IUB Journal of Social Sciences and Humanities*, 8 (1), 113–130.

Asian Development Bank. (2010). Country Gender Assessment Bangladesh.

References

Aura, S. (2008). *Women and Marital Breakdown in South India. Reconstructing Homes, Bonds and Persons*. Academic Dissertation. Research Series in Anthropology. University of Helsinki.

Aziz, K. M. A. (1979). *Kinship in Bangladesh*. Monograph Series No. 1, Dhaka: International Center for Diarrhoeal Disease Research.

Aziz, K. M. A. and Maloney, C. (1985). *Life stage, Gender and Fertility in Bangladesh*. Dhaka: International Center for Diarrhoeal Disease Research.

Bangladesh Bureau of Statistics. (2000). "Report of Sample Vital Registration System 1997 and 1998, July." Dhaka: Ministry of Planning, Government of the People's Republic of Bangladesh.

Bangladesh Bureau of Statistics. (2010). Millennium Development Goals: Bangladesh Progress at a Glance.

Bangladesh Institute of Development Studies. (2004). "Baseline survey for assessing attitudes and practices of male and female members and in-laws toward gender based violence (Final Report)." Dhaka, Bangladesh: United Nations Population Fund.

Basu, Srimati. (1999). *She Comes to Take Her Rights: Indian Women, Property, and Propriety*. Albany, NY: State University of New York Press.

Basu, Srimati. (2005). "The Imperial Origins of Dowry." *India Nest*. Com. 9 August.

Basu, Srimati. (2015). *The Trouble with Marriage: Feminists Confront Law and Violence in India*. Oakland, CA: University of California Press.

Bates, L. M., Schuler, S. R., Islam, F. and Islam, M. K. (2004). "Socioeconomic Factors and Processes Associated with Domestic Violence in Rural Bangladesh." *International Family Planning Perspectives*, 30 (4), 190–199.

Batliwala, S. (1985). "Women in Poverty: The Energy, Health and Nutrition Syndrome." In D. Jain. and N. Banerjee (Eds.), *Tyranny of the Household: Investigative Essay on Women's Work*. New Delhi: Vikas.

Beasley, M. E. and Thomas, D. Q. (1994). "Domestic violence as a human rights issue." In M. A. Fineman. and R. Mykitiuk (Eds.), *The Public nature of private violence: The discovery of domestic abuse*. New York: Routledge.

Beck, B. E. F. (1972). *Peasant Society in Konku: A Study of Right and Left Subcastes in South India*. Vancouver: University of British Columbia Press.

Begum, A. (1991). "Drug dependence problems in Dhaka, Bangladesh." *Bangladesh Medical Journal*, 20, 33–39.

Begum, S. and Ahmed, H. (1991). "Beliefs and rituals in a shrine in Bangladesh." *Journal of Social Studies, Bangladesh*, 53, 68–95.

Benmayor, R. (1991). "Testimony, action research, and empowerment: Puerto Rican women and popular education." In S. B. Gluck., and D. Patai (Eds.), *Women's words: The feminist practice of oral history*. New York: Routledge.

Bennett, Judith M. (2006). *History Matters: Patriarchy and the Challenge of Feminism*. Philadelphia: University of Pennsylvania Press.

Bertocci, P. J. (1974). "Rural Communities in Bangladesh: Hajipur and Tinpara." In C. Mahoney (Ed.), *South Asia: Seven Community Profiles*. New York: Holt, Rinehart and Winston.

Bhuiya, A., Sharmin, T. and Hanifi, S. M. A. (2003). "Nature of Domestic Violence against Women in a Rural Area of Bangladesh: Implication for Preventive Interventions." *Journal of Health, Population and Nutrition*, 2, 48–54.

Bhuiyan, R. (1991). *Aspects of violence against women*. Dhaka: Bangladesh Institute of Democratic Rights.

Bloch, F. and Vijayendra, R. (2002). "Terror as a Bargaining Instrument: A Case Study of Dowry Violence in Rural India." *The American Economic Review*, 92 (4), 1029–1043.

Blood, R. O. and Wolfe, D. M. (1965). *Husbands and Wives: The dynamics of married living*. New York: Free Press.

Boddy, Janice. (1998). "Violence Embodied? Circumcision, Gender Politics, and Cultural Aesthetics." In Rebecca Emerson Dobash and Russell P. Dobash (Ed.) *Rethinking Violence Against Women*. Thousand Oaks, CA: Sage Publications, Inc.

Bograd, M. (1990). Feminist perspectives on wife abuse: An introduction. In K. Yllo. and M. Bograd (Eds.), *Feminist perspectives on wife abuse*. Newbury Park, CA: Sage Publications, Inc.

Bourdieu, P. (1990). La domination masculine. *Actes de la recherché en sciences socials*, 84 (September), 2–31.

Bourdieu, P. (1992). *An Invitation to Reflexive Sociology*. Cambridge: Polity Press.

Bourdieu, P. (2001). *Masculine Domination*. Cambridge: Polity Press.

Bourdieu, P. (2002 [1977]). *Outline of a Theory of Practice*. Cambridge: Cambridge University Press.

Bronfenbrenner, U. (1979). *The ecology of human development: Experiments by nature and design*. Cambridge, MA: Harvard University Press.

Brown, Judith K. (1992). "Introduction: Definitions, Assumptions, Themes, and Issues." In D. A. Counts., J. K. Brown and J. C. Campbell (Eds.), *Sanctions and Sanctuary: Cultural Perspectives on the Beating of Wives*. Boulder: Westview Press.

Burnett, J. (1985). *A Social History of Housing 1815–1985*, second edition. London: Methuen.

Caplow, T. (1968). *Two against one: Coalition in triads*. Englewood Cliffs, NJ: Prentice Hall.

Capulong, E. R. C. (2012). "Mediation and the Neocolonial Legal Order: Access to Justice and Self-Determination in the Philippines." *Ohio State Journal on Dispute Resolution*, 27 (3), 641–681. http://scholarship. Law.umt.edu/faculty_lawreviews/84.

Carp, R. M. (2000). *Elder abuse in the family: an interdisciplinary model for research*. New York: Springer.

Charrad, M. M. (2010). "Women's agency across cultures: Conceptualizing strengths and boundaries." *Women's Studies International Forum*, 33, 517–522.

Chaudhury, R. H. (1987). "Dietary Adequacy and Sex Bias: Pre-School Children in Rural Bangladesh." *Social Action*, 37 (April–June), 107–125.

Chaudhury, R. H. and Nilufer, R. A. (1980). *Female Status in Bangladesh*. Dhaka: The Bangladesh Institute of Development Studies.

Chaulk, R. and King, P. A. (1998). *Violence in families: assessing prevention and treatment programs*. Washington, DC: National Academy Press.

Chen, L. C., Haq, E., and D'Souza, S. (1981). Sex Bias in the Family Allocation of Food and Health Care in Rural Bangladesh. *Population and Development Review*, 7 (1), 55–70.

Chen, M. (1983). *A Quiet Revolution: Women in Transition in Rural Bangladesh*. Cambridge, MA: Schenkman Publishing.

Chhachhi, Amrita and Renee Pittin. (1995). "Multiple Identities, Multiple Strategies: Confronting State, Capital and Patriarchy." ISS Working Paper Series No. 192. The Hague: ISS

Chodorow, N. (1978). *The Reproduction of Mothering*. Berkeley: University of California Press.

Chow, E. N. (1987). "The development of feminist consciousness among Asian American women." *Gender and Society*, 1, 284–299.

Chowdhury, A. and Bhuiya, A. (2001). "Do Poverty Alleviation Programmes Reduce Inequalities in Health? The Bangladesh Experience." In D. Leon., and G. Walt (Eds.), *Poverty, Inequality and Health: An International Perspective*. Oxford: Oxford University Press.

Chowdhury, E. H. (2011). *Transnationalism Reversed: Women Organizing against Gendered Violence in Bangladesh*. Albany, NY: State University of New York Press.

Chowdhury, O. H. (1993). *Handbook of Muslim Family Laws*. Dhaka: Dhaka Law Report.

Christians, C. G. (2000). "Ethics and politics in qualitative research." In N. K. Denzin. and Y. S. Lincoln (Eds.), *Handbook of Qualitative Research*. Thousand Oaks, CA: Sage Publications, Inc.

Cohen, A. J. (2006). "Debating the Globalization of US Mediation: Politics, Power, and Practice in Nepal." *Harvard Negotiation Law Review*, 11 (1), 295–353.

Collins, P. H. (1986). "Learning from the outsider within: The sociological significance of black feminist thought." *Social Problems*, 33, 14–32.

Comaroff, John. L. and Roberts, Simon. (1981). *Rules and Processes*. Chicago: University of Chicago Press.

Connell, R. (1987). *Gender and power*. Cambridge: Polity Press.

Counts, D. A. (1990). "Domestic violence in Oceania." *Pacific Studies*, 13 (3), 1–5.

Crapanzano, V. (1977). Introduction. In V. Crapanzano. and V. Garrison (Eds.), *Case Studies in Spirit Possession*. New York: John Wiley and Sons.

Crowell, N., and Burgess, A. W. (1996). *Understanding violence against women*. Washington, DC: National Academy Press.

Daniel, E. V. (1984). *Fluid Signs: Being a Person the Tamil Way*. Berkeley: University of California Press.

Dannecker, P. (2002). *Between conformity and resistance. Women garment workers in Bangladesh*. Dhaka: University Press Limited.

Das Gupta, M. (1995). "Life course perspective on women's autonomy and health outcomes." *American Anthropologist*, 97 (3), 481–491.

de Beauvoir, Simone. (1952). *The Second Sex*. New York: Random House.

De Haan, A. (2003). "Calcutta's labour migrants: Encounters with modernity." *Contributions to Indian Sociology*, 37, (1, 2), 189–215.

Denzin, N. K. (1986). "A postmodern social theory." *Sociological Theory*, 4, 194–204.

Desjarlais, R. (1992). *Body and Emotion: The Aesthetics of Illness and Healing in the Nepal Himalayas*. Philadelphia: University of Pennsylvania Press.

Deuba, A. R. and Rana, P. S. (2001). *A Study on the psycho-social impacts of violence against women and girls with special focus on rape, incest, and polygamy*. Nepal: Saathi.

Dhuruvarajan, V. (1989). *Hindu Women and The Power of Ideology*. Delhi: Vistaar Publications.

Dobash, R. E. and Dobash, R. P. (1978). "Wives: The appropriate victims of marital violence." *Victimology*, 2 (3), 426–442.

Dobash, R. E. and Dobash, R. P. (1983). *Violence against wives: A case against patriarchy*. New York: Free Press.

Dobash, R. E. and Dobash, R. P. (1992). *Women, Violence, and Social Change*. London: Routledge.

Dobash, R. E. and Dobash, R. P. (1998). *Rethinking Violence Against Women*. Thousand Oaks, CA: Sage Publications, Inc.

References

Dube, L. (1988). "On the construction of gender: Hindu girls in patrilineal India." *Economic and Political Weekly*, 30 (April), 11–19.
Dube, L. (1997). *Women and kinship: Comparative perspectives on gender in South and Southeast Asia*. New Delhi: Vistaar.
Dumont, L. (1980). *Homo Hierarchicus: The Caste System and its Implications*. Chicago: The University of Chicago.
Engels, Fredrick. (1884). *The Origin of the Family, Private Property and the State*. Hottingen-Zurich.
Eriksen, T. H. and Nielsen, F. S. (2001). *A History of Anthropology*, London: Pluto Press.
Espanioly, N. (1997). "Violence Against Women: A Palestinian Women's Perspective. Personal is Political." *Women's Studies International Forum*, 20 (5/6), 587–592.
Espiritu, Y. L. (1997). *Asian American women and men: Labor, laws, and love*. Thousand Oaks, California: Sage Publications, Inc.
Ewing, K. P. (1990). "The Illusion of Wholeness: Culture, Self and the Experience of Inconsistency." *Ethos*, 18 (3), 251–278.
Farrington, K. (1980). "Stress and family violence." In M. A. Straus. and, G. T. Hotaling (Eds.), *The social causes of husband wife violence*. Minneapolis: University of Minnesota Press.
Farrington, K. (1986). "The application of stress theory to the study of family violence: Principles, problems and prospects." *Journal of Family Violence*, 1 (2), 131–149.
Feldman, S. (2010). "Shame and honour: The violence of gendered norms under conditions of global crisis." *Women's Studies International Forum*, 33, 305–315.
Ferree, M. M. and Tripp, A. M. (Eds.). (2006). *Global Feminism: Transnational Women's Activism, Organizing, and Human Rights*. New York: New York University Press.
Firestone, S. (1970). *The Dialectic of Sex: The Case for Feminist Revolution*. New York: Bantam Books.
Firoze, F. K. (1996). *Women Law Code. Institute for Law and Development*. Dhaka, Bangladesh.
Flick, U. (2006). *An introduction to qualitative research*. Thousand Oaks, California: Sage Publications, Inc.
Foege, W. H., Rosenberg, M. L. and Mercy, J. A. (1995). "Public health and violence prevention." *Current Issues in Public Health*, 1 (1), 2–9.
Fox, G. L., Benson, M. L., DeMoris, A. A. and Van Wyck. (2002). "Economic distress and intimate violence: Testing family stress and resource theories." *Journal of Marriage and the Family*, 64 (3), 793–807.
Frey, J. H. and Fontana, A. (1993). "The group interview in social research." In D. L. Morgan (Ed.), *Successful focus groups: Advancing the state of the art*. Newbury Park, CA: Sage Publications, Inc.
Fruzzetti, L. (1990 [1982]). *The Gift of a Virgin: Women, Marriage, and Ritual in a Bengali Society*. Delhi: Oxford University Press.
Fruzzetti, L. (2006). "Kinship Identity and Issues of Nationalism – Female Abandonment in Calcutta." In L. Fruzzetti., and S. Tenhunen (Eds.), *Culture, Power, And Agency: Gender In Indian Ethnography*. Calcutta: Stree.
Fruzzetti, L. and Akos, Ö. (1984). *Kinship and Ritual in Bengal: Anthropological Essays*. New Delhi: South Asian Publishers.
Fruzzetti, L. and Tenhunen, S. (Eds.). (2006). *Culture, Power and Agency: Gender in Indian Ethnography*. Calcutta: Stree.
Fulu, Emma. (2014). *Domestic Violence in Asia: Globalization, Gender and Islam in the Maldives*. London and New York: Routledge, Taylor and Francis Group. Garbarino, J.

(1985). *Adolescent development: an ecological perspective*. Columbus, OH: Charles E. Merrill.
Garbarino, J. and Crouter, A. (1978). "Defining the community context for parent-child relations: the correlates of child maltreatment." *Child Development*, 49, 604–616.
Garcia, A. M. (1989). "The development of Chicana feminist discourse 1970–1980." *Gender and Society*, 3, 217–238.
Garcia-Moreno, C., Jansen. H. A., Ellsberg, M., Heise, L. and Watts, C. (2006). "Prevalence of intimate partner violence: Findings from the WHO multi-country study on women's health and domestic violence." *Lancet*.
Garcia-Moreno, C., Jansen, H., Ellsberg, M., Heise, L. and Watts, C. (2005). "WHO multi-country study on women's health and domestic violence against women: Initial results on prevalence, health outcomes and women's responses." Geneva: World Health Organization. Retrieved April 13, 2012 from www.sciencemag.org/content/suppl/2005.
Gardner, Katy. (1995). *Global Migrants, Local Lives – Travel and Transformation in Rural Bangladesh*. Oxford: Clarendon Press.
Gazmararian, J. A., Lazorick, S., Spitz, A. M., Ballard, T. J., Saltzman, L. E. and Marks, J. S. (1996). "Prevalence of violence against women." *Journal of the American Medical Association*, 275 (24), 1915–1920.
Gelles, R. J. (1972). *The violent home: A study of physical aggression between husbands and wives*. Beverly Hills, CA: Sage Publications, Inc.
Giddens, A. (1979). *Central Problems in Social Theory: Action, Structure, and Contradiction in Social Analysis*. Berkeley: University of California Press.
Giddens, A. (1984). *The Constitution of Society*. Cambridge: Polity.
Gil, D. G. (1986). "Socio-cultural aspects of domestic violence." In M. Lystad (Ed.), *Violence in the home: Interdisciplinary perspectives*. New York: Brunner.
Gilsenan, M. (1982). *Recognising Islam: An Anthropologist's Introduction*. London: Croom Helm.
Gold, A. G. (1992). "Gender, Violence and Power: Rajasthani Stories of Shakti." In N. Kumar (Ed.), *Women as Subjects: South Asian Histories*. Charlottesville: University Press of Virginia.
Gold, A. G. and Bhoju, R. G. (2002). *In the Time of Trees and Sorrows: Nature, Power and Memory in Rajasthan*. Durham, NC: Duke University Press.
Goode, W. J. (1971). "Force and violence in the family." *Journal of Marriage and the Family*, 33 (4), 624–636.
Hadi, A. (2000). "Prevalence and Correlates of the Risk of Marital Sexual Violence in Bangladesh." *Journal of Interpersonal Violence*, 15 (8), 787–805.
Hadi, A. (2005). "Women's Productive Role and Marital Violence in Bangladesh." *Journal of Family Violence*, 20 (3), 181–189.
Hampton, R. L., Gullotta, T. P., Adams, G. R., Potter, E. H. and Weissberg, R. P. (Eds.). (1993). *Family Violence. Prevention and Treatment. Issues in Children's and Families' Lives*. Thousand Oaks, CA: Sage Publications, Inc.
Hanchett, S., Akhter, S., Khan, M. H., Mezulianik, S. and Blagbrough, V. (2003). "Water, sanitation and hygiene in Bangladesh slums: an evaluation of the Water Aid – Bangladesh Urban Programme." *Environment and Urbanization*, 15, 43.
Harvey, P. (1994). "Domestic Violence in the Andes." In P. Harvey. and G. Peter (Eds.), *Sex and Violence: Issues in Representation and Experience*. New York: Routledge.
Hashemi, S. M., Schuler, S. R. and Riley, A. (1996). "Rural Credit Programs and Women's Empowerment in Bangladesh." *World Development*, 24 (4), 635–653.

References

Healey, K., Smith, C. and Sullivan, C. (1998). *Batterer Intervention: Program Approaches and Criminal Justice Strategies*. U.S. Department of Justice. National Institute of Justice.

Hegde, R. S. (1999). "Marking Bodies, Reproducing Violence: A Feminist Reading of Female Infanticide in South India." *Violence Against Women*, 5 (5), 507–524.

Heise, L. L. (1998). "Violence against women: an integrated ecological framework." *Violence Against Women*, 4, 262–290.

Heise, L. L., Raikes, A., Watts, C. H. and Zwi, A. B. (1994). "Violence against women: a neglected public health issues in less developed countries." *Social Science Medicine*, 39, 1165–1179.

Heise, L., Ellsberg, M. and Gottemoeller, M. (1999). *Ending Violence against women*. Population Reports, L (11). Baltimore, MD: Johns Hopkins University School of Public Health, Population Information Program.

Hodgson, Geoffrey M. (2004). *The evolution of institutional economics: agency, structure and Darwinism in American institutionalism*. London: Routledge.

Honeycutt, T. C., Marshall, L. L. and Weston, R. (2001). "Toward ethnicity specific models of employment, public assistance, and victimization." *Violence Against Women*, 7, 126–140.

Hornung, C. A., McCullough, B. C. and Sugimoto, T. (1981). "Status relationships in marriage: Risk factors in spouse abuse." *Journal of Marriage and the Family*, 43 (3), 675–692.

Hossain, I. M., Khan, I. A. and Seely, J. (2003). *Surviving on their feet: Charting the mobile livelihoods of the poor in rural Bangladesh*. Paper presented at the conference: Staying poor: Chronic Poverty and Development Policy, held at the University of Manchester, April 7–9.

Hossain, M. and Bayes, A. (2009). *Rural Economy and Livelihoods: Insights from Bangladesh*. Dhaka: Bangladesh: A H Development Publishing House.

Hossain, M., Afsar, R. and Bose, M. L. (1999). *Growth and distribution of income and incidence of poverty in Dhaka city*. Paper presented at the workshop: Changes and Determinants of Urban Poverty. Dhaka: Grameen Trust, Grameen Bank.

Hossain, S. (2007). "Poverty and Vulnerability in Urban Bangladesh: the case of slum communities in Dhaka city." *International Journal of Development Issues*, 6 (1), 50–62.

Inden, R. B. and Nicholas, R. W. (1977). *Kinship in Bengali Culture*. Chicago: University of Chicago Press.

Islam, M. and Ahmed, S. (1993). *Girl Child in the Family and Society. A Study on the Girl Child in Dhaka Urban and Rural Area*. Dhaka: World Vision of Bangladesh.

Islam, N. S. K., Hossain, J. K. and Ahsan, M. (2000). Sexual life style, drug habit and socio-demographic status of drug addicts in Bangladesh. *Public Health*, 114, 389–392.

Islam, Nazrul. (1996). *Urban Poor in Bangladesh*. Dhaka: Centre for Urban Studies.

Jahan, R. (1994). *Hidden Danger: Women and Family Violence in Bangladesh*. Women for Women. A research and study group. Dhaka: Bangladesh.

Jahangir, B. K. (1979). *Differentiation, Polarization and Confrontation in Rural Bangladesh*. Dhaka: Centre for Social Studies, University of Dhaka, Bangladesh.

Jain, D. and Chand, M. (1982). *Report on a Time Allocation Study: Its Methodological Implications*. New Delhi: Institute of Social Studies Trust.

Jain, D. and Banerjee, N. (1985). *Tyranny of the Household: Investigative Essays on Women's Work*. New Delhi: Shakti Books.

James, R. K. and Gilliand, B. E. (2005). *Crisis intervention strategies*. Belmont, CA: Thomson Brooks/Cole.

Jansen, E. G. (1987). *Rural Bangladesh: Competition for Scarce Resources.* Dhaka: University Press Limited.

Jansen, R., and Thornton, R. (2003). "Early female marriage in the developing world." *Gender and Development,* 11 (2), 9–19.

Jarrett, R. L. (1993). "Focus group interviewing with low-income minority populations: A research experience." In D. L. Morgan (Eds.), *Successful focus groups: Advancing the state of the art.* Newbury Park, CA: Sage Publications, Inc.

Jasinski, J. L. (2001). "Theoretical explanations for violence against women." In C. M. Renzetti., J. L. Edleson and R. K. Bergen (Eds.), *The Sourcebook on Violence against Women.* Thousand Oaks, CA: Sage Publications, Inc.

Javed, A. (1991). "Dowry Prohibition in India." *Delhi Law Review,* 13, 179–183.

Jayawardena, K. and Malathi, de A. (1996). *Embodied Violence: Communalising Women's Sexuality in South Asia.* London: Zed Books.

Jeffery, P. (1979). *Frogs in a Well: Indian Women in Purdah.* London: Zed Books.

Jeffery, P. and Amrita, B. (1998). *Appropriating Gender: Women's activism and politicized religion in South Asia.* New York: Routledge.

Jeffery, P. and Jeffery, R. (1996). *Don't Marry Me to A Plowman! Women's Everyday Lives in Rural North India.* New Delhi: Vistaar Publications.

Jenkins, R. (2002). *Pierre Bourdieu,* London: Routledge.

Johnson, Holly. (1998). "Rethinking Survey Research on Violence Against Women." In Rebecca Emerson Dobash, and Russell P Dobash (Eds.), *Rethinking Violence Against Women.* Thousand Oaks, CA: Sage Publications, Inc.

Johnston, L. and Gill, V. (1995). "Wherever I lay my girlfriend, that's my home." In D. Bell. and G. Valentine (Eds.), *Mapping desire: Geographies of Sexualities.* London: Routledge.

Junghare, I. Y. (1998). "My Home: My Parent's Place or My In-laws' House? A Cross-Cultural Comparison." In I. Glushkova. and A. Feldhaus (Eds.), *House and Home in Maharashtra.* Delhi: Oxford University Press.

Kabeer, N. (1998). "Can't buy me love? Re-evaluating gender, credit and empowerment in rural Bangladesh." IDS Discussion Paper, Sussex: Institute of Development Studies.

Kabeer, N. (2000). *The Power to Choose: Bangladeshi Women and Labor Market Decisions in London and Dhaka.* London: Verso.

Kabeer, N. (2001). "Conflicts Over Credit: Re-Evaluating the Empowerment Potential of Loans to Women in Rural Bangladesh." *World Development,* 29 (1), 63–84.

Kabeer, Naila. (2000). "From Feminist Insights to an Analytical Framework: An Institutional Perspective on Gender Inequality." In Naila Kabeer and Ramya Subrahmanian (Eds.), *Institutions, Relations and Outcomes.* New Delhi: Kali for Women.

Kabeer, N. and Mahmud, S. (2004). "Globalization, Gender and Poverty: Bangladeshi Women Workers in Export and Local Markets." *Journal of International Development,* 16, 93–109.

Kakar, S. (1994 [1981, 1978]). *The Inner World: A Psychoanalytic Study of Childhood and Society in India.* Delhi: Oxford University Press.

Kakar, S. (1997). *Culture and Psyche. Selected Essays.* Delhi: Oxford University Press.

Kalil, A. and Danziger, S. (2000). How teen mothers are faring under welfare reform. *Journal of Social Issues,* 56, 775–798.

Kamal, M. (2004). "Introducing ADR in Bangladesh." *Delhi Judicial Academy Journal,* 3 (ii). Delhi Mediation Centre, District Courts of Delhi. www.delhimediationcentre.gov.in/articles.htm#introducing.

Kandiyoti, D. (1988). "Bargaining with Patriarchy." *Gender and Society,* 2 (3), 274–290.

Kandiyoti, Deniz. (1998). "Gender, Power and Contestation: Rethinking Bargaining with Patriarchy." In Cecile Jackson and Ruth Pearson (Eds.), *Feminist Visions of Development*. London: Routledge.

Karim, A. (1999). "Advent of Islam in Sylhet and Hazrat Shah Jalal (R)." In S. U. Ahmed (Ed.), *Sylhet: History and Heritage*. Bangladesh Itihas Samiti (Bangladesh History Association).

Karlekar, M. (1998). "Domestic violence." *Economic and Political Weekly*, 33 (27), 1741–1749.

Katz, Elizabeth. (1997). "The Intra-Household Economics of Voice and Exit." *Feminist Economics*, 3 (3), 25–46.

Kaukinen, C. (2004). "Status compatibility, physical violence, and emotional abuse in intimate relationships." *Journal of Marriage and Family*, 66, 452–472.

Kertzer, D. I. (1994). Introduction. In D. I. Kertzer. and J. Keith (Eds.), *Age and Anthropological Theory*. Ithaca, NY: Cornell University Press.

Khair, S. (1995). *Changing Responses to Child Labour: The Case of Female Children in the Bangladesh Garment Industry*. An unpublished PhD Thesis. Essex: University of East London, School of Law.

Khan, M. E., Rob, U. and Hossain, S. M. I. (2001). "Violence Against Women and its impact on Women's Lives – Some Observation from Bangladesh." *Journal of Family Welfare*, 46 (2), 12–24.

Khan, S. (1983). *Spiritual Healing and Witchcraft Among the Hassan Zai of Kenar sharif*. Unpublished MA dissertation, Department of Anthropology, Quaid-I-Azam University, Islamabad.

Khan, S. (1988). *The Fifty Percent: Women in Development and Policy in Bangladesh*. Dhaka: The University Press Limited.

Khan, S. R. (2001). *The Socio-legal Status of Bengali Women in Bangladesh: Implications for Development*. Dhaka: The University Press Limited.

Khandker, S. R. (1998). *Fighting Poverty with Microcredit: Examples in Bangladesh*. New York: Oxford University Press.

Khnadker, S. R. and Latif, M. A. (1995). *The Role of Family Planning and Targeted Credit Programs in Demographic Change in Bangladesh*. Workshop: Credit Programs and the Poor, March 19–22. Dhaka, Bangladesh: Education and Social Policy Department, The World Bank, and Bangladesh Institute of Development Studies (BIDS).

Kimmel, M. S. and Aronson, A. (2000). *The Gendered Society Reader*. Toronto: Oxford University Press.

Kishwar, M. (2003). "Voices from the Economic South." *NWSA Journal*,15 (2), 111.

Kishwar, M. and Vanita, R. (1984). *In Search of Answers: Indian Women's Voices from Manushi*. London: Zed Books.

Koenig, M., Ahmed, S., Hossain, M. and Mozumder, A. (2003). "Women's Status and Domestic Violence in Rural Bangladesh: Individual and Community led Effects." *Demography*, 40 (2), 269–288.

Kotalova, J. (1993). *Belonging to Others – Cultural Construction of Womanhood Among Muslims in a Village in Bangladesh*. Uppsala, Sweden: Uppsala Studies in Cultural Anthropology.

Krishnan, S. (2005). "Do Structural Inequalities Contribute to Marital Violence? Ethnographic Evidence from Rural South India." *Violence Against Women*, 11 (6), 759–775.

Kuhn, R. (2000). "The logic of letting go: Family and individual migration from rural Bangladesh," Labour and Population Working Papers, RAND corporation.

References

Kuhn, R. (2003). "Identities in Motion: Social Exchange Networks and Rural–Urban Migration in Bangladesh." *Contributions to Indian Sociology* 37, (1, 2), 311–338.

Kumar, N. (2006). "The (No) Work and (No) Leisure World of Women in Assi, Banaras." In L. Fruzzetti. and S. Tenhunen (Eds.), *Culture, Power, And Agency: Gender In Indian Ethnography*. Calcutta: Stree.

Kurst-Swanger, K. and Petcosky, J. L. (2003). *Violence in the home: Multidisciplinary perspectives*. Oxford: Oxford University Press.

Kynch, J. and Sen, A. (1983). "Indian Women: Well-Being and Survival." *Cambridge Journal of Economics*, 7, 363–380.

Lahti, M. (2001). *Domesticated Violence. The Power of the Ordinary in Everyday Finland*. Helsinki: Research Series in Anthropology, University of Helsinki.

Lamb, S. (2000). *White Saris and Sweet Mangos. Ageing, Gender, and Body in North India*. Berkeley, Los Angeles and London: University of California Press.

Landell-Mills, S. (1992). *An Anthropological Account of Islamic Holy-Men in Bangladesh*. Ph.D. thesis (London).

Lengermann, P. M. and Brantley-Niebrugge, J. (1992). "Contemporary Feminist Theory." In George Ritzer (Ed.), *Sociological Theory* (462–463). Singapore: McGraw-Hill.

Lerner, Gerda. (1986). *The Creation of Patriarchy*. New York: Oxford University Press.

Levi-Strauss, C. (1969 [1949]). *The Elementary Structures of Kinship*. London: Eyre and Spottiswoode.

Levinson, D. (1989). *Family violence in cross-cultural perspective*. Newbury Park, CA: Sage Publications, Inc.

Liamputtong, P. (2007). *Researching the Vulnerable*. Thousand Oaks, CA: Sage Publications, Inc.

Lindholm, C. (1982). *Generosity and Jealousy: The Swat Pukhtun of Northern Pakistan*. New York: Columbia University Press.

Mabud, M. A. (1990). *Women's Roles: Health and Reproductive Behavior*. In South Asia Study of Population Policy and Programmes: Bangladesh. Dhaka: UNFPA.

Macmillan, R. and Gartner, R. (1999). "When she brings home the bacon: Labor-force participation and the risk of spousal violence against women." *Journal of Marriage and the Family*, 61, 947–958.

Madriz, E. (1997). *Nothing bad happens to good girls: The impact of fear of crime on women's lives*. Berkeley: University of California Press.

Madriz, E. (1998). "Using focus groups with lower socioeconomic status Latina women." *Qualitative Inquiry*, 4, 114–128.

Madriz, E. (2000). "Focus groups in feminist research." In Norman K. Denzin and Y. S. Lincoln (Eds.), *Handbook of Qualitative Research*. Thousand Oaks, CA: Sage Publications, Inc.

Mahmood, Saba. (2000). "Feminist Theory, Embodiment, and the Docile Agent: Some Reflections on the Egyptian Islamic Revival." *Cultural Anthropology*, Vol. 16, No. 2, 202–236.

Majumdar, Rochona. (2003). "History of Women's Rights: A Non-Historicist Reading." *Economic and Political Weekly*, Vol. 38, No. 22 (May 31–June 6), 2130–2134.

Mandelbaum, D. G. (1988). *Women's Seclusion and men's honor: Sex Roles in North India, Bangladesh and Pakistan*. Tucson: The University of Arizona Press.

Maru, V. (2010). "Access to Justice and Legal Empowerment: A Review of World Bank Practice." *Hague Journal on the Rule of Law*, 2 (2), 259–281.

McWilliams, Monica. (1998). "Violence Against Women in Societies Under Stress." In Rebecca Emerson Dobash and Russell P Dobash (Eds.), *Rethinking Violence Against Women*. Thousand Oaks, CA: Sage Publications, Inc.

McCloskey, L. A. (1996). "Socioeconomic and coercive power within the family." *Gender and Society*, 10 (4), 449–463.
McNay, L. (1999). "Gender, Habitus and the Field: Pierre Bourdieu and the Limits of Reflexivity." *Theory, Culture and Society*, 16 (1), 95–117.
Meier, J. (1997). "Domestic violence, character and social change in the welfare reform debate." *Law and Policy*, 19 (2), 205–263.
Miah, M. M. R. (1992). "The Cultural-Structural Contexts of High Fertility in Bangladesh: A Sociological Analysis." *International Review of Modern Sociology*, 22, 99–110.
Mies, M. (1982). *Lacemakers in Narsapur: Indian Housewives Produce for the World Market*. London: Zed Press.
Mies, M. (1986). *Patriarchy and accumulation on a world scale: Women in the International Division of Labor*. London: Zed Books.
Miles, M. and Huberman, A. M. (1984). *Qualitative Data Analysis: A Source Book of New Methods*. Beverly Hills, CA: Sage Publications, Inc.
Miller, B. D. (1981). *The Endangered Sex. Neglect of Female Children in Rural North India*. Ithaca, N.Y.: Cornell University Press.
Minault, G. (1981). *The Extended Family: Women and Political Participation in India and Pakistan*. Columbia, Missouri: South Asia Books.
Mizan, A. N. (1994). *In Quest of Empowerment: The Grameen Bank Impact on Women's Power and Status*. Dhaka: University Press Limited.
Moghadam, V. M. (1990). *Gender, Development, and Policy: Toward Equity and Empowerment*. Helsinki: World Institute for Development Economics Research of the United Nations University.
Mohanty, C. T. (1991). "Under Western eyes: feminist scholarship and colonial discourses." In C. T. Mohanty., A. Russo and L. Torres (Eds.), *Third World Women and the Politics of Feminism*. Bloomington. IN: Indiana University Press.
Momin, M. A. (1992). *Rural poverty and agrarian structure in Bangladesh*. New Delhi: Vikas Publishing House.
Monsoor, T. (1999). *From patriarchy to gender equity: family law and its impact on women in Bangladesh*. Dhaka: University Press Limited.
Moore, A. M. (1997). "Intimate Violence: Does socioeconomic status matter?" In A. Carderelli (Ed.), *Violence between intimate partners*. Boston: Allyn and Bacon.
Moore, H. L. (1991). *Households and Gender Relations: The Modelling of the Economy*. [draft paper] Department of Anthropology, London School of Economics.
Moore, L. W. and Miller, M. (1999). "Initiating research with doubly vulnerable populations." *Journal of Advanced Nursing*, 30 (5), 1034–1040.
Morshed, S. M. (1996). "Department of Narcotic Control: Dhaka, Bangladesh." *Narcotic control bulletin*, 8, 1–70.
Nachmias, C. F. and Nachmias, D. (1996). *Research Methods in the Social Sciences*. Arnold: London.
Nader, L. and Grande, E. (2002). "Current Illusions and Delusions about Conflict Management in Africa and Elsewhere." *Law and Social Inquiry*, 27 (3), 573–595.
Nath, J. N. (1984). *Dynamics of Socio-economic Change and the Role and Status of Women in Natunpur: Case Study of a Bangladesh Village*, unpublished Ph.D. dissertation, Department of Sociology, University of Dhaka.
National Institute of Population Research and Training. (2006). Bangladesh Urban Health Survey.
Naved, R. and Persson, L. (2005). "Factors associated with spousal physical violence against women in Bangladesh." *Studies in Family Planning*, 36, 289–300.

Naved, R., Azim, S., Persson, L. and Bhuiya, A. (2002). *Women's health and domestic violence against women in Bangladesh.* Dhaka, Bangladesh: Urban Primary Health Care Project – Asia Development Bank.

Nazneen, R. (1998). "Violence in Bangladesh." In S. French., W. Teays and L. M. Purdy (Eds.), *Violence against women: Philosophical Perspectives.* Cornell University Press. Ithaca and London.

Noman, A. (1983). *Status of Women and Fertility in Bangladesh.* Dhaka: The University Press Limited.

Nussbaum, M. C. (2000). *Women and Human Development: The Capabilities Approach.* Cambridge: Cambridge University Press.

Nussbaum, M. C. (2011). *Creating Capabilities: The Human Development Approach.* Cambridge: Harvard University Press.

Nussbaum, M. C., and Glover, J. (1995). *Women, Culture and Development – A Study of Human Capabilities.* Oxford: Clarendon Press.

O'Neill, D. (1998). "A post-structuralist review of the theoretical literature surrounding wife abuse." *Violence Against Women,* 4, 457–490.

Olavarrieta, C. D. and Sotelo, J. (1996). "Domestic violence in Mexico." *Journal of the American Medical Society,* 275, 1937–1941.

Ortner, S. B. (1995). *Making Gender: Toward a Feminist Theory of Practice.* Westermarck Lecture at Helsinki University.

Ortner, S. B. (1974). "Is Female to Male as Nature is to Culture?" In M. Z. Rosaldo and L. Lamphere (Eds.), *Women, Culture and Society.* Stanford: Stanford University Press.

Ortner, S. B. (1984). "Theory in Anthropology since the Sixties." *Comparative Studies in Society and History,* 26 (1), 126–166.

Ortner, S. B. (1989). *High Religion: A cultural and Political History of Sherpa Buddhism.* Princeton, NJ: Princeton University Press.

Ortner, S. B. (1994). "Theory in Anthropology since the Sixties." In B. D. Nicholas. and G. Eley and S. B. Ortner (Eds.), *Culture/Power/History – A Reader in Contemporary Social Theory.* Princeton University Press, Princeton.

Ortner, S. B. (1996). *Making Gender. The Politics and Erotics of Culture.* Boston: Beacon Press.

Osella, F. and Osella, C. (2000). *Social Mobility in Kerala: Modernity and Identity in Conflict.* London and Sterling: Pluto Press.

Östör, A. (1984). "Chronology, Category, and Ritual." In D. I. Kertzer and J. Keith (Eds.), *Age and Anthropological Theory.* Ithaca, NY: Cornell University Press.

Pagelow, M. D. (1984). *Family Violence.* New York: Praeger.

Panda, P. and Agarwal, B. (2005). "Marital Violence, Human Development and Women's Property Status in India." *World Development,* 33 (5), 823–850.

Pandey, G. K., Dutt, D. and Banerjee, B. (2009). "Partner and relationship factors in domestic violence: Perspectives of women from a slum in Calcutta, India." *Journal of Interpersonal Violence,* July 24 (7), 1175–1191.

Papanek, H. and Minault, G. (1982). *Separate Worlds: Studies of Purdah in South Asia.* Delhi: Chanakya Publications.

Parmar, Aradhana. (2003). "Micro-credit, Empowerment and Agency: Re-evaluating the Discourse." *Canadian Journal of Development Studies,* 24 (3), 461–476.

Patton, M. Q. (1990). *Qualitative evaluation and research methods.* Newbury Park, CA: Sage Publications, Inc.

Paudel, G. S. (2007). "Domestic Violence against Women in Nepal." *Gender, Technology and Development,* 11 (2), 199–233.

Pence, E. and Paymar, M. (1993). *Education Groups for Men who Batter – The Duluth Model*. New York: Springer Publishing Company.

Peter, Fabienne. (2003). "Gender and the foundations of social choice: The role of Situated Agency." *Feminist Economics,* 9 (2–3), 13–32.

Peterson, S. (2005). "How (the Meaning of) Gender Matters in Political Economy." *New Political Economy,* 10 (4), 499–521.

Pryer, J., Rogers, S. and Rahman, A. (2005). "Work-disabling Illness as a Shock for Livelihoods and Poverty in Dhaka Slums, Bangladesh." *International Planning Studies,* 10 (1), 69–80.

Raheja, G. G. (1994). "Women's Speech Genres, Kinship and Contradiction." In N. Kumar (Ed.), W*omen as Subjects. South Asian Histories*. New Delhi: Stree.

Raheja, G. G. and Gold, A. G. (1994). *Listen to the heron's words: Reimagining gender and kinship in North India*. Berkeley: University of California Press.

Rahman, A. (1999). "Micro-Credit Initiatives for Equitable and Sustainable Development: Who Pays?" *World Development,* 27 (1), 67–82.

Rahman, A. (2001). *Women and Microcredit in Rural Bangladesh – An anthropological study of Grameen Bank Lending*. Boulder: Westview Press.

Rahman, L. and Vijayendra, R. (2004). "The Determinants of Gender Equity in India: Examining Dyson and Moore's Thesis with New Data." *Population and Development Review,* 30 (2), 239–268.

Rahman, M. M. (1999). Population of Sylhet District During British Period. In S. U. Ahmed (Ed.), *Sylhet: History and Heritage*. Bangladesh Itihas Samiti (Bangladesh History Association), Bangladesh.

Raj, A. and Silverman, J. (2002a). "Violence against immigrant women: The roles of culture, context, and legal immigrant status on intimate partner violence." *Violence Against Women,* 8, 367–398.

Raj, A. and Silverman, J. (2002b). "Intimate partner violence against South Asian women in Greater Boston." *Journal of the American Medical Women's Association,* 57, 111–114.

Rakodi, C. (2002). "A livelihood approach-conceptual issues and definition." In C. Rakodi and T. Lloyd-Jones (Eds.), *Urban Livelihoods: A People-Centred Approach to Reducing Poverty*. London: Earthscan.

Rana, M. D. S. (2009). "Status of water use sanitation and hygienic condition of urban slums: A study on Rupsha Ferighat slum, Khulna." *Desalination,* 246, 322–328.

Raphael, J. (2001). "Domestic violence as a welfare to work barrier." In C. M. Renzetti., J. L. Edleson and R. K. Bergen (Eds.), *The sourcebook on violence against women*. Thousand Oaks, CA: Sage Publications, Inc.

Rashid, S. F. (2007). "Durbolota (Weakness), Chinta Rog (Worry Illness), and Poverty – Explanations of White Discharge among Married Adolescent Women in an Urban Slum in Dhaka, Bangladesh." *Medical Anthropology Quarterly,* 21 (1), 108–132.

Raver, C. C. (2003). "Does work pay psychologically as well as economically? The role of employment in predicting depressive symptoms and parenting among low-income families." *Child Development,* 74, 1720–1736.

Renzetti, C. M. and R. M. Lee. (Eds.). (1993). *Researching Sensitive Topics*. Newbury Park, CA: Sage Publications, Inc.

Riger, S. and Krieglstein, M. (2000). "The impact of welfare reform on men's violence against women." *American Journal of Community Psychology,* 28 (5), 631–647.

Risseeuw, C. (1988). *The Fish Don't Talk about the Water: Gender Transformation, Power and Assistance Among Women in Sri Lanka*. Leiden: Brill Publishers.

Ritzer, George. (1992). *Sociological Theory*. New York: McGraw-Hill.

References

Rodman, H. (1972). "Marital Power and the Theory of Resources in Cultural Context." *Journal of Comparative Family Studies*, 3 (Spring), 50–70.

Rodriguez, E., Lasch, K. E., Chandra, P. and Lee, J. (2001). "Family violence, employment status, welfare benefits, and alcohol drinking in the United States: What is the relation?" *Journal of Epidemiological Community Health*, 55, 172–178.

Romero, D., Chavkin, W., Wise, P. H. and Smith, L. A. (2003). "Low-income mothers' experience with poor health, hardship, work, and violence: Implications for policy." *Violence Against Women*, 9, 1231–1244.

Roseberry, W. (1994). "Hegemony and the Language of Contention." In Joseph, G. M. and D. Nugent (Eds.), *Everyday Forms Of State Formation. Revolution and the Negotiation of Rule in Modern Mexico*. Durham, NC: Duke University Press.

Roy, K. C., Tisdell, C. and Alauddin, M. (1992). "Rural–urban migration and poverty in South Asia." *Journal of Contemporary Asia*, 22 (1), 57–72.

Rozario, S. (1992). *Women and Social Change in a Bangladeshi Village*. London: Zed Books.

Rozario, S. (2001). *Purity and Communal Boundaries: Women and Social Change in a Bangladesh Village*. Dhaka: The University Press Limited.

Rozario, S. and Geoffrey, S. (2010). "Gender, religious change and sustainability in Bangladesh." *Women's Studies International Forum*, 33, 354–364.

Rubin, Gayle. (1996). "The Traffic in Women: Notes on the Political Economy of Sex." In Joan Wallach Scott (Ed.) *Feminism in History*. Oxford: Oxford University Press.

Säävälä, M. (1997). *Child as Hope-Contextualizing Fertility Transition in Rural South India*. Helsinki: Helsinki University Press.

Säävälä, M. (1998). "The 'Hindu Joint Family': Past and Present." In A. Parpola and S. Tenhunen (Eds.), *Changing Patterns of Family and Kinship in South Asia*. Finnish Oriental Society, Vol. 84.

Säävälä, M. (2001). *Fertility and Familial Power Relations: Procreation in South India*. Nordic Institute of Asian Studies Monograph Series, No. 87. Richmond, Surrey: Curzon.

Samaddar, R. (1999). *The Marginal Nation: Transborder Migration from Bangladesh to West Bengal*. Dhaka: Dhaka University Press.

Scanzoni, J. (1972). *Sexual bargaining*. Chicago: University of Chicago Press.

Schiamberg, L. B. and Gans, D. (1999). "An ecological framework for contextual risk factors in elder abuse by adult children." *Journal of Elder Abuse and Neglect*, 11, 79–103.

Schuler, S. R. and Hashemi, S. M. (1994). "Credit Programs, Women's Empowerment, and Contraceptive Use in rural Bangladesh." *Studies in Family Planning*, 25 (2), 65–76.

Schuler, S. R., Bates, L. M. and Islam, F. (2008). "Women's Rights, Domestic Violence, and Recourse Seeking in Rural Bangladesh." *Violence Against Women*, 14 (3), 326–345.

Schuler, S. R., Hashemi, S. M. and Badal, S. (1998). "Men's Violence against Women in Rural Bangladesh: Undermined or Exacerbated by Microcredit Programmes?" *Development in Practice*, 8, 148–157.

Schuler, S. R., Hashemi, S. M., Riley, A. P. and Akhter, S. (1996). "Credit Programmes, Patriarchy and Men's Violence against Women in Rural Bangladesh." *Social Science and Medicine*, 43 (12), 1729–1742.

Scott, J. (1990). *Domination and the Arts of Resistance: Hidden Transcripts*. New Haven: Yale University Press.

Scott, J. W. (1988). *Gender and the Politics of History*. New York: Columbia University Press.

Scott, R. W. (2001). *Institutions and Organizations*. London: Sage Publications, Inc.

Sen, A. (2001). "Many faces of gender inequality." *World Economic Forum*, 2009. The India Gender Gap Review 2009. Geneva.

Sen, A. K. (1990). "Gender and Cooperative Conflicts." In I. Tinker (Eds.), *Persistent Inequalities: Women and world Development*. New York: Oxford University Press.

Sen, A. K. and Sengupta, S. (1983). "Malnutrition of Rural Children and the Sex Bias." *Economic and Political Weekly*, 18 (19–21), 855–864.

Sharma, M. K. (2004). "Conciliation and Mediation." *Delhi Judicial Academy Journal*, 3(ii). High Court of Delhi. www.delhimediationcentre.gov.in/articles.htm#introducing.

Sharma, U. (1986). *Women's Work, Class, and the Urban Household: A Study of Shimla, North India*. London: Tavistock.

Silva, M. C. (1995). *Ethical Guidelines in the Conduct, Dissemination, and Implementation of Nursing Research*. Washington, DC: American Nurses Publishing.

Skeldon, R. (1997). *Migration and Development: A Global Perspective*. London: Belhaven Press.

Spivak, G. (1988). "Can the Subaltern Speak?" In Nelson, C. and Grossberg, L. (Eds.), *Marxism and the Interpretation of Culture*. Urbana: University of Illinois Press.

Sprey, J. (1979). "Conflict theory and the study of marriage and the family." In W. R. Burr., R. Hill, F. I. Nye and I. Reiss (Eds.), *Contemporary theories about the family* (Vol. 2). New York: Free Press.

Squires, Judith. (2007). *The New Politics of Gender Equality*. London: Palgrave Macmillan.

Srinivas, M. N. (1979). "The Fieldworker and The Field – A Village in Karnataka." In M. N. Srinivas., A. M. Shah and E. A. Ramaswamy (Eds.), *The Fieldworker and The Field – Problems and Challenges in Sociological Investigation.* Delhi: Oxford University Press.

Srinivas, M. N. (1984). *Some Reflections on Dowry*. New Delhi: Centre for Women's Development Studies.

Stake, R. E. (1978). "The case study method of social inquiry." *Educational Researcher*, 7 (2), 5–8.

Steele, F., Amin, S. and Naved, R. T. (1998). *The impact of a micro-credit programme on women's empowerment and fertility behavior in rural Bangladesh* (Policy Research Division Working Paper 115). New York: Population Council.

Stockard, Jean and Johnson, Miriam M. (1980). *Sex Roles: Sex Inequality and Sex Role Development*. Washington, DC: Prentice Hall Sociology Series.

Straus, M. (1994). "State-to-state differences in social inequality and social bonds in relation to assaults on wives in the United States." *Journal of Comparative Family Studies*, 25, 7–24.

Straus, M. A. (1980). "Sexual inequality and wife beating." In M. A. Straus. and G. T. Hotaling (Eds.), *The social causes of husband wife violence*. Minneapolis: University of Minnesota Press.

Subedi, P. (1997). *Nepali women rising*. Kathmandu: Sahayogi Press. Nepal.

Tan, J. (1981). *A Comparative Study of the Marital Fertility of Older Women in Nepal, Bangladesh and Sri Lanka.* Unpublished PhD dissertation. Princeton University.

Tenhunen, S. (1997). *Secret Freedom in The City-Women's Wage Work and Agency in Calcutta*. Helsinki: Helsinki University Printing House.

Tenhunen, S. (2006). "Transforming Boundaries: Women's Work and Domesticity in Calcutta." In L. Fruzzetti and S. Tenhunen (Eds.), *Culture, Power, and Agency: Gender in Indian Ethnography.* Calcutta: Stree.

Tenhunen, S. (2009). *Means of Awakening – Gender, Politics and Practice in Rural India.* Calcutta: Stree.

The World Bank. (2012). *Gender Equality and Development.* World development report.

Therborn, G. (2004). *Between Sex and Power: Family in the world, 1900–2000.* London: Routledge.

Tjaden, P. and Thoennes, N. (2000). *Full report of the prevalence, incidence, and consequences of violence against women: findings from the National Violence Against Women Survey.* Washington, DC: National Institute of Justice, Office of Justice Programs, United States Department of Justice and Centers for Disease Control and Prevention.

Todaro, M. P. (1993). *Economic Development in the Third World.* Hyderabad: Orient Longman.

Tolan, P. H. and Guerra, N. G. (1994). *What works in reducing adolescent violence: an empirical review of the field.* Boulder, CO: University of Colorado, Center for the Study and Prevention of Violence.

Tolman, R. and Rosen, D. (2001). "Domestic violence in the lives of women receiving welfare." *Violence Against Women*, 7, 141–158.

Trautmann, T. (1981). *Dravidian kinship.* Berkeley: University of California Press.

Trawick, M. (1996 [1990]). *Notes on Love in a Tamil Family.* Berkeley: University of California Press.

Tucker, Kenneth H. Jr. (1998). *Anthony Giddens and Modern Social Theory.* London: Sage Publications, Inc.

Turner, R. J., Wheaton, B. and Lloyd, D. A. (1995). "The epidemiology of social stress." *American Sociological Review*, 60 (1), 104–125.

Udayagiri, Mridula. (1995). "Challenging Modernization: Gender and Development, Postmodernism Feminism." In Marianne Marchand and Jane I. Parpart (Ed.) *Feminism/Postmodernism/Development.* London: Routledge.

Uddin, M. J. (2003). "Resettlement and Social Structure of a Slum in Greater Dhaka: A Case Study," *Social Science Review*, 20 (1), 57–72.

United Nations Children's Fund. (2009). *A Perspective on gender equality in Bangladesh. From young girl to adolescent: What is lost in Transition? Analysis based on selected results of the Multiple Indicator Cluster Survey 2009.* UNICEF.

United Nations Development Fund for Women. (2005). *Progress of South Asian women, 2005: A series for the fifth South Asia regional ministerial conference celebrating Beijing plus ten.* New Delhi: Institute of Social Studies Trust. Unnithan-Kumar, M. (2003). "Spirits of the womb: Migration, reproductive choice and healing in Rajasthan," *Contributions to Indian Sociology*, 37, 163–188.

Uusikylä, H. (2000). *The Other Half of My Body: Coming into Being in Rural Bangladesh.* Research Reports No. 236, Department of Sociology, University of Helsinki: Helsinki University Printing House.

Van Schendal, W. (1981). *Peasant mobility: The odds of life in rural Bangladesh.* Assen: Van Gorcum.

Vatuk, S. (2006). "Domestic Violence and Marital Breakdown in India: A View from the Family Courts." In L. Fruzzetti. and S. Tenhunen (Eds.), *Culture, Power, And Agency: Gender In Indian Ethnography.* Calcutta: Stree.

Wahed, T. and Bhuiya, A. (2007). "Battered bodies and shattered minds: Violence against women in Bangladesh." *Indian Journal of Medical Research*, 126, 341–354.

Walum-Richardson, Laurel. (1981). *The Dynamics of Sex and Gender: A Sociological Perspective*. Boston: Houghton Mifflin.

Weismantel, M. (1988). *Food, Gender and Poverty in the Ecuadorian Andes*. Philadelphia: University of Pennsylvania Press.

White, S. C. (1992). *Arguing with the Crocodile: Gender and Class in Bangladesh*. Dhaka: The University Press Limited.

Whitehead, A. (1990). "Rural Women and Food Production in Sub-Saharan Africa." In J. Dreze and A. K. Sen (Eds.), *The Political Economy of Hunger, I: Entitlement and Well-Being*. Oxford: Clarendon Press.

Whyte, R. O. and Whyte, P. (1982). *The women of rural Asia*. Boulder: Westview Press.

William, S., Gustavo, A., Peter, M. L., Naved, R. T. and Thornton, J. (2011). "Prevalence and Correlates of Physical Spousal Violence Against Women in Slum and Nonslum Areas of Urban Bangladesh." *Journal of Interpersonal Violence*, 26 (13), 2592–2618.

Wilson-Williams, L., Stephenson, R., Juvekar, S. and Andes, K. (2008). "Domestic Violence and Contraceptive Use in a Rural Indian Village." *Violence Against Women*, 14 (10), 1181–1198.

Wolfe, D. M. (1959). "Power and authority in the family." In D. Cartwright (Ed.), *Studies in social power*. Ann Arbor: University of Michigan Press.

Wood, G. and Salway, S. (2000). "Policy Arena – Introduction: Securing Livelihoods in Dhaka Slums." *Journal of International Development*, 12, 669–668.

World Health Organization. (1997). *Violence against women: a priority health issue*. Geneva: WHO. (document WHO/FRH/WHD/97.8).

World Health Organization. (2002). *World report on violence and health*. Geneva: WHO.

World Health Organization. (2010). *Preventing Intimate Partner and Sexual Violence against Women: Taking Action and Generating Advice*. Geneva: WHO.

www.bbs.gov.bd/dataindex/Millenium percent20Development percent20Goals.pdf.

Index

Page numbers in **bold** denote tables.

abandon/abandoned: abusive spouses 84; by husband 86, 94
abandonment 148, 151
Abdullah, T. 47, 81
adolescent girls 31, 45; arrangement of marriage 44; chastity protected 52; father taking no responsibility 142; married at 16, 122; not allowed to discuss husband selection 57; sick and thin 77
ADR (Alternative Dispute Resolution) 15
abuse 143, 150; of bride 65, 88; divorce on grounds of 13; extreme cases of 93; failure in dowry promise 65; with filthy language 85; mental or emotional 89; minor 96; by mother-in-law 122, 133; outside help to stop the 126; physical 5–6, 150; physical and mental 116; reduces risk of 81; sexual 151; by sister-in-law 138; spouse 90; verbal 6, 87–89; wife 5, 85, 87, 125; wife can seek an injunction 15; women suffering from 84; of young women 123
abused women 4, 6, 17, 73, 105, 130, 146
abusive: adults 17n7; behavior 91; husbands and in-laws 126–127, 136; language 87; marriages 96; names 33; spouses abandoned 84; words 77, 88
advocates 22, 25, 117, 136; advise to file a suit 143; advise returning to husband's house 144; of both sides 134–135; counseling center 131, 133–134, 144; decision of 142; empty promises of husband 133; engaged in ADR processes 145; female 26, 134; free of charge 131; help to get maintenance costs 142, 145; human rights 130; orders 139; power asymmetry with clients 146; see sufferings of divorced women 135; take a lot of money to file a case 115; try to stop quarrels 140, 142
affinal family 15, 60, 63, 67, 75; demands for money 111; new wife 122; return to 145
affinal home 22, 109; does not want to return to 135; return to 134, 138, 144; taken from 138; violent 137, 151; vulnerability in 133
affines 59, 64, 67, 79; attending *shalish* 139; demand of dowry 66; domestic violence by 3, 16, 18–19, 23, 77–78, 92, 105, 136–137, 150; empty promises 135; entitled to make demands 145; giving poison 144; living with 92, 122; living separately from 137; no wedding feast arranged 108; violent 85, 133–134
Afia 60–61, 91; woman grocer 74
Afsar, R. 27–28, 30–31, 36–37
Agarwal, B. 1, 12, 69, 77–78, 81, 143
Agnes, F. 1, 4
Ahmed, S. 43, 45, 47–48, 51, 54, 56
Ali, S. 4, 14, 107
Ali Noor 137, 139–141
Ameen, N. 4–5, 15, 36, 54, 65–66, 107, 111, 128
arranged marriage 36, 52, 54, 58–60, 66, 75, 108–109, 113, 120, 122, 124, 137
Ashrafun, L. 46, 128
Asian Development Bank 17n6
attiyas (kin) 37
Aura, S. 3, 12, 43, 88, 101, 123
Aziz, K.M.A. 43, 56, 59, 68n4

Bangladesh Bureau of Statistics 2, 17n4, 42n4

Bangladesh Family Court Ordinance 1985 14
basti life 86–87, 149
Basu, S. 1, 4, 19, 132
Bates, L.M. 3–4, 147, 150, 153
Beauty: divorced by second husband 75; living alone in an urban *basti* 76; patriarchal repression 77; widowhood 74
Begum, A. 120
BegumAfia 60–61
belonging: affected by shift in space at marriage 60; cannot be guaranteed 35; feelings of 106; to lower socio-economic class 152; natal and marital 62; sense of 68n4
belongingness 106; women deprived of 117
Bertocci, P.J. 44, 59
Bhuiya, A. 4–6
Bhuiyan, R. 4, 13–14
birth 57, 59, 61, 137; child 43, 55–56, 87, 94; of a daughter 44, 46, 75, 100, 122, 125; to a dead child 56; family 62; first child 54–56, 116, 124; mother died after 35; order 109; place of 22, 27–28, 34, 36, 75; skewed sex ratio 1; of a son 46, 56, 117, 138; stillborn children 77
Bourdieu, P. 9–10, 54, 67, 107
bride(s) 57, 141; abused by senior women 88; assimilation to husband's family 62–63; devalued status 65; dreams of 147; educational status 59; faults 90; formally says *kobul* 60; gifts from family 64; meet and talk with groom 58; mismatch in ages with groom 114; Muslim 60; natal family 60, 64–65, 124; new (*notun bou*) 62, 65; newly married 56, 60; parents and kin 61; presents 109; price/dower (*Den Mahar*) 95, 108, 127, 131, 141; *stridhan* 64; subordinate to husband/senior men and to mother-in-law/senior females 48–49; vulnerable in Bangladeshi society 124; wedding gifts 110; young 88, 124

caste 101, 147; inequalities 88, 118, 125; inter-caste marriages 55; low-caste Hindus 24, 32; lower 125; marriage within 54; no system 36; occupation 33, 40; position 47; scheduled 116, 118; system 32, 55
chastity 50–52, 124
Chaya 113; early marriage 124; first child 116; son 117; unfaithful husband 113, 116, 126; violent mother-in-law 125; vulnerability 126
Chen, L.C. 47–48
child marriage 115; restrictions on 131
Child Marriage Restraint Act 1929 115
Child Marriage Restraint (Amendment) Ordinance 1984 13, 54
Chowdhury, E.H. 4, 128, 152
Christians, C.G. 22, 42n2
conjugal life 55, 64, 74, 87, 102–103, 137, 139; disorganized 120; dominance of a mother-in-law 123; rearrange 135; slum women 97–98
contraception 56, 87
contraceptives 87, 100
counseling center 16, 21, 23, 25–26, 117, 137, 143, 153; advice on divorce 121; advocates 22, 115, 131, 133–135, 144; BLAST 16; clients 106–107; facilitators 128; female victims 150; file a suit 144; formal support 108; help to rearrange marriage 112; inside the court arena 20; legal help 119, 127; maintenance costs for children 117, 142; maintenance payments 145; mediations 152; no long-term supervision available 146; non-governmental 7, 18–19; registration file 109; to resolve divorce case 113; *shalish* (mediation) 128, 132, 136, 139, 141–142, 144
co-wife/co-wives (*sotin, sotiner sangsar*) 9, 97, 99–101, 125–126, 142; domestic violence 125
Crapanzano, V. 76–77
cross cousins 54, 59; paternal 108–109
Cruelty to Women (Deterrent Punishment) Act 1983 14

daughter-in-law 12, 43, 53, 75, 104, 108, 125, 133–134; contested relationship with mother-in-law 88; in marital home 152; member of affinal kin group 136; traditional power relationship with mother-in-law 72
death: attempted murder 66, 144–145; attempted murder of children 122; dowry murders 1; homicides 3; murder 65, 131; murderer 46; *see also* suicide(s)
de Beauvoir, S. 151
Demographic Health Survey 54
Den Mahar (bride price or dower) 95, 108, 127, 131, 141

developing countries 18–19, 120, 147
discrimination 5, 9–11, 85, 104, 123; against women 131, 148; in the family 15; protect women from 12
discriminatory food and health care practices 1; laws governing women's private lives 131
dishonor/dishonored 94; abusers may feel 127; affected other daughters 109; family 117, 138; husband feels 142; rescue parents from 61; wife 111
Dissolution of Muslim Marriage Law 1939 15
divorce 13, 59, 61, 78, 82, 90, 99, 121, 131, 137, 141, 143, 151; benefits from 136; civil law remedies 15; dissolution of marriage by death or 14; encouraged/forced by parents 36, 77; family appeal for 134; family pressure on husband 138; filing for 127; granted 150; initiated by wife (*khula* or *mubara'at*) 13; legal 15; letter 123; limited powers of Union Councils 128; Muslim rights 135; no provision in Hindu religion or law 13, 92–94, 131; papers (*Talak nama*) 115, 140; practice in Islam 92, 140; rate increased 148; social stigma 152; *talaq* 13, 94, 112; threats of 6; views of Muslim women 94; views of natal families 96, 105; views of slum women 16; women's rights of 94–95, 131, 136; *see also* Muslim Marriage and Divorces (Registration) Act 1974
divorced man 94–95
divorced woman/divorcee 52, 93, 95, 113, 143; creates problems for natal family 90; guardianship by male relative 47, 74; held in low regard 105, 112–113; living alone 75–76; no defined place 137; rural 123; sufferings of 135; vulnerability 96
Dobash, R. 7, 59, 105
domestic violence 53, 84, 107, 131, 142, 149–150; contested relationship between spouses 87; coping strategies 16, 20, 86, 89, 96, 104; by co-wife 125; effects of 148; emergence and practice of 108; freed from 137; long-term 15, 127; on lower socio-economic strata 18; lower in urban populations 19; maintenance payments 144; in marriages between relatives 111; in Nepal 89; perpetrators of 4; resist 85; stand up against 123; tough punishments for 14; typical features of 97; victims of 1, 5, 16, 108, 126, 145, 149; widespread 147; women's voices raised against 152–153
domestic violence by affines (in-laws) 19, 74, 77–78, 92–93, 136, 143; by female in-laws or a co-wife 125; in marital home 112–113; by mother-in-law 16, 18, 66, 77–78, 105, 111, 122–123, 125, 133, 136, 138
domestic violence causes 6, 22, 106, 128; conditions that encourage 151; dowry 108; factors associated with 5, 7; factors contributing to 123; potential 64
domestic violence by husbands 82, 105–106, 143; addict 121; extra-marital relationships 113
domestic violence mediations 132, 144; friends try to mitigate 73; Hindu women's process of solving 92; informal 150; informal help commonly fails 16; legal remedy socially undesirable 141; try to resolve 126; working to combat 128
domestic violence, risk of 4, 126; increased 5, 71; reduced 143
domestic violence against women 1, 22, 84, 147, 150; by affines 3, 23, 78; attitudinal problem of men 89; causes 7, 16, 85, 106, 113; contributing factors 123; coping strategies 147; critical problem 4, 6; in the home 107; law enforcement and state intervention required 153; legitimated 4; no specific law for 15; providing legal advice 128; regular events 87; rural 5; women's description 85
domestic violence against young wives 19; culturally rooted 74; impoverished conditions encourage 151
dowry (*joutuk*) 64, 77, 117; cause of domestic violence 108; deaths, murders 1, 3, 66; demands 5, 14–15, 55, 61, 65, 113, 124–125, 150; insufficient 89; marriage without 67, 120–121, 137; none given 65, 125; not demanded 61, 113, 137; practice(s) 64, 66–68, 148, 152; pressure to pay 111, 144; Prohibition Act 1980 14; provided by natal family 47; refusal to give 6; system 14; *see also Den Mahar*, marriage gifts
drug addict 94, 120–122
drug addiction 120, 122, 150; *see also* heroin
Dube, L. 62

early marriage 5, 49, 54–56, 68, 109, 124
education 101; children's 72; daughter's 72; formal 68, 120; levels 72; marriage as barrier to 124; minimal level 124; poor 124; religious 122; of spouse 59
educational attainments 20, 49; backgrounds 29; backward 147; institutions 2, 124; poor standing of women 1; status 59
education daughters' 50, 55–56; between first and eighth grade 40; girls' 49–50; higher 49; at home 50; level 22, 40; levels of wife and husband 20; limited 19; primary school 20, 50; religious 50; secondary 41; university 23; women's 36; women's participation 2
extended households 38, 48, 88

family honor 15, 144; destroy 54, 139, 144; dishonored 138; importance of chastity 50–51; losing 50; daughter's marriage 114, 124; primary education for daughters 50; protect 55; rebuild 35–36; tarnishing 6
father-in-law 16, 18, 43, 47, 63, 125, 133–134, 136, 144–145
Feldman, S. 2, 148
female infanticide 1, 46
Flick, U. 21–22
Fruzzetti, L. 11, 37, 58–59

Garcia-Moreno, C. 18–19
Gardner, K. 53–54, 58–59, 62, 76
Giddens, A. 10–11
Golapi 119, 125; elopement 118; marriage not approved 117
government shelter home 119
groom 61, 63; friend of 118; garments 66; gifts exchanged 64; good 44, 54; helped to establish future economic security 65, 109; made no demand for dowry 113; meet and talk with 57–58; older 113; personal life 61; photo 57; register the marriage 60; suitable 55, 61; *varadakhshina* (gift of the groom) 64; well-to-do 114
groom's family 61, 65, 122; demand larger dowry 124; demands gifts 64, 66, 68; gifts to **110**; marriage proposal from 61; may not accept the bride 117; payment of dowry to 111; send photos 57; social commerce of marriage gifts 65
gushti (localized patriline) 59, 62, 68n1, 68n4

Hadi, A. 4, 84, 107, 116
Hadith of prophet Mohammad (SM) 79
Hampton, R.L. 5, 17n7
Heise, L.L. 18–19, 91
heroin 120–122
hidden resistance power 104; transcripts 103–104; *see also* resist, resistance
Hindu 52, 64; community 13, 67; deities 33; dowry practices 67; laws 13, 144; man 32, 118; man of different caste 118; parents 67; society 45, 67, 92; sons 45–46; student mess 40
Hindu families 33; low-caste 32; selling lands 67
Hindu girls 50, 55, 67; bride newly married 57; daughters 46, 67, 92; teenage 117
Hindu religion 13, 44, 46, 92–93, 116; *Dharmashastra* (code of religion) 64
Hindus 50; approved marriage 64; *jamai sasthi* 63; low-caste 24; marry within their caste 54
Hindu Widow Remarriage Act 1856 13
Hindu women 13, 24–25, 45–48, 50, 55–56, 67, 84, 87, 92–94, 116, 131, 144
HIV infection 120
Holy Quran 50, 76, 79; verses used to support oppression of women 92; wedding gifts **110**
honor 58; in affinal family 67; of bridegroom 64; daughter's (*izzat*) 109, 112, 114, 124, 139; to daughter's married life 67; family 6, 15, 35–36, 50–51, 54–55; of the husband 59; position of 46; of the son-in-law (*jamai sasthi*) 63; tarnishing women's 71, 73; work of 70
honor, family 144; happiness at cost of (*shomman*) 125; husband's 107; through marriage 150; protect 76–77
Hossain, M. 27, 41
Hossain, S. 30–32
human rights 3, 128, 130, 153; activists 14; advocates 130; women's rights as 152

immigration 29; status 59
incest relationship 114, 126
insecurity 19, 37, 114, 151–152; forces marriage 116; limits women's lives 51; physical 32; social and economic 15, 30, 126, 136
Islam, M. 45, 47–48, 51, 54, 56

Jahan, R. 4, 36, 54, 56, 107, 111, 128

Jain, D. 11
Jansen, E.G. 27, 35–36
Jansen, H. 18–19
Jeffery, P. 1, 3, 43
Jenkins, R. 10
Joyfull 142; blamed for going to legal system 141; mediation case 137; quarreling sister-in-law 139; right to legal justice 140; violence by husband and mother-in-law 138

Kabeer, N. 2, 8, 69, 82, 148
kabin (marriage registration papers) 95, 109, 113, 131, 137
Kandiyoti, D. 2, 48, 77
Karim, A. 28
Kaukinen, C. 73, 82
Khan, S. 63, 77
Kimmel, M.S. 7–9
kinship 4, 8, 123, 149; alliance 66; based societies 43, 59; bonds 44, 109, 127; connections 34; fictive 37, 73; gender inequality 9; ideology 53; structures 43, 125; terms 37, 68n4, 68n5, 68n6, 73; ties 60; traditional safeguards 18; in the urban setting 16
kinship systems Dravidian 54; patrilocal 3; processes of 8; South Asian, structural asymmetry 136
Koenig, M. 3, 6, 107
kosto (pain/difficulties) 85, 87, 104, 133, 137
Kotalova, J. 44–45, 53–54, 56, 59, 62, 68n3
Krishnan, S. 88–89
Kuhn, R. 27–28, 35
Kumar, N. 12, 37, 74

laborers 130; agricultural 36, 98; casual day 33, 38, **40**, 91, 108, 113; immigrants with insufficient skills 29; seasonal 40; in tea gardens 29; women, building construction 70; women, casual day 38, **40**, 80, 101, 108, 137; women, wage 97; young female, migration 27
Lahti, M. 104, 106–107
Lengermann, P.M. 9
Lerner, G. 8
Levi-Strauss, C. 54, 59
Liamputtong, P. 25, 147
love marriage 34, 36, 51, 58, 117–118, 125

Macmillan, R. 73, 82
Madriz, E. 20

maintenance 89; child 117, 127, 134, 140–142, 146; costs 117, 127, 134, 142–145; Hindu women have a right to 13; household 38; problems 5; religious-based laws 13
maintenance payments 144–145; husband not giving 85; regular 143
maintenance suit 14, 144; expensive 15
male domination 1, 9, 11
marital violence 26; become regular and severe 90; parents shocked 111; relationship with structural inequalities 88; risk factors 19
marriage *see* arranged marriage, early marriage, love marriage
marriage gifts 58, 64–65, 109; pressure to give 68; voluntary 66–67; *see also* dowry
marriage proposals 60–61, 108–109, 113, 124
marriage registrar 109, 140
marriage registration papers (*kabin*) 95, 109, 113, 131, 137
marriage transactions 59; gift 65, 68
McNay, L. 10
mediation see *shalish*/mediation
Miah, M.M.R. 63
micro-credit: borrowers 5; lending 38; organizations 5–6; participation 82
migrants 28; agricultural laborers 36; climate 35; face severe problems 32; family 37–38; internal 2; rural poor 37; in urban areas 27
migration 148; causes of 16, 34, 36, 39; to the city 80; family 28, 35; history 34; increased rate of 35; internal 2, 20, 27–28, 35–36, 88; labor 37; lives after 36–37, 132; more scope for women 92; national and international 1, 20; of poor households 16, 34, 39; rural-urban 27–28, 35, 45, 69, 152; stages of 27; trend and flow of 29; urban, effects of 44; women's lives after 21; *see also* immigration
Miles, M. 18
Moni 113; conditions of marriage 109; domestic violence 111–112, 125; early marriage 124; marriage to paternal cross cousin 108; natal family's economic hardship 126; wedding gifts **110**
Morzina 23–24, 32, 75, 77; daughters 46–47, 55–56; economic resources 73; family 37; migration 36; mother-in-law 72; quarrels over water collection 31;

works in bachelor's dormitory of university teachers 23, 71–72
mother-in-law/mothers-in-law 2, 12, 32, 62, 74–75, 108, 125, 134–135; abuse with foul language 133; angry over birth of girl baby 116; bride subordinate to 48, 63; close-kin 112; contested relationship with 88, 150; domestic conflicts with 73; domestic violence by 16, 18, 66, 77–78, 105, 111, 122–123, 125, 133, 136, 138; dominance in conjugal life 123; greed for dowries 109, 126, 144; habit of quarreling 88; happy over birth of boy baby 117, 140; harsh with neighbours 112; important role 123; interference 56; negative role of 84; power relationship with daughter-in-law 72; pressure on new wife to bear children 56; provoke their sons 88; relationships with daughters-in-law 11; tried to poison son's wife 145; wants to take son's wife back 133, 135; young wife disobeys 79
Multiple Indicator Cluster Survey 54
Muslim 24; bride 60; daughter 52; divorcee 75; families 33; girl's education 50; high value of sons 45; husband 13; man 142; oral divorce 112; *pardah* 79; religion 112; religious education 122
Muslim law 47; family 13, 95; personal 13
Muslim Family Laws Ordinance 1961 13–14, 128
Muslim Marriage Act 13
Muslim Marriage and Divorces (Registration) Act 1974 13
Muslim marriages 13, 95; alliances between relatives 111; cross cousin and parallel cousin 54, 59; early 55; equal is desirable 59
Muslims 36, 50; Holy Quran 79; sex of newborn baby 44
Muslim woman/women 23, 45–46, 48, 50, 52, 55, 57, 71, 74, 79–82, 84, 87, 90–92, 94, 108, 113, 131, 135, 142; casual unskilled laborer 80; right to divorce husband 94

Nahida 116, 124; divorce papers 115; husband's incestuous relationship 126; marriage forced by natal family 114; older husband 113, 124
natal family 116; causing stigma for 118; change of residence 120–121; contact by mobile phone 90; contact not allowed by husband 47, 52; divorce problematic for 127; dowry from 65, 67; experience of girlhood in 44; husband economically dependent on 141; husband's 119; inheritance from 47; large 108; left after marriage 34, 54, 60; limited resources to support 109; married couple staying with 60; members 26, 90, 92, 107, 115, 126–128, 130–131, 134, 136, 142; no marriage arranged 99; offer advice 127; oppressors of husband's 131; poor 91–92, 144; poor economic condition 113–114; pressure to bring dowry from 68; protection 125; rarely supports divorce 93; return to (*naior*) 47, 52, 75, 94, 122; seek help from advocates 142; socio-economic condition of 22; unequal treatment of sons and daughters 152; viewed as place of refuge 63; wedding presents from 33; woman's dependency on 124; would not accept daughter back 99
natal home 75, 111–112, 114, 118, 120–121, 138, 151
National Institute of Population Research and Training (NIPORT) 2, 17n5
Naved, R. 4, 107, 147
Nazneen, R. 3, 123
Neharun: maintenance costs 143; polygamous husband 142
Nepal female children 46; violence by husbands 89
Nirmola poisoned 144–145; vulnerable condition 144
Nurjahan 120–121, 124, 126; drug addict husband 120
Nuru Miah 97–99
Nussbaum, M.C. 74, 149, 151

obedience 50; obedient 94; to husband 116
oppression of women 11, 15, 69, 130; resistance to 78, 104
Ortner, S.B. 9, 11–12, 103

parallel cousins 54, 59, 75; *see also* cross cousins
pardah 52, 77, 79; *see also* veil
Parul 55; domestic violence from affines 77–78
Parvin 97; daughters 100; depends on husband's income 101; head injury 98; husband's second marriage 99; *see also* Renu

patriarchal: bargains 2, 148; contract 148; despotism or equilibrium 8; social structures 11, 38, 75, 91
patriarchal social structure 38, 149; challenge to 75; code of conduct 101; laws not strong enough to protect women 131; open resistance to 104; protection and relatedness for women in 103; religion as strongest weapon 92; South Asian 11; *Talaq* as threat 94; traditional 127; women's vulnerability 91, 103, 117
patriarchy 9, 114; blow against 101; classic 2, 48; ideal model of 101; male is superior to female 104–105; overarching power 4; social and religious beliefs in favor of 123; subordinates women in gender relations 11
patrilocal 49; culture 62; extended household 48; kinship systems 3; residence system 47, 151
Patton, M.Q. 21
Peter, F. 69
physical violence 6, 89; higher level 5; *kosto* 104; patriarchal domination 150; prevalence 19; vulnerable to 151
poison 66, 114; in food 144–145
polygamy 5, 15, 41, 131, 148
poverty 1, 27, 31, 37, 63, 82, 104, 116, 152; acute 67; because of daughter's marriage 112; causes for migration 34, 38; cause of violence 84; dream of escaping 35; forced end to formal education 120; gender inequality correlated with 149, 151; lack of work 38; loss of agricultural land due to 28; severe, extreme 113–114, 122, 137; stricken 46, 49, 70, 86–87, 96; sufferings of 34; trapped in 41; in urban slums 29; vicious circle 64; vulnerability of 87; work outside home 70–71, 79
pregnancy 87, 94, 115, 118; deserted during 119; unaccepted 125; violence during 134, 150
pregnant 56, 100, 119; after the divorce 115; beaten while 138
protect: daughter-in-law, sworn to 133; family honor 55; human rights 130; husbands' honor in the home 107; marital bonds 150; right to legal justice 140; workplace 73
protection of adolescent girls 44, 52
protection of women 76, 95; difficulties 143; from economic crisis 28; employment cannot 143; family-based, loss of 96, 125; family courts 14; honor 76–77; husband failed to 141; against husbands seeking revenge 131; identity 22; laws enacted 12, 15, 131; from legal agency 122; male 95, 103; by secret resistance power 77, 103; sexual 73; strategies 19; from violence 121, 125, 131, 136
puberty 51, 124

Raheja, G.G. 53
Rahman, A. 3, 5
Rahman, M. 29, 42n5, 97
rape 1, 3, 14, 116, 121; sexual assault by the husband 115
Rashid, S.F. 30–32, 107
Rashida 51–52
Renu 98; natal family would not accept her back 99; second wife 97; sons 100–101
reproductive: age 4; capacity 8; organs 56
resist 78; the code of conduct 69; domestic violence 85; oppression 104
resistance 103, 148; to intra-family power structures 78; open 104; power 77, 104; secret 76–77; spirit forms 83n1; *see also* spirit, supernatural powers
Roy, K.C. 28
Rozario, S. 63, 65, 148
Rubin, G. 8
rural communities 18, 46, 88
rural poor 36; migrants 37

Säävälä, M. 3, 12, 43, 46, 88, 101, 112, 123, 128
Samaddar, R. 35
Schuler, S.R. 3, 5, 82, 95, 107, 127
Scott, J. 8, 103–104
secret: extra-marital relationships 94; resistance 76–77; savings 81
self-divorce right in the *kabin* 95
Sen, A.K. 12, 17n1, 74, 93
senior: men 48; wife 101, 133; women/womanhood 43, 49, 84, 88
separation 53, 131, 137, 151; children suffer most 94; increase in 148; of Muslim bride from natal family 60; never wanted 90, 105; not seen as solution 96; physical 47; problem in woman's life 93; social stigma of 152
sexual harassment 68n2; in public (eve-teasing) 1
sexuality 8–9, 54–55, 116
sex workers 126; street-based 94, 116–117

Index   179

shalish/mediation 19, 22, 131, 137, 152; ADR 15, 129–130; advocates 134; advocates arrange 26; affects bargaining position of battered women 132; attempted murder case 144; BLAST 130; cases returning again 146; changing practices 7; gender roles in 22; husband did not come 115, 131; informal community 128–129; inside the family 15; kin-based 136; by legal aid workers and professionals 131; maintenance costs 144–145; mini-trial 129; not always the best solution 131; polygamous husband not providing maintenance costs 142; practiced by the NGO 136; sessions 25; socio-cultural factor affecting 132; traditional practices 16, 128; without success 136; women's voices suppressed 146
Sharma, U. 12, 82, 107, 129
Silva 151
sindur 94, 117
sister-in-law/sisters-in-law 12, 37, 74, 76, 104, 108, 133–134; contested relationship with 150; domestic violence by 16, 18, 122, 125, 136, 138–141; interfering 137
slum woman/women 16, 20, 23–25, 38, 46, 56, 97, 102; believed husbands should beat their wives 6; hidden resistance power 104; impoverished 151; lives limited by insecurity 51; marriage negotiations 57; middle-aged 49; not protected from domestic violence 125; pressure from mother-in-law 56; problems of dowry practice 66; share conjugal problems 150; try to resolve domestic violence by informal tactics 126; working outside their homes 39, 75–76
son/male child 44–45, 49, 51, 56, 80, 108, 112, 116–117, 138, 140–141; birth welcomed with loud prayer 44; dutiful to wife and children 144; education 49; failure to bear 142; guardian of widowed mother 47; from lower class family 59; maintenance payments 145; marriage to sister's 109; marry again for dowry 77; mother of 17n7; orphaned 35, 75; parent-child bond 88; preference syndrome 45–46; rebuked 133; son-in-law 63, 91, 133; violence to wife 134
spirit 76; exorcism 83n1; possession 76–77, 83n1

spousal violence 5; physical 6, 19; *see also* domestic violence, marital violence
stigma (*kolonko*) 91, 118–119; social 96, 107, 113, 117, 152
stigmatized (*kolonkito*) 105, 112, 115, 119, 124; situation 125
suicide(s) 66, 75, 114; in marital home 3
supernatural powers (*giin*) 76, 101; spirits 76; spiritual powers 83n1

talaq 94; Three *Talaq* 13, 94, 112
talaq-e-tawfeez 13
Taslima 122; early marriage 124; mother-in-law's violence 122–123, 125
Tenhunen, S. 11, 73, 81, 101
Therborn, G. 9, 53
tip 94; *sindur* 117
torture 67, 78, 92; denial of 134, 138; by husband or in-laws 95, 111, 121, 125, 133–134, 138, 141, 144, 150; inhuman 126; neighbours rescue from 112; physical 3, 120; psychological 52; reasons behind 93; by relatives 109; resistance 103; by sister-in-law 137–138

Uddin, M.J. 30–32, 46
unemployment 149; level among young males 65; problems 27
UNICEF 2, 4, 17n2, 17n3, 41, 49, 54, 147, 150
United Nations 148; Conference on Women 1
Urban Health Survey 6, 19
urban poor: breakdown of marriages 96; communities (*bastis*) 18; populations 19; slums 29, 37–38, 56, 132; surplus labor 27
USA 59; ADR developed 129
USAID 129
Uusikylä, H. 44, 53, 56, 62–63

Vatuk, S. 12, 88
veil (*pardah* or *burkha*) 52, 76, 118; modesty marker 77; work outside the home 79
victim women/females 22, 26, 145–146, 150; came to seek help with relatives 128; counseling center 146; deterred from seeking formal legal support 127; divorce generates loss 137; efforts to stand up against domestic violence 10, 153; fear and shame of detection 52; free legal support 19; poor 153; rebuked by parents or elder brothers 151; seek support from ADR 15

violent husband 52, 77, 85, 89, 102–103, 113; addicted 122; divorce from 136; regular maintenance for children from 146; wife failed to free herself 137

wedding gifts **110**; *see also* dowry
White, S.C. 2–3, 12, 78, 80, 148
William, S. 3–4, 6, 147, 150, 153
women: poor and lower-middle-class 148; working 69–70, 73–74, 79–80, 82, 86
Women and Children Repression Prevention (Amendment) Act 2003 116
women laborers 29; building construction 70; casual day 38, **40**, 80, 101, 108, 137; wage 97; young, migration 27
women's honor 150; in affinal home 109, 112; low status work tarnishes 71, 73; protecting 76–77

women's rights 3, 17, 93, 130, 148, 152
women's voices 23, 70, 142; opportunity to be heard 130; raised 4, 153; shameful 97; suppressed 146
work/working outside home 2, 23, 45, 54, 56, 69–72, 75, 80–82, 95, 100, 107, 152; changes among *basti* women 79; depend on husbands 81; laborious jobs 86; no suitable work 40; not allowed 82, 91; poorly paid jobs 38, 70; prevented 52, 82; searching for 73
World Bank 129
World Health Organization (WHO) 4, 126; Multi-country Study on Women's Health and Domestic Violence 18

Zakia 101–103; hidden resistance power 104